And One Fine Morning

And One Fine Morning

Memories of My Father

Nick Hayes

NODIN PRESS

ISBN: 978-1-932472-98-1

Library of Congress Control Number: 2010921860

Photo credits:
Photographs of Christ Church Lutheran on page 157 used by permission of Peter Seeger and Tom Dolan.
Photograph of Harry's Cafe on page 163 used by permission of the Minnesota Historical Society.

Design: John Toren

Nodin Press, LLC
530 N. Third Street,
Suite 120
Minneapolis, MN
55401

To My Parents, Mark and Vivian

Introibo ad altare Dei.
Ad Deum qui laetificat juventutem meam.

It eluded us then, but that's no matter—tomorrow we will run faster, stretch out our arms farther … And one fine morning—So we beat on, boats against the current, borne back ceaselessly into the past.

– F. Scott Fitzgerald, *The Great Gatsby*

In death, there is always hope.

– An Irish proverb

Contents

And One Fine Morning

Memories of My Father

Prologue
Photograph, 1954

The best way to introduce my father is with a photograph. It was 1954. He was at the top of his game. His eyes looked straight into the camera. He smiled in anticipation. A new suit added a touch of style. The newspaper had recently described him as an award-winning architect.

Nothing in his expression gives us an inkling that a few months later a series of heart attacks and strokes would cut him down, cost him his left leg, impair his speech, and cripple his gift for painting and drawing. Two years after the photograph was taken, a final heart attack killed him.

The suit was the only thing the undertaker got right. At the wake, I remember looking at the open coffin and thinking the smile was wrong. The undertaker knew better. He had known my father since they were kids on the play grounds of Minneapolis's North Side. The undertaker had never liked that smile. My father was mocking him, he might have thought. He had wired my father's lips shut and closed in a straight line. Everyone knew my father's smile sloped up to the left as if he were about to wink. By straightening out his lips, the undertaker gave him a frown. The part in my father's hair was also wrong. Only the suit and double Windsor knot were right. My father took the suit and tie away with him.

In the photograph, his lips parted in his characteristic smile as if he is about to tell another story. My father loved nothing more than to tell a good story. When he said of someone that he had nothing to say, it was an insult. It was a fault that could not be corrected and an admonishment to us. Be polite but don't expect much of this guy.

More than fifty years later, I can still see my father smoking a Camel, martini in hand, holding forth to the smiles and laughter of his friends and family. I loved nothing more than to sit beside him in the living room, on lawn chairs in the backyard, or at a table at Harry's, his favorite bar and restaurant. I would smile or laugh, pretending to comprehend the stories of old priests, his Irish-American boyhood on the North Side of Minneapolis, his days as a man about town when both he and Minneapolis came of age together. Sometimes he lectured on architecture, ridiculing a rival's work or explaining how the curvature of the woodwork in a certain church conveyed the concept of grace.

Memory is life's second act. My father's started on an afternoon in June 1956, the day of his funeral. After his burial, his memory rode home with the crowd that came to our house. I was eight years old. My ears took in everything. There were his friends, a clan of relatives, and all those priests and nuns—all of them laughing and re-telling stories my father told and the stories told about him.

That was when I began collecting the pieces of this story. Throughout my childhood and youth, family gatherings revolved around stories about him. My mother's stories mixed fondness with a few unresolved issues, providing a counter-balance to my Aunt Eileen's undiluted adoration of her brother. In the Catholic schools of my youth, priests and nuns would stop me in the hall. They would begin, *Your father was such a great guy* ... and add yet another anecdote to my growing collection. His things remained in my childhood home. Watercolors and drawings, clothing, diaries, letters, and a navy locker full of memorabilia lived with us for decades, until my mother finally re-married, sold the house, and divided his things among her four sons and the Goodwill.

I am now older than my father ever was. My doctor tells me that I have less time left than I had thought. I spent my life searching for things of the past. I made a career out of the pursuit of the past as an historian of a foreign country and another time. All the while, I have carried my father's memory with me. My father is forever forty-something in the memory I have carried and in the course of time I have become his older companion.

It's time to tell our story. Along the way, I have opened a few archives, dusted the silverfish off old documents, sorted through legends, letters, paintings and photos, and made a bit of sense out of his life and times.

I had a girlfriend in college who said I had more of a father in my dead one than she had in her living one. She said I should write a book about him. This is it.

1
A Powerful Vise

> *... it seemed as though the entire region around my chest*
> *became constricted as if it were held by a powerful vise that*
> *was slowly tightened.*
>
> – Charles Yale Harrison,
> *Thank God for My Heart Attack* (1949)

THE SUMMER OF THE HAYES-DIEHL WARS

In 1947, when we first moved to the neighborhood, there had been plenty of territory. The gangs of neighborhood kids each claimed as theirs a vacant lot or the rights to one of the new houses under construction. The discarded lumber from those construction sites went into our tree houses and play forts, and those sites also yielded the precious metal of our currency in the form of steel slugs the size of quarters that the workers cut from electrical boxes and wiring installation. But by 1954, the free space in our neighborhood on the southern fringe of Minneapolis was running out.

August had given way to September that year, but the summer refused to surrender to fall and lift the burden of heat and humidity. The Hayes–Diehl Wars started because my brothers, young Mark, Brian and Tom, built a tree house in a stand of trees on an old farmstead that passed for the neighborhood forest. The Diehl kids claimed the territory. The Diehl's lived on the other side of Penn and had been in the neighborhood for years when we moved in. They acted like they owned it. Sometimes, they were nice. When they got a TV, for example, they let the four of us watch it through the living room window. The Diehl girl, Barbara, once even opened the front door a bit so that we could hear *The Lone Ranger*.

No one remembers why the Diehls decided to make a stand over the tree house in Irwin's forest, but they began to launch surprise attacks on our games in a vacant lot and ambush us in the alley. There were four Diehl boys just like us except none of them was as young and worthless in a fight as I was. To make the sides even, my three older brothers recruited Mike Flannery. Like Rusty and Rin Tin Tin on TV, I was allowed to tag along with our dog, Doby. On the last day of summer vacation, the Diehls proposed a peace conference. We met in the alley on Queen. The oldest Diehl boy pulled out a Big Five Tablet and read aloud, *It was a tie.* My brothers and Flannery nodded their heads. Then the Diehl boy added, *but the Diehls won.*

War! shouted Flannery, who always tended to push my brothers a bit too far. Young Mark said that we should quit anyway—we had to get ready for school—but Flannery and Tom immediately charged the older Diehl boy who screamed to his cohorts, *Retreat!* They took up a position in a dry patch within the swamp at the edge of Armitage Park. The Hayeses and Flannery took up a position on the piles of sand and cinder blocks dumped on the edge of the swamp. *Hey, Nickey!* Flannery said to me, *Look at this!* He smiled as he held up a cinder block and added it to the ammunition intended for the Hayes's artillery barrage against the Diehl positions. Soften them up before the infantry. *Remember, Pearl Harbor,* Flannery yelled and motioned to Tom to attack.

Just then, our mother pulled up in our green '53 Ford Fairlane. We thought she was mad at us. She had parked on the wrong side of the street and too far from the curb. Nobody ever parked on this street. She left the car running, took a few steps toward us and raised her voice just enough so that her message was clear. *Boys! You got to come home,* she said. *Your Dad's very sick.*

It's Pounding, My Chest

It was all because Lucy cooked with bacon grease, my mother has repeated over and over again. *Everything! She cooked everything in bacon grease.* From my father's first night in the hospital to today, my mother has blamed her husband's heart attack on her mother-in-law's cooking. The accusation has only helped me keep alive my memory of how Grandma Lucy's peanut cakes tasted like sweet bacon.

My mother overlooked a more obvious cause: Her husband smoked two packs of Camels a day. In 1954, the surgeon general's report on smoking was still a long way off; at that time Joe DiMaggio advertised Camels in *Life* magazine. Joe's three-pack-a-day Camel habit wasn't holding him back at the plate or checking his mighty swing, nor had smoking hurt my father's jump shot in his basketball heyday. Camels were made to prove that certain men—gentlemen and athletes like Joe DiMaggio and Mark Hayes—intuitively understood how fine tobacco goes with grace and style. My father's Camel was a trusted friend with a knack for style, always there when you needed him, saying "go ahead, relax, that's it, cool and easy," and never letting on that he was taking my father down a shortcut to the grave. A lot of men in my father's generation had friends like that.

Sometimes, my mother remarked that she should have known. She was a nurse.

Ever since he came back from the war, there were signs that something was wrong. He had night tremors and fevers that came with the heat of summer. One night he woke up screaming, *Viv! I'm on fire!* His perspiration had soaked the bed sheets. My mother took his temperature and gave him some Schweppes with ice cubes. He went back to sleep. He wondered if he had gotten the malaria during the campaign in the Philippines in 1944, or perhaps much earlier when he first landed in Liberia. He would sometimes sit in his lawn chair in our front yard on Queen Avenue on summer days, wearing his Munsingwear pocket polo shirt and light weight gabardines, sipping gin and tonics. He said the quinine helped his malaria. *Oh, Mark, that's just your excuse,* his sister, Aunt Eileen would say with a laugh, *you just like gin and tonics.* All I ever knew about malaria was that it had something to do with my father's fondness for gin and tonics on warm summer Saturdays.

Another troubling symptom—he would sometimes experience a mortifying pause in mid-sentence, unable to speak. One glaring episode took place during a visit with my parents' friends from down the block, Frank and Polly Butler. Frank was the host of a popular radio show on WCCO, and he often pestered Mark on weekends for a new joke to tell on his show Monday morning. On this occasion my father was adding a few wrinkles to the time-honored joke about Mr. Rabbit, Mr. Lizard, and Mr. Turtle. Mr. Turtle had just gone into a bar to ask the bartender … At this point I was settled in on the couch waiting patiently for the last word (which rhymes loosely with Rabbit) when my father paused awkwardly. His half-parted lips stayed tense. His face trembled in a silence that seemed to last a minute. When he resumed the joke, relief took over. The Butlers laughed nervously, too loud and well ahead of the punch line.

Earlier in the summer, my parents had taken a weekend vacation to Chicago, staying at the Palmer House—their favorite hotel. My father's arm froze in place as he was writing on the bill during checkout. He couldn't speak. My mother asked what was wrong. Finally he spoke and signed the bill.

It happened again in front of a crowd of people at a reception in St. Paul for the opening of a new residence for the Sisters of St. Joseph—Bethany Convent. My father had designed the new convent and my parents brought me to the event. There were dozens of priests, a handful of bishops, and a sea of the Sisters of St. Joseph. The Mother Superior said some nice things about Mark Hayes and asked him to say a few words. He started with a half-stutter. Then, for a moment that seemed more like a day in school he was unable to speak. On the way home, my mother insisted he see the doctor. *I'll decide when and if I need to see a doctor,* he replied.

You could say the heart attack had nothing to do with the war. You could say my father died because that was just the way things were in our family. His older sister, the Aunt Anna I knew only from a photo on my bedroom wall, had problems with varicose veins. She was two years older than Mark, black Irish, pretty and smart like her younger sister Eileen. Their mother, our Grandma Lucy, always talked about the expensive cars Anna's boyfriends drove—Packards and Hudsons. She was thirty-one years old when she died during an operation.

Our favorite uncle, Jim, died in the winter of 1953 at the age of thirty-nine. Jim had been a "blue baby" and lived under the shadow of a weak heart. He lived with Grandma Lucy. The family doctor had told him that there was a new type of surgery that could correct his heart problem. He went to Gillette Hospital in St. Paul for the operation and stayed overnight for tests. The phone rang early the next morning, and doctors told my father that they found his brother dead in the hospital bed. Jim died from the tests. He never had the operation.

Jim's was my first wake. The Richard Gill Funeral Parlor was on the corner of Franklin and Chicago. Mr. Gill greeted my father by name as he led me by the hand. *And here's the latest edition to the Hayes family,* Gill said, addressing me. It seemed perfectly normal to me that the undertaker was keeping count of the members of the family. *It's time to say good-bye to Uncle Jim,* my father said to me. We knelt together facing Jim's casket. I wondered why Jim did not have his car keys. His hands lay folded on his chest. His fingers wrapped around a rosary. I had never seen Uncle Jim with a rosary in his hands. His right hand always held his car keys that he twirled on a chain until they wrapped around his index finger. His face was the color of cigarette ash. My father's suit stretched tightly over his shoulders as he hunched forward, elbows on the rail, hands clasped, thumbs pressed against his mouth, his body quaking. His face was the same color as Jim's. As we stood up and turned around, I saw Lucy. There was no expression at all in her face, just her eyes fixed on something far away.

THE NEXT THING I REMEMBER after my mother's sudden appearance at the swamp was the sight of my parents in our house. Shoulder to shoulder, my brothers and I stood at the edge of the living room. When our mother told us to go to another room, we complied by stepping a few feet backward into the dining room that extended out from the living room. Our father lay on the couch. Our mother sat on its edge. Realizing his young sons were nearby, he tried to raise himself up but quickly gave up even that small show of dignity, collapsing back down hard on his back. His right hand holding his chest, his words trembled. *Viv, it's pounding, my chest,* he stammered, repeating the words *my chest* until they were lost in an inaudible whisper.

His problems had started the day before. In the morning, he had chest pains at the office and came home. The pain continued. The family physician, Dr. Donatel, came to the house. He said that it was only a bad case of heartburn. But just to be sure, he told my father to come over to the clinic for an EKG. Donatel had a small practice a few blocks away. The office was equipped with little more than an examination table and the doctor's little black bag. My father insisted on driving himself to the clinic for the test. Donatel said he would call him the next day with the results. My father had other plans for the following day. He was going to buy a new house.

Donatel called early in the morning and spoke to my mother, telling her that her husband had had a heart attack, and she must get him to the hospital immediately. My father flatly rejected the idea, saying, *I'm not going to the hospital. I'm going to buy a new house for my family.*

He said nothing more about the doctor's call. He dressed himself in a light grey worsted wool suit, white shirt, and tie in a double Windsor and left without a word. He drove downtown to the First National Bank to pick-up a cashier's check for $20,000. From there he drove back to meet the owner at the new house. My father turned over the cashier's check, signed the papers, and drove home to the house on Queen. The job done, he surrendered to the living room couch and the pain that had never left his chest.

My Aunt Eileen drove Grandma Lucy over to our house. My parents had already left for the hospital. When I saw Grandma Lucy arrive, rather than Mrs. Winter, the babysitter who stayed with us when my parents went out for dinner or a cocktail party, I knew that they would not be back soon.

The first night went well. My mother stayed overnight at the hospital and came home in the morning. Dr. Donatel had told her she might as well go home; he would call if anything came up. She decided to go ahead with the plan she and Aunt Eileen had made for the day and took the four of us along with Eileen's daughter Mary to the State Fair. To save money on parking, Eileen came over to our house and we all packed into the Fairlane. But none of us was interested in the fair that day. We blamed the heat and dust. As my mother drove the Ford back into the driveway at Queen we were ready to burst out the doors. As soon as she opened the car door, she heard the telephone ringing. She jumped out, and, not noticing that my hand was already on the door post, slammed the door on the fingers of my right hand. I screamed. My mother turned her head first to me and then back to the kitchen where the phone was still ringing. Eileen said, *Get the phone, I'll take care of Nickey.*

Standing in the doorway, my mother leaned to one side while on the other side she held the telephone receiver by its cord, swinging the telephone like a limp pendulum. *Mark's gotten much worse.* Eileen led me by the hand, ignoring my screams about how my finger hurt. *I'll get Lucy*, she said. We knew our mother would not be back that night.

My father had suffered his second heart attack. When my mother arrived at the hospital, our parish priest, old Fr. Driscoll, was giving him his Last Rites. Eileen called us from the hospital and spoke to Lucy, who knew what these things meant.

Boys, your father is going to heaven, she told us, *and we need to say the rosary.* Our rosaries came down from the crucifix in the front entry. The five of us knelt down on the living room carpet. *The First Sorrowful Mystery,* Lucy began, *the Agony in the Garden.* We weren't the family rosary type. Young Mark and Brian said the Hail Marys. Tom mumbled. As the youngest, I got away with sitting on the floor and not saying anything. We finished the five decades and were relieved when instead of starting in with the Joyous or the Glorious Mysteries, Lucy said it was time for dinner.

The next morning I overheard a conversation about my father's leg. *We almost lost Mark last night,* my mother told Lucy, *they were going to amputate his leg below the knee.* They were going to cut off his leg, I thought. A wooden leg is not a leg. I remembered his basketball photo. He stood on the far left of the line-up of his high school team. Basketball jersey, shorts, legs long and slim. But he didn't lose his leg that night. He was still my father, Mark Hayes, who stood a head above the other fathers at Sunday mass and walked into a room as if he was taking over a basketball court. Although the immediate danger retreated, it was not gone. It was not the words *heart attack,* but *amputate his leg,* that had meaning to me and threatened to take away the father I knew.

THE NEXT WEEK my brothers and I underwent a childhood trauma that was not uncommon in the post-war era of social mobility. We reluctantly made the move to a new house and stepped up the social ladder. Left behind was the boisterous sub-division on Queen Avenue, ahead was a new house standing amid an ensemble of silently elegant homes that ignored us the way that old money ignores new. The move was our father's idea and he was not with us. His absence added to our distress and put in our heads quickly repressed thoughts of a mutiny.

The timing of the move coincided with the start of the school year. Thus, on the morning of moving day, four recalcitrant boys conspired to disguise their opposition to the move by protesting against the first day of school. Our mother took charge. We were told to get in the car while movers carried boxes from our bedrooms to an ominous Mayflower moving van. In place of our familiar bus ride to school, seated comfortably in two rows of seats respected by all but a few uninitiated kids, our mother drove us to school that morning while we listened without enthusiasm to her upbeat announcement that we would now have a lovely eight block walk to and from school each day. That afternoon a hard rain drove home the message that the long hot summer was finally over and turned our first walk home into a fast and wet sprint.

Our dog Doby didn't make the move. There was a man in a truck trying to take our dog. Doby turned and leapt with hope when Brian showed up. *Mom, help, someone's taking Doby*, Brian yelled as he ran into the kitchen. She lied, telling him not to worry. Doby was just going away for a day. Later, she said she had to get rid of Doby because on the first day in the new house he lifted his leg on the delicate Japanese wallpaper in the front entry. (Years later, she admitted she had always disliked Doby.)

Prosperity had moved my father's friends to new homes on Lake Minnetonka and in the forested suburbs west of the city. He would not live outside the Minneapolis city limits and looked for a new home in those neighborhoods where the city's elite of the previous generation lived. He explored the listings in the Kenwood area north and east of Lake of the Isles, and the handsome dwellings in Tangletown that looked down from a hilltop to Minneapolis's fabled Minnehaha Creek and Parkway. One Sunday morning, he saw a newspaper ad for a house on the street of his dreams. It was called Forest Dale. The cul-de-sac ambled along the Minnehaha and hid its homes under the cover of pines, cedars, and maples.

Double rows of evergreens marked off the four sides of the yard that was now ours. The house itself had three floors. The third floor was an old attic. You pulled down a trap door in the ceiling to reveal an old set of wooden stairs with a hand rail that rolled down. Our father had told us boys that this third, secret floor was ours. It could hold our Lionel train set, its villages, bridges and towns. There was also room for our boxing bag and the pool table. The first thing I did in the new house was run up the stairs to the second floor and pull the chain that brought down the magic staircase. When I hurried up the wooden steps, my head was barely over the landing when a deer's head with antlers and moths buzzing around it greeted me. I remembered the rumor that the owner's wife had gone crazy in this old house. Maybe she hadn't really left. A few times I was sure I heard her laughing and hiding in the dormers of that third floor. It was a good thing, I thought, that I could still walk the mile back to the old neighborhood at Queen.

Our other grandma, Elsie, had come from Vancouver to help our mother with the move and with us kids while our father was in the hospital. A few nights after Elsie came to stay with us, my mother returned home unusually late from the hospital. I was standing in the doorway between the kitchen and dining room where I often watched Elsie make dinner. My mother took a few steps into the kitchen, stopped, and sobbed, *Mother, I can't take it anymore. I don't know what I am going to do.* This was the first time I had ever heard my mother crying. Together with the whispers about amputating my father's leg, the hushed murmurs that had replaced the fond laughter at the mention of my father's name, and the silence that in place of his voice had furnished this spacious new house—bit by bit the story of my family's new life was unfolding like the beads of a newly added mystery to the rosary.

It came in threes. A few days later, my father suffered a stroke. Elsie had made dinner for us. My mother called to say that my Aunt Eileen was coming to bring us boys to the hospital and to say goodbye to our father. They had amputated his leg in the afternoon and he was getting weaker and weaker. When we stepped out of the elevator onto the floor, it was full of people who formed a line of sorts leading up to my father's room at the end of the hall. Just as we arrived our parish priest, Fr. Driscoll, went past carrying a wooden box and white cloth. The corridor walls were a cheerless green. My mother led me toward the room. Uncle John stepped out into the hall. He covered his face with one hand and was crying. We didn't say anything to him. There were priests and nuns; at the end of the hall an old priest stood with Lucy, saying the rosary. The crowd in my father's room stepped aside as my mother entered with us—her four sons. An overhead light glared down on him. He was in an oxygen tent, and didn't move or look at us even though his eyes were open. I wasn't sure if it was him. I didn't recognize the skin on his face. He lay under a white blanket, and when I looked at where his legs should be, I felt some relief. I told myself it was not true about the amputation. A lump in the sheets deceived me into believing he still had two legs.

Back in the hallway, Sr. Rita Claire, the director of the hospital, waited for us. She gave us a pleasant and simple explanation for everything. She told us not to worry. Our dad was such a great guy God couldn't wait to have him in heaven. We knew she liked him. He had worked with her as the architect for the expansion of St. Mary's Hospital. She arranged for my mother to spend the night in a guest room, and put my brothers and me in a vacant room across the hallway from our father's room. We slept two to a bed. The last thing I remember that evening was Sr. Rita Claire saying, *Don't worry, Mrs. Hayes. We'll keep an eye on them.*

Early the next morning, Sr. Rita Claire woke me saying, *Good morning, Mr. Hayes. Did you sleep well last night?* Then, she added, *We have some good news for you.* She brought us into our father's room. My mother was there. My father was weak, unable or unwilling to speak, but I recognized his face.

For the rest of the fall and into the winter months, my mother took me to my father's hospital room every day after school. I had set up toys in the corner by the armchair. Socko the monkey lived on the chair. My favorite toy was a hook and ladder fire truck in red enamel with M.F.D. for Minneapolis Fire Department in gold lettering on the door. The ladder swiveled around and easily went up. A small crank could raise the extension ladder another foot in case an imaginary fireman needed to save Socko from an imaginary fire on the armrest of the chair.

A constant stream of visitors—old friends, architects, and especially all those priests—came and went. Every day, in the late afternoon, Vic, his longtime friend and co-partner in the architectural firm, paid him a visit. Uncle John came every day while Grandma Lucy respected her oldest son's insistence that she not come to the hospital. A steady stream of other visitors whose names I did not know contributed the comfort of a daily routine to our lives in the hospital room. The scene was almost normal, except that my father never spoke—the visitors did all the talking.

Outside the hospital's walls, tragedy struck my father's close friend, Loren Abbott, who often came to visit. My brothers and I knew his three sons from our school. The playgrounds were cruel to his oldest boy, Michael, a slow child too easily humiliated, teased, and driven into a mad rage. Because he had rather large protruding ears, the kids at our school called him Peter Rabbit. One day, when he was thirteen, he asked his dad if he could drive the car. No. Michael went to the gun cabinet in the family's den, took out his father's shot gun, walked back to the living room and shot his dad. It was on the front page of the newspaper the next day. When my mother saw the newspaper, she told us not to say a thing about this to our father. She called the hospital to make sure that he did not see the newspaper. He had to stay calm. No one ever told him why Loren stopped coming to visit.

All those afternoons, I ran the Minneapolis Fire Department. Day after day, a fireman climbed the extension ladder to save Socko's life one more time. As long as my father stayed in the hospital bed, he was my tall father nimbly dribbling the basketball down the court and dropping in another bucket for two more. Afternoons in the St. Mary's hospital room were like Sundays with my father except there were no martinis, my father didn't tell his jokes anymore, and we would never get back to Queen Avenue.

THE MAPLE TREE AND ROPE SWING

On Christmas Day 1954, my father came home for the first time to the house on Forest Dale. The doctor had said the excitement and noise of Christmas Eve would be too much for him. Late Christmas morning, my mother brought him home. My brothers and I waited in the living room by the Christmas tree.

Even on crutches, he was still tall. His grey and white Pendleton was buttoned at the neck. On his left leg, the gabardine slacks folded at the knee and were pinned to the thigh. With my mother helping him along, he swung his way across the living room and toward a chair. The davenport and cocktail table from the old house on Queen waited for him on the far side of the room. The piles of opened gifts and the extra ornaments on the tree over-stated the message. His family had its first Christmas Eve without him.

He did not speak a word, but looked intently at his sons and this room he did not recognize. I started talking to him about the toys I got for Christmas and wanted to show him how my new Remco Robot moved its arms and walked. Then he broke the silence. *Viv, I need to lie down.* I followed as she helped him up the stairs and to their bedroom on the second floor. She anticipated his fear of the stairway by telling him that they could install a small elevator. They paused on the stairway landing where he gasped for air. In the bedroom, he let his crutches fall to the floor. He stood on his right leg, his arm draped over my mother's shoulder as she slumped toward the bed. Her knees buckled under his weight as she bent him forward and slid him off her and onto the bed. She stood and turned him over to lie on his back. She reached for his half-leg, which stuck out pointing over the edge of the bed, and tucked it under the covers. As pain shot across his face he turned away from his wife and youngest son and stared at the blank bedroom wall. The day at home for Christmas was not working. Before dinner, she drove him back to St. Mary's.

A few weeks later he left St. Mary's for Veteran's Hospital. I did not like to go there because he shared the room with another man. The guy was a bit crazy. He kept telling my father—and anyone who came in the room—how he had been bald but the drugs had brought back his hair, which was thick, curly and black. *Never mind him,* my father once said to Uncle John. *The other day he told me a Hershey bar came out when he crapped.* It wasn't my father's kind of humor but everyone smiled at the first signs that he was talking and making jokes again.

Next, he went to the heart clinic at the University of Minnesota Hospital. They fitted him there for an artificial leg. It was made of a light weight wood in a shade of pale yellow, in three parts, with joints at the knee and ankle. He would only let my mother put it on. When it was done, she helped him into his slacks and slipped socks and shoes over his feet, both real and wood. She pinned up one sock to his calf with a tack. In the physical therapy room, she helped him practice walking. Like a parent setting a child off on a bicycle with trainer wheels, she would hold his arm for a bit and guide his hands to the safety hand rails as he took his first steps on his own.

When he could walk on his own with a cane, he came home. It was late winter. His heart attacks had left him with a partial paralysis of his left hand and vocal cords. Even when he was relaxing, he squeezed a rubber ball in his left hand trying to bring back its muscles. The trembling in his hands never stopped. Most of the time, he sat on the living room couch with his back to the watercolors he had painted in Africa. His pen and ink drawings, framed in the hallway in black and white, were windows looking back to another time. He was no longer an artist and no longer left-handed. He spent long hours at the dining room table forcing something out of the pencil in his right hand. It insistently acted out the role of the contrary fraternal twin of his left hand and made a mockery of his efforts to draw a straight line or form the letters of the alphabet. Once I saw him crush a pencil in his right hand.

He had lost his gift of speech. More often than not, he would utter a single word that lacked the phrase or sentence required to complete the thought. His speech therapy consisted of practice on a first-of-its-kind recording device. It looked like a small record player. You recorded on a thin, round, plastic disk with a hole in the center that spun around a turntable. On good days, we talked together into the microphone. *Well Nickel plate*, he said, using his favorite nickname for me, *what's better, Skippy's creamy or crunchy peanut butter?* On the many bad days, he started with long *aaah's* or just held on to the sound of the first letter of my name, repeating *nnnn* like Morse code. When his voice came back, anger had taken over the sentence. With a loud *Oh, shit,* he shut off the recorder.

He had forgotten things he learned at school. His slide rule stayed in the drawer of his study desk that young Mark had taken over on the second floor. At the dining room table he practiced multiplication tables and division. His eyes were failing. Gone were the Mickey Spillane novels, detective stories, and copies of *True Magazine*. He did read the *Minneapolis Star* and *Wall Street Journal* with thick tortoise shell reading glasses aided by a magnifying glass. His friend, Fr. Breitenbeck, had given him a book called *Thank God for My Heart Attack* that he never opened. I often opened the book up and stared at drawings of a man in a swimming pool. He was doing a hand stand on the diving board. He was in swimming trunks. One leg was missing below the knee.

On Sundays, Vic came over. When his friend tried to stand up from the couch, Vic would say, *No, no, Mark, don't bother getting up.* But my father had his pride, and stood up. His athletic strength had survived in his right leg, which on its own raised him up to stand erect and straight in the shoulders. For all of this effort to stand, his posture was unnaturally still. A rigidity came from a fear of falling and gave him the appearance of a tall, immobile wooden soldier.

Vic brought blueprints from the office. My mother made them a pitcher of martinis. Vic pointed out details on the blueprints and made jokes about people they knew. My father seemed to smile. One Sunday in early summer, Vic said that it was time my father started coming back to the office. On Monday, Clarence Harkins, who worked as their draftsman at the firm, came to pick him up and took him to the office. He was back home before lunch.

But gradually things got better. My mother had bought a new car, a 1955 Ford Country Sedan. It was a two-toned station wagon in the colors of a dreamsickle and fudgesickle that Ford called Coral Mist and Sierra Brown, with a fold-out seat for two in the way-back. The summer of 1955 was a good time to have a new car. One night, we went to a drive-in movie theater to watch *Battle Cry*. There was a new type of place to eat called Henry's. The radio and television ads endlessly chanted, *Henry's, Henry's! Forty-five cents for a three-course meal. Sounds to me like that's a steal.* One night, all six of us went in the station wagon to *Henry's* out in the suburbs. We ate in the car. The French fries tasted the best. A sweet pickle and mixture of ketchup and mustard took over the taste of the small, limp hamburger. The malt came in a plastic cup without the extra in the steel canister from the blender. *Sounds to me like that's a schmeel*, my father said after one bite and stuffed his hamburger back into the paper bag. I thought he was having trouble with his words again.

The doctors had said that a psychiatrist could help to lift the cloud of anger and sadness that had descended on my father, and he agreed to see an old friend from his Catholic grade school days who had taken up the profession. The car trips were his idea. He said my father needed to go out more on simple expeditions and see his friends. That was all there was to the therapy except that on many Sunday afternoons we drove out to the psychiatrist's home in the suburb of Wayzata. My father had de-signed the house, which seemed to be made of glass. On those Sundays, the psychiatrist and his patient sipped martinis and looked at art books and prints strewn across the cocktail table.

By late summer, my father was taking walks. In the early evening he would pick up a cane in his left hand and he and I would walk from our house along Forest Dale, which sloped down a hill to Minnehaha Creek. More often he sat silently in a lawn chair in the back yard. In the center of the yard stood a white maple with its lowest branch about ten feet from the ground and stretching out at a right angle from the trunk. He no longer wanted to go to his once-favorite neighborhood store, Settergren's Hardware. He asked my mother to go there and buy rope and a swing seat. She brought back two pieces of thick hemp rope and a round, red metal seat. Young Mark hung it from the maple tree.

Every kid needs a tree swing, my father told me. *My Dad made a rope swing for Anna and me in Williston,* he continued. *It's the first thing I can remember.* They had died long ago. His dad. His sister Anna. He had never before said a word to me about them or his childhood in North Dakota. I was afraid it made him sad to think about them. Now, sitting in the lawn chair, he was smiling as the memory of his dad took turns with the memory of his sister giving the swing a push and lifting me up and back, up and back.

JUST LIKE IKE

I had thrust upon me the unpleasant fact that I was indeed a sick man.

- Dwight D. Eisenhower

In the fall of 1955 America's fear of the Russians and communists gave way to a new threat: heart attacks. In September, one struck President Eisenhower. For weeks on end, we saw images of Ike in his hospital room. We talked about Ike and said prayers for him at Christ the King Grade School. Though I knew more than the other kids about heart attacks and hospital rooms, I didn't talk about it in class. No one knew my Hail Marys were not for Ike.

One Saturday in October, my father and I watched the Army-Navy game on TV. The fans on the Army side held up signs in the air that read *Get Well Ike.* I watched the whole game waiting for Navy to hold up *Get Well Mark* signs. By February, Ike had recovered. The danger, however, still lurked. On St. Patrick's Day, March 17, 1956, our family's favorite comedian, Fred Allen, went out for an evening stroll and a heart attack left him dead on the streets of New York. Sr. Marie Claire told my third grade class there was a lesson to be learned in the story of Allen. He did not even have enough time to say the Act of Contrition. *It is so important to always be in the state of grace*, she said and hinted that this should be a lesson to those households in our parish where families had not celebrated St. Patrick's Day in the right way. Not knowing much about New York, I imagined Fred Allen ambling down the walk through our front yard of grass and clover, turning by the tall evergreens to the street and falling over dead as a door nail on our sidewalk.

Later in the spring, on the Sunday before my First Holy Communion, I sat at the dining room table all afternoon and memorized sections of my Catechism. My father sat beside me and worked on a letter, his feeble cursives scratched out and barely connected the letters of the words of two sentences. *Dear Fr. Breitenbeck, I want to thank you for your help. I think I am beginning to see why God let this happen to me. Sincerely yours, Mark.*

The next Sunday, a photo captured the last real time my father and I had together. It was 1956, the Sunday of my First Holy Communion. My father stood behind me. Like the fifty or so eight-year-old boys at Christ the King Catholic School that Sunday, I was all dressed up in my First Holy Communion outfit—a white shirt, silk tie, and pants with a military-style cloth belt with a brass buckle. I was relaxed, with both hands in my pockets as I looked directly at the camera. My hair was "short," not because I wanted it that way but because my mother wanted it that way. The top of my head barely reached my father's waist. Behind him an empty lawn chair—the simple aluminum tubing and green-and-white fiberglass weave was the new look for summer that year—stood ready to catch him if he were to tip backward. He stood a step away, trusting his balance to one hand placed on my right shoulder and the other on a cane. He stared away from the camera over his right shoulder. There is more bone than skin on his face; his lean body is visibly weak. He stands directly behind me. His secret is safe. The camera does not see that his leg is missing.

Later that afternoon, my friend Kevin Dolan showed up at my house on his bicycle. Both of us were still in our First Holy Communion outfits. *I want to go beat up George Crone*, Kevin said. *Do you know where he lives?* I knew. We went off together, Kevin giving me a buck on his bike. Soon, the art of throwing rocks at street lamps distracted us. George Crone had one more day in peace.

My father's last heart attack came the next day.

My father and me. My first Holy Communion Day, 1956.

Part 2:
Before My Time

A road in Kilrossanty Parish, County Waterford, Ireland.

2

The Irish Flag in the Closet

There are things
that are not forgot
in a generation.

— Brendan Behan, *Irish Sketchbook*

My family belonged to the Minnesota Irish, one of the more lost of the lost tribes of Eire. We Minnesota Irish spoke English with the faint trace of a Scandinavian accent. It was largely in our habit of overusing reflexive pronouns and talking a bit too much that our Irish linguistic roots were disclosed. Our beacons of light shone from the East to the West in the form of movies and stories that were meant to teach the lost Irish of the Plains about the lives of the real Irish-Americans in Boston, Brooklyn, or Chicago.

Some of us were more lost than others. In Protestant Minneapolis we were always on the defensive. We had to explain to our neighbors why we didn't live in St. Paul and also to accept our second-class status in the eyes of St. Paul's Irish, who clustered in the shadows of the grand cathedral Archbishop John Ireland had built overlooking that city.

My Grandma Lucy led us to believe that there was something to be proud of in the family's Irish history. This seemed a bit funny to me because if it were so, our parish priest, old Father Driscoll, should have liked us better than he did. As far as I knew, being Irish had something to do with Father Driscoll at Christ the King. Every St. Patrick's Day, the whole grade school wore something green and went to the gym in the morning where the eighth graders sang songs for Father Driscoll. As Sharon McNulty sang "Over in Killarney," Father Driscoll started to cry. *A living saint she was,* he sobbed as Sharon crooned "Tu-la-ru-la-ru-la-tu-la-ru-la-lie." This lasted a minute or two until the Irish lullaby had put the old priest to sleep. Then his sister, who was also his housekeeper, nudged him awake and walked him back to the rectory. Even though it was still early in the morning, the nuns told us Father Driscoll was tired and needed a nap because he had said the 6:40 mass that morning. After he left, we watched a movie about a boy with green hair.

The pride of which Lucy spoke evidently meant that we were some other kind of Irish than Father Driscoll. Maybe the Hayeses were the kind of Irish I saw on TV. Yet something told me Grandma Lucy didn't want us compared to Ed Norton in *The Honeymooners*, even though she laughed as hard as anyone when we watched the show. She must have meant the family in the movie about the Irish in Brooklyn.

One Sunday all of us had crowded together on the chesterfield in front of the TV and watched Dorothy McGuire and James Dunn in *A Tree Grows in Brooklyn*. My mother cried at the end. She probably had a reason. When I compared my life, played out on the lawns and streets claimed from the drained swamps of south Minneapolis, to the Nolan's world of asphalt, fire escapes and a two-room flat in Brooklyn, theirs seemed to be the better one. I belonged there with the Brooklyn Irish, even if the only thing my father had in common with Johnny Nolan was that they were both good dancers. To me, the color of Ireland was not green but the black and white of our Sylvania Blonde Console TV. I imagined my bedroom was just like Francie Nolan's, with one window and a fire escape looking out to the streets of Brooklyn, though mine had two sets of windows shaded by Venetian blinds looking out on a field of blue spruce, poplars, and a honeysuckle hedge. I had to pretend that outside I saw a scrub elm struggling to grow out of the cement of an urban sidewalk.

One Sunday, Lucy was saying something to us about the glories of our Irish selves when I made one of my rare attempts to get my grandmother's attention. *You mean like in* A Tree Grows in Brooklyn? I asked. *No, they're shanty,* she replied irritably. It was not until much later that one of the nuns explained to us at Christ the King the difference between the "lace curtain" and the "shanty" Irish. The windows in our house on Queen Avenue had Venetian blinds but Lucy's house did have curtains on its windows. I guess that was enough to make us "lace curtain."

She was vague about the reasons. On her side, there were the O'Briens. This meant that we belonged to one of the royal clans of ancient Ireland. Maybe so, but half the kids in our grade school must have also been kings and queens because they were named O'Brien. On her late husband's, our grandfather Nick's side, our cousin was Helen Hayes, she told us. We took her word for that. The famous actress did look like old photos of my Aunt Anna.

In my high school days, the "wisdom" of adolescence prompted me to make jokes about Lucy. In my telling of the Helen Hayes story, my knowing smile let you know that this young man knew a thing or two about the theatre and movie stars. What my grandmother didn't know, I would say, was that, of course, Helen Hayes was a stage name. What I didn't know and had never bothered to check was that Helen was her Christian name and Hayes was a middle name taken from her mother's maiden name. The actress kept these names for the stage. Helen Hayes was in fact just as she looked—a distant cousin. I only learned this much later when I browsed through her autobiography. What I suspected, however, was that Lucy, who never cared much for or had anything to do with her husband's family, didn't actually know that and had made a lucky guess. Why not assume that the most famous Hayes of her time was family? And who among the Hayeses wanted to be the jerk who would ruin a good story with a few facts? It was a good thing for Lucy's telling of the family's glory that she did not live long enough to hear the name of Isaac Hayes. When asked where in Ireland the family came from, Lucy replied with one word, *Waterford,* leaving the inference that, matters of theatrical talent aside, the Hayeses had something to do with expensive cut-glass crystal.

Lucy kept an Irish flag in the closet of her dining room. It never came out, even on St. Patrick's Day. The Irish tricolor of green, white, and orange stayed in Lucy's closet as her way of making a statement about our Irish heritage. Her father had made the same point by naming his favorite son Parnell* and starting a family tradition that each

---

* Often celebrated as the uncrowned king of Ireland, Charles Stewart Parnell (1846-1891) was the dominant figure in the late nineteenth century in the movements for Irish home rule and land reform. Although an Anglo-Irish landowner, Parnell enjoyed strong support among the Irish peasantry for his advocacy of land reform and opposition to forced eviction of the tenants. The revelation in 1889 that he had a long-standing affair with a married woman with whom he had fathered three children brought his political career to an end in scandal. The Irish Catholic hierarchy had long distrusted the Protestant Parnell and issued a resolution in 1890 condemning as immoral his personal life. Incidentally, Parnell visited Minnesota in 1880 where he met with the Coadjutor Bishop (and future Archbishop) John Ireland.

generation gave a son the name of Ireland's most celebrated (and contro-versial) national hero, and with it the ambivalence the name implied. It was the point Lucy tried unconvincingly to make in 1959 when she ridi-culed all the Irish who were voting for John F. Kennedy simply because he was Irish, and then, after having voted twice for Eisenhower, cast her ballot for Kennedy too.

THE HAYESES OF KILROSSANTY

A few place names mentioned without context, an inexplicable fam-ily pride, and an otherwise impenetrable silence were all that passed from one generation to the next regarding our family's Irish history. At any rate, that's all I was given. Baptisms, marriages, and deaths waited in the records of the Church of St. Brigid for anyone willing to make the trip back to my great-grandfather Hayes's place of birth, Kilrossanty Parish, County Waterford. I made that trip. Archives in Dublin and Waterford, I later learned, documented a great-great grandfather's ten-ant contracts for land and condemned a few distant relatives to death for treason against the crown. And I came upon a book written by an Irish historian describing the forced evictions or "clearances" of peasants from the region during the famine of 1845-48. My family was one of them. Local records placed my family on one of the ships that sailed from New Ross to Quebec, one of the most well- documented and infamous routes of the transatlantic passage of the Famine Irish. In Kilrossanty, a mass grave dating from the Famine summed up the place of the Hayeses in Irish history. The muteness of the boulder on the site of the mass grave made a point. The story of my family's Irish history is better told by its stone silence than by all the facts I uncovered in scholarly monographs and the crypts of archives or by anything I can tell you by breaking their code silence and telling their story now.

In the spring of 1846, early on in Ireland's Great Hunger, the word came down from a Lord Fitzwilliam that the Hayeses were to be evicted, along with many other tenants on his lands spreading across Waterford, Wexford, and Wicklow Counties. It made no difference that they were contract tenants for two lots, or that they had paid their rent even though the potatoes had come up black in the last harvest, or that for as long as anyone could remember they had raised oats, barley, and livestock for Lord Fitzwilliam and the potatoes for themselves in fields along the Mahon River. If they were at fault, it lay in the hubris of the belief that the beauty of the valley, with its crown of the Comereagh mountains and the Mahon River keening like a song from the waterfalls above to the parish below, was God's promise that Kilrossanty was blessed. The parish's Holy Well of St. Brigid, they further believed, had preserved the Hayeses during other times of trouble, as when Cromwell's army had been quartered in nearby Kilmacthomas, and when the English troops later took away and hanged an uncle for his part in the rebellion of 1798. St. Brigid would see that they could last this one out too. But she wouldn't. The water in her holy well turned black in 1846.

For my great grandfather James ("Big Jim"), the youngest of the four Hayes brothers of that generation, leaving was not so bad. His father's contract for two lots gave the family more than twenty acres. It was more land than most had even when subdivided. Nearly half had already gone to Big Jim's older brothers Tim and John, who were married and had children. A few corners here and there had to be given to some cousins on his mother's side of the family–the Walshes. Someday, when they married, Big Jim and his brother Mick hoped to work what land was left.

But in the fall of 1845, the drills had been black with rotted potatoes, and the winter had been hungry. By early spring the green hills of Comereagh were black with fear. In March, Lord Fitzwilliam's agent told the Hayeses they must leave before the rent came due in early May. By April, there had been talk of what was happening to the west, where the farmers were being forced off the land, sent like cattle to the ports, and shipped off to God knows where. The Hayeses fared a little better: Lord Fitzwilliam would provide an allowance of food, clothing, and a pittance of schillings, see that they got to New Ross, and pay for their fares to Canada, where they would be given land.

Staying on in Ireland wasn't a choice. The Hayeses had seen what had happened the previous year, with evictions in nearby villages and royal troops stationed in the Mahon Valley to see that the starving and now-homeless Irish didn't touch their landlords' crops and livestock, or try to live on in the piles of rocks that had once been their cottages. They had seen what happened to those who refused to leave and were forced out at gun point by the sheriff on eviction day, to be followed by a bunch of local louts who had become adept at "tumbling" and could utterly destroy eight houses in three hours and get paid five shillings, no less, for the job.

Going to the work house wasn't a choice either. Others were chasing rumors of public work at the work house in nearby Dungarvan, but it was so over-crowded that families were sleeping in the halls. And they were the lucky ones. The warden had closed the doors saying they could take no more.

When, later in '46, the Relief Commission in Dungarvan declared that there would be no more public work, riots broke out. The royal troops fired at the crowd, wounding several and leaving at least two dead on the streets. The story made it into the English newspapers. Things were no better at the work houses in Cork, Limerick, and Skibberdeen. With the work house closed, the only other choice would be to take to the roads living like homeless wanderers and ending up on the streets of Cork, Limerick, Waterford, or Dublin in such poverty that it made the tinkers look like lords.

For the choice they *did* make there was something of a precedent. Since the 1830s, Lord Fitzwilliam had lured tenants off his estate lands with promises of "passage and support" and land in Canada. They also knew that something worse than the poor house was all that was left for them in County Waterford. By taking Fitzwilliam's offer, the older brothers, Tim and John, could tell their wives that they knew what they were doing. They didn't. But neither did they know how much worse it would soon become for those who were spared the disgrace of the first evictions. What seemed like a better fate in 1846—to stay on the land—became a curse in 1847, the worst year of the famine. By winter, the black fever, the "bloody flux," and even cholera struck Kilrossanty and the other parishes of the Mahon Valley.

My great grandfather, uncles and aunts left before the plagues finished off the work of the famine. Had they stayed, their future in Kilrossanty would have been a short journey to a mass grave. Their parents, my great-great grandparents, John and Mary, were left behind, protected only by the landlord's agent's flimsy promise of soup and Indian meal. They died of the "black fever" early in the spring of 1847. They lie now in an unmarked mass grave in the northeastern corner of a cemetery by the ruins of the Church of St. Brigid, in ground so close that they might almost touch the healing waters of St. Brigid's Well.

For five generations, nothing was said of these Hayeses who stayed behind. A hundred and sixty years later, when I made the journey back to Kilrossanty, I discovered I was not the first Hayes in recent times to make the trip. Another Hayes, a distant relative, had made the journey before me. Her name was Ellen Hayes. In 1982, she came home to rest with the family. Beneath her name on the grave stone were added the names of more than twenty other Hayeses who had perished during the Great Hunger and been laid to rest there anonymously. Until then, from 1847 to 1982, only the occasional anonymous remembrance that came when strangers above ground whispered the Sorrowful Mysteries of the Rosary acknowledged my family's presence in the unmarked mass grave of Kilrossanty.

In 1846, my great grandfather, uncles and aunts, sailed from New Ross to Quebec, one of the most well-documented and infamous routes of the transatlantic passage of the Famine Irish. They were fortunate to be sailing when ships still kept their passengers in steerage to the legal limit of 176; the next year the "coffin ships" began to disembark with more than three hundred passengers stuffed into the hold. The following April the *Dunbrody* sailed out of New Ross carrying such a load of passengers already racked with "ship fever." More than half died at sea and the rest arrived at Grosse Isle in the St. Lawrence only to be welcomed by quarantine in a stone infirmary ironically called "The Lazaretto." Most died there and were buried in mass graves on the island.

A century and a half later, I find some consolation in the knowledge that my great grandfather Big Jim escaped such horrors, though his were bad enough. Big Jim himself didn't know at the time, and could take no consolation from the fact that he had survived Ireland's Great Hunger, which cut her population in half, killing at least two million and casting another two million out to foreign shores. He would have only known that life as he knew it had come to an end from hell.

Before the family departed there was one last night in Kilrossanty, with songs, dancing, and more than a drop of home-brew—poitín—in the hall of St. Brigid. Father John Casey, who had baptized all the local Hayeses, stayed until dawn. In the morning, a mass was said on the ruins of the Church of St. Brigid and Father John blessed them one last time. They were loaded into a wagon and escorted by soldiers who were there to prevent them from fleeing, thus becoming a roadside spectacle during the day's ride from the Comereagh Mountains to the harbor at New Ross. They slept on the docks there and left the next morning. The ship's captain let them stand on the deck as they sailed down the Barrow into Waterford Harbor, past the ruins of the monastery at Churchtown and the lighthouse at Hook Head. It was the last piece of Ireland they would ever see. By that time the sense of loss had already set in and they stared back as the Ireland of their wretched poverty sank below the horizon and in its place rose the new Ireland of their nostalgia. And who could blame them for overlooking that it was their dear Ireland that had given them the shame of eviction and the stench of seven to eight weeks in foul steerage? Who could blame them for wanting instead to believe that they were part of another Ireland that their grandchildren would know through the songs of Bing Crosby?

A Yeoman in Ontario

Not much was said in our house about the Hayeses life in Ontario, though there was a story about three ancient aunts who arrived from Toronto dressed in black, prayed the rosary night and day, and drove Grandma Lucy up a wall. Somewhere in the back of my head, I also seemed to recall that my grandfather Nick had been a lawyer in Toronto.

The way things turned out my life had its own Ontario chapter. My childhood summers were spent visiting my mother's sister, Aunt Eva, and her husband, Uncle Keith, in Ottawa. A childless couple, they doted on me, taking me to just about every tourist attraction in Ontario and Quebec that they thought might entertain their American nephew or persuade him that there was life outside Minnesota. Uncle Keith brought me to the yacht clubs of Toronto, the marina, and the neighborhood of the city's old establishment where he had spent parts of his childhood, and where his aging father stretched out a graceful retirement wearing his son's generosity to clothe his genteel poverty. I put my Grandfather Nick's childhood there. I made him an honors graduate in law from the University of Toronto and placed his family home among the stately late-Victorian mansions of Toronto's Anglo-Scot gentry. In fact the Ontario Hayeses never set foot in those old Toronto clubhouses, or belonged to any *other* club, for that matter. But my exaggerated version of my grandfather's biography could be forgiven. Information was scanty. Grandfather Nick let a few photographs of sisters in Toronto do the talking about the family's Ontario lives and they didn't say much.

One aspect of the Ontario story could be taken as evidence that just maybe St. Brigid was keeping an eye on Kilrossanty's children. It was a miracle that all of them—four brothers, two wives, and four children—made it across the ocean alive. The phrase "coffin ships" was coined to describe these ships carrying the Famine Irish from New Ross to Canada. St. Brigid also spared my family from the quarantine that detained tens of thousands on Grosse Isle and left 6,000 of them in a mass grave. They travelled on without interruption along a route that since the 1820s had transported the Irish up the St. Lawrence to York and on to the frontier of "Upper Canada." Land was waiting. Each of the four Hayes boys received a homestead grant for 100 acres of rolling hills, woods, and prairie meadows about five miles from Barrie at Oro Township along the shores of Lake Simcoe. How they survived the first winter is anybody's guess, though it probably owed something to the kindness of strangers—and to Lord Fitzwilliam's shillings.

According to provincial records, in the first year they raised cabins for the two older brothers and their families. Over the next ten years they added barns and two-story wood frame farm houses with lumber felled from the pines that covered almost half their lands. In time, Big Jim took a fancy to a Mary Balfe, who had come to Barrie with her folks from Carnew in County Wicklow. The Balfes claimed they had once been lords, though during the Famine they had come over like everybody else. Anyway, they weren't Hayeses. Mary brought a touch of pretense along with her wedding chest when she married Big Jim in 1858, using the contents to furnish not only her household but also the belief that she and Jim were a little better than all those other Hayeses.

Big Jim and Mary had reason to take pride in the farm they created out of a hundred acres of wilderness along the eastern shores of Lake Simcoe. The census of 1871 documented that they had a farmhouse, barn, a plough, and a horse-drawn wagon called a "democrat" that could carry twelve people. It also exposed a bountiful land that folks back in Kilrossanty would not have believed. One acre could produce 150 bushels of potatoes, six cultivated acres yielded 150 bushels of wheat, and other fields produced an abundance of turnips, hay, and grazing lands for a livestock herd that counted two oxen, 33 milking cows, 10 heifers, five sheep, and five pigs. Not bad for those times. For a tenant from Kilrossanty who would have shared two lots of stones with his three brothers and could not have even called the thatch roof over his head his own, Big Jim had made it. The census tipped its hat to this cottager from Kilrossanty. The census taker wrote down that Big Jim was not a cottager, nor a tenant, but a "yeoman." But the inability of Big Jim and Mary to read or write, some three decades after they had left Ireland, was also duly noted in the census. When the time came, Big Jim marked his will with an "X."

In 1861, a daughter, Alice, was born. Mary gave him eight more children over the next two decades, five sons and three daughters, before she was gone in 1886.

The farming was good. The work was hard. Yet for all his work, Big Jim felt his reward was a lack of respect and gratitude from his sons, and a cloud of recrimination cast a shadow on the last years of the Hayes farm. Big Jim never let drop a grudge against his sons, who seemed to like every place in Canada but the family farm. The oldest, John, went all the way to Vancouver, luring a younger brother away with him. The next eldest, Tom, wasn't much good at the farm work anyway. It was just as well that the Blessed Virgin appeared to him in a dream and called him to be a priest and teach people in Michigan how to pray the rosary. One by one, all his sons left. Of his girls, only Kate, his youngest (and favorite) married. She and her husband Frank moved to Toronto.

Big Jim was hardest on his youngest son, Nick, who had gotten the idea that he was too good to farm. Mary put that idea in his little head before she died in 1886. In 1893, Big Jim sent Nick to a fancy school—St. Michael's College in Toronto. He didn't see much point in it but he had made a promise to Mary. When Nick graduated in 1895, he had top marks for "piety, regularity, application, neatness" and near the top in "religion, Latin, and English." His grades dropped a bit in math and history. A son who wrote, read, and spoke Latin wasn't going back to the farm.

In 1895, Nick enrolled in the Osgoode Hall Law School—Law Society of Upper Canada. He only stayed for one term. The last of Big

Jim's sons had decided to try his luck out West. In the summer of 1897, he bought a ticket from Toronto to Chicago, from there to Minneapolis and the Great West beyond. He had a friend in a place called Bismarck, and not the one in Ontario. He would try his luck there, and if that didn't work, he would see if there was any truth to the stories his brothers in Vancouver had sent back home.

With his sons gone and daughter Kate in Toronto, Big Jim settled into an old age on the farm with his three older daughters. He lived longer than most Hayeses and when he died in 1904, Father O'Malley laid him down to rest beside Mary in the Cemetery of St. Mary in Barrie. In his will, he left a share of the farm to Father Tom; it ended up in a mitered felon's pocket. To his other six sons he gave one dollar apiece. The girls got the rest. The farm was sold and the three older daughters moved to live near Kate in Toronto where they settled in to the life of maiden ladies. The three lived together, spending the rest of their days in widow's black and mumbling the rosary making their final years a lengthy expression of grief and a rebuke to Nick, who needed to be continually reminded what a good father he had.

THE *POLONAISE* OF THE PRAIRIE

In the Midwest, every place has to have another place nearby that it looks down upon and compares itself favorably to. When you live in Minnesota, you're surrounded by them. The one that figured prominently in our family lore was North Dakota. Growing up in Minneapolis, we listened to Grandma Lucy's stories of her North Dakota winters—the snows, the winds, and more about the winds. It made Minnesota seem like a tropical paradise. It was only much later that I was drawn to the romance of our family's version of *Little House on the Prairie*.

When the story of Lucy's mother, my great grandmother Anne O'Brien, showed up in a young professor's National Endowment for the Humanities grant proposal, the historian in me suspected that a modern day feminist had made it all up and planted the evidence in the archives in Bismarck. There she was—a single mother on the North Dakota prairie in a time when her neighbors were more likely to be Ojibwa or Lakota than Irish, the manager of a farm, and a hotel proprietor whose guests arrived by covered wagon, horseback or stage coach. Perhaps she knew that generations later we would question her story. So, she wrote it all down for her skeptical great grandson to read nearly a century later.

The story of the O'Brien's emigration from Ireland was similar to the Hayeses, though they left earlier—in 1845—with a group of families evicted from plots of land near Limerick. They were shipped out of Galway and settled in Belleville, Ontario. Yet somehow, Anne's telling of this familiar story comes off sounding more like Moses leading the Israelites across the Red Sea than the slave's tale of the Hayeses and just about everyone else that Ireland had dumped in Canada. By the same token, if Big Jim was determined to show that his Ontario farm was about as good as things can get in an Irish life, Anne's tale showed that things could be better.

At the end of the 1870s, the O'Briens gave up on three decades of farming in Belleville, Ontario, and took another try at emigration. Three of my great uncles settled in Michigan's Upper Peninsula; one great aunt chanced to settle in the most beautiful landscape anyone in my family had seen since they left Ireland—Grand Marais, Minnesota; and, my great-grandfather Michael, accompanied by his wife Anne and his father John, homesteaded just across the Canadian border in the Dakota Territory.

The move to the Dakota Territory was my great grandparents' honeymoon. They left shortly after their wedding in 1879. Michael told his bride that he was taking her to the most beautiful place God had created in all the land between Ontario and Utah. The jewel of God's creation was the Pembina Hills or, as Michael called it, "the mountain" of the Dakota Territory. In 1877, Michael had travelled west from Ontario in search of land in the U.S. to homestead somewhere along the proposed railroad lines. He went as far west as Salt Lake City. The visit only confirmed his Catholic skepticism about the theological foundations behind the endless proliferation of Protestant sects since Martin Luther's day. Michael happened to be in Salt Lake City the day Brigham Young died, August 29, 1877. Pandemonium broke loose. Better to have the Sioux, Chippewa, Cree, and Métis for neighbors than Mormons, Michael decided, and he retreated back to a homestead claim on land at the westernmost edge of the platted world in the late 1870s—a place in the Dakota Territory that sometimes belonged to a township

Above: Michael O'Brien;
Right: Anne Halloran O'Brien.

called St. Joseph, sometimes to Leroy (and "new" Leroy), and, most of the time, to a town named after the mother of Russia—Olga. He might have oversold Anne on his Dakota paradise. His in-laws, the Hallorans, invited themselves along when the family moved in the summer of 1879 from Belleville to the Pembina Hills.

You could have written a book about Anne's first winter in the Dakota Territory. In fact, someone did. A century later my sons read the story of that first winter as told by Laura Ingalls Wilder in *The Long Winter.* Wilder's family moved in the same year as Anne's to the Dakota Territory and faced, like my great grandparents, a grim struggle for survival in the longest and cruelest winter in the history of the northern prairie.

The O'Briens were not the first to claim the land Michael had chosen. In 1848, the last and most deadly battle between the Pembina Chippewa and the Sioux tribes bloodied the hills over the hunting rights to land that in a generation became the pastures and timberland of the O'Brien's. An abandoned Catholic Church, a log framed building, served as Anne's nuptial bower for her first days in the Dakota Territory. They divided the building into three rooms. The front and entry room served as a small store. Two other rooms made do as their living quarters.

The O'Briens were not alone. The structure had a two-room lean-to. One of the lean-to rooms housed a Métis woman and her children. She was the healer of the river valley, dispensing medicinal herbs, potions, roots, and other cures to the ailing. A French-Canadian priest lived in the second room of the lean-to. He brought the sacraments and interceded with the saints on behalf of the Métis and the handful of new Irish Catholic immigrants in the area. Unable to speak English, the priest resorted to Latin when he addressed the O'Briens. They silently nodded their heads in agreement no matter what the priest said and did their best to maintain the fiction that all Catholics were at home in the native tongue of ancient Rome.

That fall Michael laid claim to 80 acres of timberland standing about three miles from their first home. He cleared a few of the pines and then trimmed and planed them into boards to construct a makeshift one room hovel. His original idea was to use the log hut as a shelter and storage room while clearing the land and then to construct a more proper place to house his wife and their first child, who was due in April. But winter arrived early that year, intent on going down in memory not just as a season but as a myth. And as the hard winter set in, another settler filed a competing claim to the land. In February, Michael left his wife to make the trip to Pembina on the Minnesota border and assert his right to the land. To substantiate his claim, Michael had to swear that his family lived on the land. For a few days, during which temperatures dropped to minus 50 degrees, Anne O'Brien, seven months pregnant, stayed alone in an improvised log shack.

Four decades later, she re-told the story in the Langdon newspaper. *The house was not yet completed*, she wrote, *and the door was not yet finished so as to close entirely. With the thermometer registering between forty and fifty below zero the house was almost uninhabitable.* In the late afternoons she could make out the profile on a hill of three Chippewa on horseback, wrapped in blankets. She did not know if they were there to protect her, or if were they waiting for her to die … or if she had really seen them at all.

Michael defended his claim successfully, and the next year the shack grew into a comfortable log home. Within three years, the O'Briens moved to a finished wood frame house and farmlands higher up in "the mountain." French priests performed and recorded in French the baptisms of their six children and confirmed the sacred legitimacy of their marriage. A French priest gave the last rights, said the funeral mass, and

The O'Brien family home, Langdon, North Dakota. Left to right: Anne, Parnell, Lucy, Maud, Tess, Lil, Mark

blessed the grave of the family's last living tie to Ireland when Michael's father, John, died and was buried in Olga in 1890.

As far as Anne could remember, virtually every night their farm home served as the overnight lodging for farmers moving grain and supplies by oxcart to and from Canada. Often pioneers in covered wagons, firm in the belief that just a little further west there had to be better land, also stayed and rested a few days at the O'Brien farm. There were others, some of them found half-frozen in the snow, who found temporary refuge at the O'Brien's farm.

This constant stream of lodgers, who were expected only to pay with an evening of conversation, gave Michael the idea of buying a hotel in nearby Langdon. Not long afterward, the murder of a neighboring farm wife and the lynching of the suspect moved him to public outrage. Wasn't it about time for the law of savagery to end and the rule of law to begin? His passion and, no less, his impressive vocabulary, resulted in his election to two terms as the local sheriff.

Michael had made his mark on the local community, and eventually he put his name on the map as well. Part of his farm on "the mountain" became O'Brien's Coulee and O'Brien State Park, known to tourists, hunters, back-packers, and skiers far and wide. The Lakota and the Pembina Ojibwa continued to call the O'Brien's land by another name and returned to "the mountain" from time to time to venerate the blood of their ancestors.

The American chapter of Michael's life was short. Anne gave him six children. He gave her a prosperous farm, a thriving hotel business in Langdon, and the honor of a family pew in the front of that prairie parish church. Her life without him was described as that of a living saint, she being a widow at the age of 38 with four girls and two boys to raise on her own. In 1895, the story of Michael's untimely death from "apoplexy" at the age of 43 made it to the front page of the newspaper in Bismarck. To recognize that a pillar of the Church of St. Joseph in Olga had been lost, the parish took up a collection to commission his portrait in stained glass. To this day, placed among the elongated windows of the Church of St. Joseph, Michael still looks down on the praying Catholics of Langdon, North Dakota. From the day of Michael's death in 1895 to her own death in 1923, Anne wore a widow's black. With elaborate matching hats, ruffles and hints of crinoline in her dresses, she wore her sorrow with panache. It found its perfect detail in the cameo brooch she wore on her neck, which held an inlaid photograph of her late, dear husband. Without her husband and with only two sons, a twelve-year old with a bad heart and an eight year old who spent most of his time in church, Anne had to make it on her own. She sold the hotel in Langdon. Her money and heart went into making her home into the cultural standard for North Dakota gentry.

Meanwhile, my grandfather Nick had been keen on cutting his ties to Canada. His great railway adventure in the summer of 1897 turned into a one-way ticket to Langdon, North Dakota. A friend set him up with a banking job in the one horse, store-front street that passed for the town of Neche. He wasn't going back to Ontario where Big Jim and his sisters blamed him, not his older brothers, for the inevitable end of the family farm. A job in hand in the semblance of a bank in Neche was a better bet than the two or more dreams in the bush that his brothers chased in the Yukon and British Columbia. He decided to stay. He acquired U.S. citizenship in 1902 and let everyone know he wasn't going back to Canada.

An iron safe with a desk beside it passed for the bank in Neche. But things picked up. Nick moved to another bank in Dresden which had a teller's window.

Nearly six feet tall, broad in the shoulders, with piercing blue eyes and chestnut red hair, Nick had stepped off the train in Langdon as if sent by central casting in Dublin to play the lead in a melodrama about a handsome lad who had all the Irish girls' hearts atwitter in those dusty North Dakota towns. When he first showed up one Sunday at mass and filed into a pew at the Church of St. Joseph, more than a few bonnets spun his way and drew sharp looks from parents watchful of their daughters' reputations. The rumor that he was bachelor and a lawyer from Canada had made the rounds of the pews by the time people were mumbling the Prayers at the Foot of the Altar. As the faithful beseeched God's intercession on behalf of their good and holy Bishop Shanley in Fargo and the even better and holier Archbishop Ireland in far away St. Paul, normally pious young women prayed, *Oh, God make him look my way.*

The youngest of Anne O' Brien's children, Tess, wrote in her diary that her three sisters—Maude, Lucy, and Lillie—took a little more time and squabbled a bit more each Sunday as they fussed about and readied themselves for church.

When Nick finally did pay a call one Sunday afternoon at the O'Brien's farm in Olga, they had a lot to say.

And it was there that Nick found something that Big Jim, Mary, and his brothers and sisters lacked. Anne and her children knew how to read and write. Anne had sent her girls and son Mark to be educated at the Catholic academies for girls and boys, St. Mary's and St. Paul's, in far away Winnipeg. By the time Nick showed up, Anne had made their farm home in Olga into a matriarchy with culture. They had a grand piano in the parlor. Anne's girls had access to a family library, and could quote more than one or two poets; they played something called a "Polonaise" on the family piano. They had a certain something. To drive the point home, Anne's youngest son was named Parnell, as if he were destined to be the president of the Irish Free State of North Dakota. As if to redeem the name, Parnell O'Brien accepted God's call at an early age and, after graduation from eighth grade, entered the novitiate of the Passionist Fathers.

Nick set his heart on the second oldest of the girls, Lucy—the one with a laugh that crackled like a prairie fire in August and long fingers that played the piano like it was a harp. By Irish standards, theirs was

Anne O'Brien and Parnell

a short courtship. It was only nine years. Finally, it happened that Nick came to call on Lucy at the farm in Olga with some sense of urgency. A job offer from a bank in the oil boom town of Williston forced Nick to make his intentions known. With Michael O'Brien casting a kaleidoscope of light on them from the Church window, Nick and Lucy were married in the Church of St. Joseph and headed west to Williston.

In 1907, Lucy named her first born Anna, after her mother; her first son, my father, was born in 1909. Lucy named him after her brother Mark—the one with a weak heart—thinking, perhaps, that her brother might not be around much longer.

Williston was as far west as Nick got. This restlessness had to stop. He had brothers who pushed as far west as you could go only to flounder about in Vancouver. He took to heart the lesson of the uncle on his mother's side who found his pot of gold out West in the form of a gold claim in the Yukon, only to be murdered by a claim jumper. It was time to retreat east. Minneapolis, Minnesota was as good a place as any for the long road of the Hayes from Kilrossanty to end.

3

The Parish Dunphy Built

My job is to carve men out of boys.

          – Father John Dunphy (1884-1963)

We thought that when we came face to face with
Almighty God on that final judgment day.
He would not be long haired, like the statues,
but bald-headed, like Father Dunphy.

          – Bernard Casserly, *The Catholic Bulletin* (1963)

During the long afternoons when my father was in St. Mary's Hospital, I did not know the old priest's name. I only knew that he had a special place in my father's life. He came to the hospital every day to see my father. Other priests came too. They walked in the room with a hearty, *Well, how's everyone doing today?* They stepped to his bedside and started a conversation with, *Mark, how do you feel today?* Silence hung in the air for a moment, finally broken with a sentence about how this or that church building project was doing or how Father So-and-So said to say hello. The other priests quickly shifted gears and drove the conversation past my father to the easier task of making small talk with my mother or with me, the little boy playing on the floor with a new red fire truck. *I suppose you want to be an architect when you grow up,* Father Novak once asked me. When I replied, *No, I want to be a fireman;* the priest fumbled for words and settled on an annoyed, *Ah, huh.*

The old priest was different from the others. He ignored me, letting me concentrate on my fire truck. He greeted my mother properly with a *How are you, Mrs. Hayes* in a tone that let her know that no reply was

Father John Dunphy

necessary or expected. He pulled up a chair beside the hospital bed. *Mark,* he said so slowly and kindly that the one word seemed in itself to be a long, fondly remembered story. He didn't let an instant pass because he knew how a fraction of a second would bring on the agony that lay behind my father's silence. The old priest jumped ahead with sentences that started with, *Remember when, you used to...,* or, *Now, there was a character if I ever knew one ...* swiftly transporting the two of them out of the hospital room at St. Mary's and into in another place and time of boxing gyms, basketball games and stories from the old neighborhood that my mother and I didn't know.

1602 Dupont Av N

> *The North Side has never been a glamorous past of Minneapolis. It has no lake district or scenic river gorge to recommend it, and it is literally on the other side of the tracks, separated from downtown Minneapolis by the city's oldest rail corridor along Third Avenue North. ... However, the North Side has a few pockets of exceptional homes, including a group of elaborate Queen Annes around 16th and Dupont Avenues.*
>
> – Larry Millett, *AIA Guide to the Twin Cities*

By the time I came to visit the old neighborhood of my father's youth, the Irish-Americans had been gone for more than a generation. Mass at old Father Dunphy's Church of the Ascension was said more often in Spanish than English and the old Latin was reduced to cameo appearances in the Holy Week services. Old timers, who long ago moved out of the neighborhood, returned for Mass on Saturday afternoons, milled about in the vestibule for a few minutes afterwards, and left their childhoods behind in their rear view mirrors as they drove back to the suburbs. These days I often join them. Inside the church, heads seem to turn in my direction, making me believe for a moment that they spot some family resemblance in my face until I correct myself. My face is older than any remembered image of my father, aunts and uncles they might have.

Elsewhere in the neighborhood, I look over my shoulder as I walk down the main street, West Broadway. The "No Loitering Police Order" sign at the entrance of Brix's grocery tells me that no one inside the store remembers the Hayeses.

It was not always so. In March 1942, about to depart for Africa, my father wrote down his address in his diary as 1602 Dupont Avenue N, Minneapolis, Minnesota, U.S.A. It didn't matter that he had lived for the past year with his wife and first child in an apartment in south Minneapolis, or that for the previous five years he had lived in St. Louis and Rochester, Minnesota. 1602 Dupont Avenue N was the address of his heart and his title to a piece of the parish he had never really left. Whenever he used the phrase "back at the house," you knew he meant the house on Dupont that his father had bought for the family in 1919.

Anna, Jim and Mark Hayes

If Nick ever called any place home, it certainly wasn't North Dakota. In the spring of 1914, having spent seventeen-odd years in that largely flat and somewhat desolate state, his employment inquiries paid off with a job offer as a claims adjustor with the Hartford Fire Insurance Company in Minneapolis. He and Lucy moved into a house in the southeast section of the city along with daughter Anna and son Mark. Two more children, Jim and John, were born there. But it was the house he bought five years later—the house on Dupont Ave N—that became fixed in memory. From 1919 on, the family was known as the Hayeses on Dupont.

Minneapolis was going somewhere and leaving St. Paul behind. The capitol city would be the lost Midwest of Nick Carraway's childhood. Most people would know it only from images in the novels and short stories of its most famous literary son as a place of innocence and grandeur lost. Minneapolis had no time for nostalgia and rushed ahead to a future as a "modern" city. Back East (and for Minneapolis this meant east of the Mississippi) cities pandered to themselves with world class dreams. With the Columbia Exhibition, Chicago had thrown down the gauntlet to out-do New York. Minneapolis passionately embraced the second rate dream of outdoing St. Paul, Fargo, Omaha and whatever else dared to call itself a city out on the Great Plains.

The waves of Scandinavian immigration had come to an end. Protestant Minneapolis had to put aside its scruples and turn to second generation Catholics—the Irish, Germans and even some Poles—who had to be enticed from the farms to provide the mill city's manpower. The city still drew the line on some things. It went out of its way to make its handful of Jewish immigrants unwelcome and to cultivate a national reputation for anti-Semitism. It steered the newcomers to neighborhoods on the North Side or across the river in the city's Northeast and Southeast neighborhoods. On the South Side, Minneapolis drained its swamps and wetlands and re-routed the flow of water into a chain of lakes and creeks. They gave the parks and waterways names from Henry Longfellow's "Song of Hiawatha" and bequeathed them to the city's Lutherans. They were the heirs of the scenic core of a fabled City of Lakes. On the North Side, Minneapolis had decided that the population of second generation working class immigrants never had and never would read Longfellow and didn't need parks and waterways anyway. Instead, the city filled in the wetlands of the North Side and ran its unsung waterway, Basset Creek underground through a culvert that flowed beneath cheap, newly erected housing and businesses on its way to the Mississippi.

Nick's choice of a neighborhood showed his knowledge that even the North Side had its social pecking order. He moved within a heartbeat of the Church of the Ascension, the hub of Irish-American Minneapolis. He chose to live among the respectable families who clustered in the two and three story homes along the avenues west of Lyndale. This was the North Side's answer to the South Side's presumptive claim to a monopoly of Minneapolis's middle class. The lifeline of the neighborhood was 20th Street, though the completion of the streetcar line in 1914 had sparked a boom and also inspired a name change to West Broadway. The cluster of businesses on Broadway had lost out to Hennepin and Nicollet Avenues in the race to be the city's downtown. Never mind, West Broadway was giving its best shot at becoming Minneapolis's thriving mid-town. The street proliferated with clothing and fashion shops, movie theaters, restaurants, its own department store, and four groceries. The Hayeses shopped at Brix's Grocery, where the owner, Richard Brix, boasted that there wasn't a grocery store on the South Side that could match his—not even that fancy pants Hove's store in Edina.

The house that Nick bought was right in the heart of it all—six blocks west of Lyndale, three blocks south of West Broadway, a block away from Ascension, and a

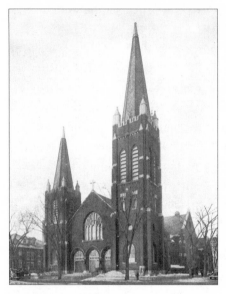

stone's throw away from North Commons Park. It was a corner house standing back and away from the street, surrounded by a lawn approaching the size of two city lots with clusters of oak, evergreens and birch. You entered through the large screen porch that faced Dupont. The living room invited you to lounge in stuffed davenports and arm chairs with your feet resting on an ottoman. A closet held four seasons' worth of the family's coats and jackets, with space left over for the O'Brien's

Church of the Ascension, Minneapolis, ca 1934.

heirloom Irish flag. A guest bedroom just off the dining room was home to a steady stream of North Dakota expatriates. Across from the dining room, a den provided space for culture with a library shelved in Lucy's dark walnut bookcases, her beloved piano, the Victrola and its '78's, a writing desk, and the Crosley cathedral radio. The telephone hung on a wall in the den. It rang constantly, and not only because it was a party line, or because my aunts, first Anna and then Eileen, were so pretty and popular. It rang so often because the Hayes' telephone number was only one number off from Richard Brix's grocery. Usually, the Hayes boys were helpful when folks called in for groceries to be delivered and gave them the correct number. Then again, it always got a laugh when one of them decided to take down the order, go over various requests, and offer a few suggestions of their own. Jim in particular thought this was funny. Lucy held back laughter and with feigned irritation made one of the children call in or run over to Brix's with the delivery order.

The kitchen was the largest room of the house, and on weekdays meals were served at the kitchen table by the stove. At the other end of the room, an ice box stood in the corner where a wooden door for the ice man opened from the outside. The back door went out from the kitchen into another screen porch and from there to 16th Street. For the children, the best part was the secret stairs leading to the second floor. Instead of using the appropriate main mahogany stairway that ascended from the living room, they preferred to race up and down the back stairs that took off from the kitchen. This was called the escape route when fights started upstairs.

Though demography was the natural enemy of extra sleeping space in any Catholic home, my father could recall a time of luxury uncommon in Catholic family homes when Anna and he had their own bedrooms. The younger boys, Jim and John, shared a room. Lucy and Nick's master bedroom was large enough for three. Eileen was born in 1921 and, in 1924, fourteen years after my father's birth, the youngest of the family, Dave, was born. Sleeping arrangements adapted to the new realities. The girls, Anna and Eileen, took one room. Jim moved in with my father. Dave shared John's room. The family's collie, Ginger, laid claim to a piece of all the bedrooms by making the rounds and stopping in each for a little rest every night. Two kids to a bedroom was a high standard for the neighborhood. Few Irish families could indulge in the Hayes's extravagance of reserving its linen closet for nothing other than linens, or not pressing the den into service as an additional bedroom. You did not even have to count the extra bed in the master bedroom to make the arithmetic work. Two girls, four boys, and three bedrooms allowed the Hayeses the propriety of segregating their sons and daughters in separate rooms. This was an era when the concept of a second bathroom had not yet entered the minds of Midwestern city dwellers. The upstairs bathroom at Dupont, with its sink, commode, and tiger claw bathtub, met the Minneapolis standard for modern.

The guest room on the first floor was proof that Lucy was an inn keeper's daughter. She never knew how many North Dakota relatives she had until the rumor spreads across the northern prairie that they had

The House on Dupont, circa 1920. (Left to Right) My grandfather Nick, Uncle Jim, my Father (who is holding up the toddler, Uncle John).

a place to stay at her home in Minneapolis. The Lord had blessed the extended O'Brien clan with an inordinate number of vocations. There was a holy host of travelling priests—her second cousins or nephews twice removed—who appeared at her doorstep more often than anyone else ... and stayed longer.

The priests did not catch the hint that Lucy's house was a bit over-crowded or object when their accommodations were downgraded from the single suite of the guest room to a double occupancy in the bedroom of one of Lucy's boys. In 1934, Lucy's youngest sister, Tess, took over the guest room. The explanation for Tess's arrival was brief. Lucy told her children that their Aunt Tess would be staying with them for a while. Nothing was said of why Tess had left her own home on Minneapolis's South side or why her husband Arnie was not with her. He had in-vested his wife's inheritance in a short-lived enterprise that was in part a Minneapolis version of the Fuller Brush Company and in part a pyra-mid sales scam. Lucy herself seemed to have been his only customer. One winter morning in 1934, Arnie told Tess he would have a long day ahead peddling mops, brooms, and cleansers and wasn't exactly sure when he would be home. You could say there was a bit of honesty to his statement. He walked out of the house and never returned.

Uncle Arnie was seen again only once. Tess's nephew, my Uncle

John, one afternoon spotted his uncle Arnie standing in the line at the back door to the parish's rectory. Every afternoon, these men with broken lives could find a meal without a sermon in the rectory kitchen. By that time, Aunt Tess was a long-standing resident at Dupont. She supported herself by baking pastries in Lucy's kitchen and selling them at Brix's on Broadway. Her husband probably enjoyed these pastries, which came with the meals at the rectory and served as Arnie's way of staying in touch with his wife.

With time, things not mentioned become things that never happened. The "poor Tess" of the broken marriage was hushed into oblivion and in its stead appeared the "Oh, you know your Aunt Tess" who traded in consignment baking for a certificate from secretarial school and a working girl's life in Oklahoma City.

When Tess left Dupont, her brother Parnell took his turn at making the guest room his weekend home. He was Lucy's favorite sibling. He had entered the novitiate of the Passionist Fathers in his high school days, and the Passionists ordained him "Father Michael" and assigned him to the Monastery of St. Gabriel in Iowa. Most weekends, however, his ordained name and roman collar were left behind in Iowa, and the guest room at Dupont became his personal priory. When Parnell died in 1944, another Passionist, Father Pendergast, appeared at the door. Pendergast bore a striking resemblance to Parnell, which worked to his advantage when he introduced himself to Lucy's children—*You can just call me, little Parnell*—and then moved his overnight bag into the guest room.

Other changes were afoot. The stable in the backyard that had once been home to a pair of horses, a carriage, a two-seat wagon and a hay loft became the garage for Nick's Model T. Every morning around 7 you might have thought Lucy was blessing the garage. After hurrying out the back door, she would make the sign of the cross as she passed the garage and rushed down the alley reciting to herself the opening prayers of the mass. She always arrived a minute or two late but was invariably in sync with the congregation's responses to the priest.

Inside the house, the family's early life on the prairie was preserved in black and white studio photographs hanging on the walls. There were the posed Williston studio photos of Anna and my father as country bumpkins, an O'Brien family photo of Anne and her six children on

51

their farm house porch, and the somber photo of Nick's three maiden sisters back in Ontario in their spectral black dresses keeping an eye on little Nick.

The images on the fireplace mantle in the living room were snappier. New photos from Nick's Kodak Brownie showed Anna in a smart jumper and his oldest boy, Mark, in knickers, cardigan, and a tie. Another exhibited Anna as a pretty and sophisticated-looking eighth grader, standing beside Parnell, who held young Eileen in his arms. Parnell was now Father Michael to the rest of the world. A photo taken at his ordination showed the priest with a jaunty straw hat, a smile, and a wink reminding the family that though his name had changed, he was and would always be Parnell. There was one compromise among the portraits on the mantle: A portrait photo of Nick's brother in Michigan, Father Tom, stood as a reminder that there were two sides to the family and Nick better not forget where he came from.

My father used to say that Nick was a family man but he was not home much. His job as a claims adjustor for Hartford sent him on the road every week, Monday through Friday. He had a traditional sense of the chain of command in a family. My father was barely twelve when Nick took him fishing a few miles north of the city at Bass Lake one Saturday morning. My father's brothers Jim and John were left at home so Nick could talk to his oldest son. *You're the man in the house when I'm away*, he said. It was a statement of fact, not the start of a conversation.

Lazy-Ike was his next word. *They call this a Lazy-Ike, a guy in Iowa makes them.* He held the hand-carved wooden lure between his thumb and index finger. He held it in the same way the sisters had told my father at school a priest is consecrated to hold the Holy Communion Host.

Nick's attire that day indicated he was a gentlemen first and a sportsman second. He wore a white shirt, a tie knotted in a double Windsor, and dark summer-weight wool trousers. He wore a hat—not the round-brimmed felt banker's hat he favored for work days but a straw one with a short brim and a black silk band. (The next day, he would dress the same for Sunday mass, but substitute a grey felt hat and add a light-weight coat confirming that the Saturday trousers belonged to his summer suit.)

Nick dangled the Lazy-Ike on the line a moment to make sure his son was paying attention and after two or three swings sent the lure in a looping cast some thirty feet out into the lake. The lure plunked into the water with a splash, telling his son that everything was as it should be and the time for talk was over. Quiet. Lazy-Ike was listening to the fish.

After that, his siblings remember, my father always wore a tie. He usually loosened the knot by the neck and rolled his sleeves up to signal that he dressed well but was not a stuffed shirt.

He also decided that the time had come to let his siblings know that he smoked. Outside the house, my father's height and athletic talent gave him a free ride into the cliques and gangs of the neighborhood. It wasn't so easy for the younger and slighter brothers Jim and John. Jim had heart trouble. He lived under Lucy's caution not to exert himself. The neighborhood jerks were quick to tease Jim and he would return the compliment with quick twists of phrase that made fools out of them.

In another time, I retraced my father's steps through the old neighborhood. The house at 1602 Dupont N had been torn down and a HUD rambler built in its place. Lucy's blessing had worked. Only the old stable by the alley had survived and was there to welcome old family members back and share a few laughs over the old jokes.

THE PASTOR AND HIS PARISH

Fate was kind to Father John Dunphy putting him to rest in Calvary Cemetery before anyone in the Ascension Church choir had suggested singing "Kum-bye-ya", seven years before the interstate ploughed under the heart of the parish he had built in Minneapolis' North Side, and, as if to prove the infinite wisdom and mercy of Divine Providence, eleven days before the death of John F. Kennedy.

The rectory from where Dunphy ruled Ascension Parish is now empty except for two small offices for parish workers on the first floor. In 2006, while I was researching my father's involvement with the church and neighborhood, they kindly offered me the use of Dunphy's old office for the summer. At his desk, I sorted through the old records, newsletters, photographs, yearbooks, diaries, letters, and memorabilia left behind in the closets and storerooms that had become Ascension's version of the Vatican Archives. The windows of Dunphy's office looked out on the parish school, playground, Ascension Club, and the nave of the church. A block away, at the intersection of Dupont and West Broadway, the summer began with a brutal and senseless murder that put the old neighborhood back in the news. Sometimes it's true, things were better in the past.

When Bing Crosby played Father O'Malley in the 1947 movie *Going My Way*, the talk at the Ascension Women's Sodality was all about just how that sweet Father O'Malley reminded the ladies of their own dear Father Dunphy. The men of the parish had a different take on the movie. Dunphy never had the time of day for wimps in Roman collars like Bing Crosby's Father O'Malley.

There are only a handful left from my father's generation at Ascension, and they have lived more years outside of Ascension than within the parish. Yet, ask them a question about Dunphy and the past becomes the present. Their faces shine, laughter trips up their narrative and imitations of Dunphy's mannerisms give their stories a theatrical flair.

Everyone had their favorite Dunphy story. My father's came from his days as an altar boy. It happened during the 9 o'clock, the main Sunday mass. My father and his best friend, Garrity, were the altar boys. Dressed in their white chasubles and black cassocks, they waited in the sacristy. Dunphy was late. A few minutes after nine, his clothes disheveled and trousers only partially buttoned up, a bleary eyed Dunphy fluttered into the sacristy. He hastily threw the rich green vestments of the Easter season over his clothes, pivoted and speaking for the first time said, *Boys, let's go*. They led the priest through the sacristy doors and to the foot of the altar. By that time, Dunphy detected that his pants were slipping down around his knees. At the foot of the altar, in the last second, with my father on his right as the Bell and Garrity on his left as the Book, Dunphy improvised his own liturgical reform. Back to the Faithful, Dunphy paused and said, *Ah, what a glorious summer morning the Lord has given us! Let us all bow our heads for a moment to thank the Lord for the beauty of this day.* Only the altar boys knew what happened next. Dunphy hastily lifted his vestment robes up, hoisted up his pants, let the robe fall back in place, and, raising his voice on high, he intoned, *In Nomine Patris, et Filii, et Spiritus Sancti* as a cue to the good men and women of Ascension that it was time to lift up their heads and the time for liturgical experiments with the vernacular was over.

He never spoke from the pulpit. Instead, he paced back and forth in the center aisle, rocking to and fro from his left to his right foot. At least once every sermon, he pointed his finger at a nodding head and called a snoozing parishioner by name, telling him to wake up or find another church for Sunday mass. He did tend to go on. If, however, he caught someone sneaking a glance at their watch, he would say, *You down there, am I keeping you from something?* You never missed his point. He would stand still, slap his bald head for emphasis and, leading with *Ooooh! This old bald head may have a small brain but . . .*, drive in a few more for you to take home.

One time after reading the Gospel, Dunphy stepped away from the pulpit and stood at the center aisle, stared mutely at his congregation for a moment, then slapped his head and shouted, *I need a woman!* No one knew how to respond. A few eyebrows were lifted. Wives elbowed napping husbands. Laughter escaped out of tightly shut lips. In the awkward moment of silence, the little Kolb girl said too loudly, *Mommy, I have to go pee- pee.* It took a while before the Faithful understood that Dunphy was talking about hiring a new housekeeper.

Dunphy's sermons were short on theology and long on solutions to the "Irish Question," sports, politics, and funding drives. *Where there is a now a dollar to spare*, he never tired of saying, *there is only one place to deposit it, in the coffers of the Ascension Building Fund.* In the weekly *Ascension Messenger,* he set down in plain English his "do's" and don'ts" for Catholics. From his list of "don'ts," my favorite took aim at the pikers who pretended *to be in an ecstatic condition of devotion when the contribution box approaches.* He periodically published his formula for how families should calculate their parish giving based on a fixed percentage of their weekly income, and also disseminated quarterly reports on each parish family's donation. My Grandfather Nick, I was pleased to discern, had done the right thing where it mattered most. He gave in "9's"—ninety cents to the Sunday collection plate and nine dollars a month to the Ascension Building Fund. The consistent pattern of 9's and other occasional special gifts suggested that Nick took seriously the Dunphy percentage formula while enjoying an annual income, quite respectable for the 1920s, of about $4000.

When Dunphy decided too many Ascensionites were not taking seriously one of his "don'ts"—"NOT to be late for Mass," he taught them a lesson. At the beginning of the mass, as the two altar boys opened the sacristy doors and Dunphy entered the sanctuary, one of the assistant priests would, on cue, lock the doors to the church. One parishioner who worked for the fire department snitched and the fire marshall showed up one Sunday to put a stop to it. Or, as a few of the Ascension guys said with a chuckle, the fire marshall just wanted to make sure that the rare parishioners who might have a good word to say about the Republican Party had an escape route.

On a typical Sunday, when other parishes of the diocese heard sermons on why Archbishop Dowling in St. Paul had banned dancing at Catholic schools, the Faithful at Ascension might hear Dunphy's proposal for a just and fair settlement to the Irish Question. He often presented his long-time friend Tommy Gibbons as a role model for the men of the parish. Gibbons had been a contender for the heavyweight title, and had once gone fifteen rounds with Jack Dempsey. He later became the Ramsey County Sheriff. Keep in mind, the men were told, there is seamless cloth woven of a good Catholic upbringing, grace and strength in the ring, and being a good family man.

In the dark days of the Depression, Dunphy urged his parishioners to vote for Floyd B. Olson in the gubernatorial race. The Republican Lutheran pastors were condemning the Farmer-Labor candidate to hell, even though he was Norwegian, because of his alleged communism, atheism, and a few things about his personal life that decency forbade the Lutherans from mentioning. Dunphy turned his parish into a get-out-the-vote machine. On the Sunday before the election, he ended his sermon with, *You're all working class Irish men, get out there and vote for Floyd B. Olson!* Later in the 1930s, Dunphy often went on a rampage against the radio priest and fascist sympathizer Father Coughlin, and cast a suspicious eye on anyone in the congregation who might have been tempted to turn the radio dial to Coughlin's nonsense about Mussolini or Hitler.

A few aldermen on the North Side had not supported Dunphy's pet project. He wanted the city to build a bridge connecting the downtown with Seventh Avenue North. The aldermen went down in the city elections and the bridge went up.

The truth was that by the time *Going My Way* hit the American movie theaters, Dunphy's best days were behind him. It was the same year the Church gave him the royal purple and elevated him to the level of monsignor. The gesture was the St. Paul hierarchy's way of suggesting that it was time he thought about retirement. Dunphy was a holdover from the Depression era, working class Catholics who were being supplanted by the going-Eisenhower's-way Catholics of a more affluent time.

John Dunphy was born in 1884 in Kilmacow, County Waterford, Ireland, not far from the Hayes' parish in Kilrossanty. Archbishop Ireland recruited him and a generation of other priests from Irish seminaries to be the builders of the churches and parishes of the Archdiocese that spread across the Upper Midwest. Dunphy finished his seminary studies and was ordained in St. Paul. Ireland appointed him Dean of Students for the seminary and the fledgling College of St. Thomas.

At St. Thomas he was known as "the Dean of Discipline" or "the King." (His reputation for warmth and humor came later.) He meted out swift punishment for those guilty of the sin of tardiness. More than once, he threw a chair at a student who came to class late, and anyone who questioned his regime was welcome to meet him in the boxing ring. One challenger turned out to be a ringer—a former professional fighter that the students recruited. Dunphy duked it out with the kid for the full three rounds, and when it was over both fighters were still on their feet. Dunphy was exhausted and admitted to another priest that the kid was pretty tough.

On another occasion, a bad call by the umpire at a baseball game sparked a riot. Fans poured from the bleachers out onto the field and chased the umpire down the third base line and into the outfield. Dunphy was leading the pack, rubber hose in hand. *What are you doing, John?* One of his fellow priests asked. *I was only trying to protect him from the crowd,* Dunphy replied.

The rubber hose came with Dunphy from the College of St. Thomas to Ascension. He found it useful in the morning when he joined the Sisters to monitor the playground, holding it in his right hand as he jumped through the puddles and herded the older boys back to order. To the younger kids, and especially the girls, he often stooped down, made funny faces, and dared them to make a wish while rubbing his old bald head three times. Dunphy also carried the hose as he made the rounds on report card day. He would occasionally scowl at a report card, look the kid in the eye, and say, *Wait in the hall for stricter attention.* No further explanation was necessary. A few moments later a wail would erupt from the hall, which inspired the other students to study harder.

IT WAS NEVER COMPLETELY CLEAR why the diocese sent Dunphy across the river, though Minneapolis was experiencing a surge in Catholic population at the time, and perhaps in the eyes of the newly installed archbishop, Austin Dowling, too many of them were of a rather unruly working class sort; he was loathe to have the Minneapolis newcomers play Visigoth to St. Paul's Rome. New York-born and a graduate of Manhattan College, Dowling probably saw himself as several rungs above Dunphy on the Irish American social ladder. Whatever the motivation may have been, Dowling sent Dunphy on a part-time basis to Ascension, telling him that the aging Father Harrington needed help with the boys in his parish.

Harrington was Ascension's second pastor. The first, Father Alexander Christie, had built a small wooden church on the site of an old farm field in the 1890s. He was remembered most of all for his failed attempt to recruit men into a Temperance Society. When Harrington took over in early 1894, he quietly dropped that initiative and turned his energies toward a bricks-and-mortar Catholicism. He was a builder. First came the school, which opened in 1897. When the doors of a new church opened six years later, they led you, not into the twentieth century, but back in time, as if the old Irish priest had reclaimed Ireland's gothic cathedrals lost to the Anglicans and Penal Laws in the seventeenth century. A spire on the south side rose to a cross, and a bell tower on the north side called parishioners to prayers and daily mass. The center aisle led across the nave to the sanctuary and the altar, a masterpiece of Carrara marble and Mexican onyx crafted by the sculptor Conbradi of St. Louis. The entire interior was bathed in light descending from above through a stained glass window honoring the Ascension of Christ. Large, ornate, stained glass windows adorned the walls. One depicted the gift of the rosary by Our Lady to St. Dominic under the watchful eyes of Pope Leo XIII, and, on the south wall window in spectacular tones of green, St. Patrick was forever driving the snakes from Ireland. Harrington added a convent in 1916.

The basement of the new church was cramped but big enough to host the parish's first basketball games, musicals, and plays, and meetings of those Catholic clubs—the Sodality Society, the Rosary Society and others—that provided the social glue of the parish and strengthened the faith.

In 1921, the parish fathers answered the priest's call and found the money to raise a new building to house the Ascension Club. They were reluctant to call it a "settlement house" because it evoked associations with the protestants at Hull House in Chicago, but the Ascension Club did serve as an Irishman's settlement house. When its doors opened in 1922, a full basketball court, a swimming pool, a bowling alley, and a boxing ring also made it the finest athletic complex of the North Side.

A new rectory added the finishing touch. The red brick manor had three full floors. On the first, there was ample room for a kitchen and a dining room, office space, study rooms, and French glass doors that opened to the pastor's study—a generous and comfortable library with easy chairs, writing desks, and a welcoming fireplace. The second and third floors housed sleeping rooms, lavatories, and records. A two-story brick porch leading out from the first and second floors provided a view west and north of the church to the school, playground, and Ascension Club. The porch might well be a portico for the pastor to greet and bless the faithful gathered on the grounds of Ascension. One might not have been surprised if the rectory announced the selection of new pastors by sending white smoke up the chimney.

ON HIS FIRST NIGHT as the new pastor, Dunphy discovered what a financial albatross Father Harrington had left him. The Ascension Club carried a price-tag of $193,764.76, some of which Harrington had concealed from the bishop. It would take more than church basement bingo to fix this.

Dunphy had learned a bit about business from his old mentor, Archbishop Ireland, and he had soon arranged for the parish to sell the Ascension Club for $1 to a separate foundation. Dunphy was the chair of the foundation but he played a clever hand in picking the other members of the board, which included not only eminent Catholic businessmen but also a rabbi from Temple Israel, a Lutheran minister, and an African American from the newly opened Phyllis Wheatley House a few blocks south of Ascension on 10th Avenue. This new arrangement brought forth several revenue streams that city hall would not ordinarily have allowed to flow through the coffers of a church, and did not have to be reported to Dowling in St. Paul.

Almost immediately the limits went up on cash prizes for bingo, raffles, and the Wheel of Fortune at the annual Ascension Bazaar. This four day event was held each year in November or December, and among its offerings was a turkey dinner with all the fixings for fifty cents that went through three or four seatings a night. Brix's Grocery gave the church a deal on the cost of the food. The proceeds from the dinners combined with the ticket sales from games and rides insured a good profit, even with cash prizes of up to $700 being handed out. If there was not a musical or a play, there were picture shows for twenty cents a ticket. Nell Shipman in the 1921 silent movie *The Girl from God's Country* was a perennial favorite.

But boxing events were the finest jewel in the Ascension crown. Dunphy introduced Golden Glove matches in 1922, and three years later he brought in a sports promoter from Plymouth Avenue who put up the prize money. The semi-amateur prize fights on Saturday night were hosted by Tommy Gibbons. The prize was eight dollars. Admission was twenty five cents and there was never an empty seat.

The Ascension Club, Harrington's financial albatross, had found its wings. There were additional sources of revenue, best not discussed, trickling in from the card and billiard tables of the Men's Club on the second floor. There was also a membership fee of ten dollars a family. The fee was only a suggestion, as Dunphy knew enough about his congregants' finances not to press the issue and not to bar the door on any Ascensionite.

Dunphy's sickle had brought in a fine harvest. The parish grew to 1,800 families; the school enrolled more than 1,200; the Ascension Club was the pride of the North Side; and best of all, Dunphy did not have to bother the archbishop about money, though clergy from neighboring parishes complained occasionally to His Grace that Dunphy merely winked when Catholics slipped across parish boundaries to become members of Ascension.

PROHIBITION COINCIDED WITH Dunphy's early years at Ascension, inspiring discretion in the observance of certain customs. When Dunphy took over the rectory, the archbishop reminded him that he had long been disappointed in Father Harrington's failure to renew Father Christie's efforts to promote sobriety. The archbishop acknowledged that Father Christie's earlier choice of the Temperance Society played into Protestant hands and encouraged Dunphy to follow the lead of Catholic parishes in New York that were endorsing the Matt Talbot Society, an Irish precursor to Alcoholics Anonymous. His Grace looked forward to the day of Talbot's inevitable canonization. The archbishop reminded Dunphy that the Eighteenth Amendment was the law of the land and, especially in Protestant Minneapolis, he enforced a strict tea-total only policy in the rectories of his diocese. One wouldn't want to give Minnesota's own Congressman Volstead cause to make waves in the Protestant mill city with evidence of papist priests who turned their rectories into places of mockery for the Constitution and his own Volstead Act. Mindful of His Grace's admonition, Dunphy took the precaution of locking the French doors to the rectory library. Behind those doors, he continued Harrington's custom of housing a fine collection of whiskey, bourbon, and gin, and often invited the parish assistants in for after-dinner cocktails.

For the curates, dinner with Dunphy was a formidable and stiff affair. The pastor required that they dress in their black cassocks and Roman collars, except on those rare occasions when the temperature rose above 100 degrees. On those days Dunphy would cordially suggest that the curates come to the dinner table in black trousers and a white shirt opened at the collar. Most evenings, there was a special invitation. It was not to be taken for granted, however, and not extended to every assistant or visiting priest. You never knew. Some of them were probably Dowling's stooges. Even so, after the evening meal on most nights, and always on Saturdays, Dunphy would put on a wry smile and suggest that perhaps Father would care to join him in the library. There, behind the closed French doors, Dunphy unlocked the liquor cabinet and offered his guest a cigar and his drink of choice, adding, *I prefer bourbon, don't you?* Of course, the curate always preferred bourbon, and the priests settled in for a long evening of drinks, cigars, conversation, and freedom from the fuddy-duddy archbishop in far-off St. Paul.

The Holy Name Society was Dunphy's answer to Dowling's suggestions on promoting sobriety. The official purpose of the Holy Name

Society was to continue the Church's battle against the Albigensian heresy of the thirteenth century. Dunphy saw it as an answer to the blasphemies and heresies of Minneapolis's Protestant evangelical leader, Reverend W. B. Riley, a Baptist preacher who was the Billy Sunday of Minneapolis. Riley was the pastor of the First Baptist Church in Minneapolis and founder of the Northwestern College of Bible and Missionary Studies, which churned out a national legion of fundamentalist evangelical preachers. Riley turned Minneapolis into a national stage from which he showcased campaigns against modernism, the teaching of evolution, alcohol, which The Reverend called "the mother of all vice," and "harmful foreign elements." His rants against alcohol and "foreign elements" didn't fool Dunphy, who knew old time American anti-Catholicism and anti-Semitism when he saw it. Although never strong on the finer points of Catholic theology, Dunphy saw a new Albigensian in Riley. He would point out in his talks to the Holy Name Society that even this evangelical's use of the name "Jesus" was a sacrilege. Good Catholics only rarely uttered the Holy Name and reverently bowed their heads and crossed themselves when they did so. On the big issue, Dunphy would ask, *Do the Baptists not know the lessons of the Wedding Feast of Canaan?* If wine with family and friends was good enough for Our Dear Lord to have blessed it, is it not fitting and right that the men of Ascension, their families and friends enjoy the same?

Dunphy answered Riley's rallies across the Upper Midwest by outdoing him with his own annual show at the Minnesota State Fair Grounds. Each year, working with parishes throughout the diocese, Dunphy organized the annual rally of the Holy Name Society. Numbers were on his side. The Catholics could always turn out a bigger show than the Protestants. Every year during Lent, Dunphy led a procession of Catholic men and their sons to the stadium of the fair grounds where they consecrated themselves to the devotion of the Holy Name of Our Lord Jesus Christ, the sacraments of "His One, Holy, Catholic, Apostolic Church," and, in rather vague terms, condemned blasphemy, profanity and immorality. Back at Ascension, the Holy Name Society organized the men into social activities held regularly at the Ascension Club and sponsored an annual summer father/son fishing trip and picnic to Bass Lake, for which the Holy Name Society had raised the funds to purchase a bus. And on the second Sunday of every month, the men and their sons took

Father Dunphy enjoying a cigar with the nuns

precedence at the mass by stepping forward together as the first to take Holy Communion. As for the pesky question of temperance, the men's devotions would yield them the grace of God to overcome temptation and, if they should on occasion fall off the wagon, the partial indulgence for their participation in the monthly mass and communion gave them forgiveness and a fresh start.

Dunphy believed in the gospel of salvation by sports. His calling was to mold boys into men on the athletic field, and from his first days at Ascension, he took on the mission of revealing the grace that sent a basketball through a hoop, that lifted a fly ball across left field and out of North Commons Park, that guided the double reverse hand-off in the backfield which befuddled a defensive line.

One sport above all others was sacramental. Boxing. Dunphy saw to it that the boys of his parish had a backup plan when turning the other cheek failed. He took it as his personal responsibility to see that every Ascension boy knew how a left should jab, how a fighter's fist tucked in the thumb, and how God often spoke through a well-placed right hook.

The boys and girls of Ascension learned to appreciate the finer things as well. The Ascension Club was home to theater groups, evening movies, musical ensembles, and the unforgettable Dorothy Lundstrum School of Dance. Mrs. Lundstrum and her three daughters lived across the street from the church. She sold milk and candy in the school cafeteria. The idea started early in the 1920s. Lundstrum offered classes in square dancing as part of the grade school's physical education program. Later dances in the gym became part of the social activities for married couples. When Dunphy took charge of Ascension, he made it official. Dorothy Lundstrum's School of Dance took over the third floor of the Ascension Club. From there, she and her three daughters gave to the Broadway Avenue boys and girls the gift of dance. Lundstrum's classes ranged from the Virginia reel to ballroom dancing. She and Dunphy were smart enough not to fight the Jazz Age but to join it.

Dowling was not so smart. He probably had the goings-on at the Ascension Club in mind when he issued a statement banning "indecent dancing" from Catholic schools. Dunphy printed Dowling's letter without comment in the *Ascension Messenger*. *Indecent dancing is not only dancing of mixed couples*, Dowling wrote, *but exhibitions of so-called artistic dances in which performers, sometimes children and sometimes young women, appear indecently.*

The letter prompted Dunphy to raise his eyebrows and ask Mrs. Lundstrum, *Dorothy, he couldn't have us at Ascension in mind, could he?* Of course, not, she replied, and Ascension went on dancing through the Jazz Age, producing the only Catholics kids in town who knew the Jitterbug and Charleston as well as the Baltimore Catechism.

THAT STUFF'S NO GOOD AT ALL

My father fit in at Ascension. School work came easy. He was never sent into the hall by Dunphy for stricter attention at report card time. He excelled in art. The nuns put him in charge of the class art projects, and he oversaw the drawings with colored chalk of a frieze on white rolled paper depicting scenes from geography and history lessons. As for his one major short-coming—he was left-handed—the sisters had a cure. Through long and repetitive practice, they trained him to curl his left hand so that the nib stroked to the right and rolled out perfect right-handed Palmer cursives.

He was a natural for Dunphy's sports teams. His height made his jump shot from right guard the weapon of choice for the Ascension Cubs on the basketball court. A left hander, he batted clean-up. He swam. A halfback in football, he ran like a gazelle, nimbly bounding past the defensive tackles.

Dunphy left the task of saving the troubled marriages in the parish to his assistants. In his office, he kept a file box on marriages. Each new assistant would receive a folder from Dunphy that broke down the cases into those capable of fixing and those beyond repair. This was an Irish parish. Most of the men strayed for their love of the bottle, not in pursuit of other women. In the marriages that still had a chance, the husbands received the brunt of the priest's advice. They were told to join the Holy Name Society. In the case of those that Dunphy concluded had gone beyond hope it was the wife who received the attention. Dunphy directed the assistant to be mindful of her need to stay a part of parish life, invite her to meetings of the Women's Sodality Society, and see to it that whatever social help the parish could offer was made available to her.

When the Hayeses moved into Ascension parish, their neighbors the Frankmans were in the first category. They lived in a fourplex just across the alley. Old man Frankman, however, ignored the curate's advice to join the Holy Name Society. One night, after a few too many at the Railway Workers Fraternal Association, he came home, climbed the stairs to the second floor, stood in front of his apartment door, and fell backward down the stairs. The concussion killed him. After that, the parish assistants were always inviting Mrs. Frankman to all kinds of things. She didn't go to Dorothy Lundstrum's dances, however. That would have been inappropriate for a widow. But her two daughters did.

The oldest, Ceci Frankman was always hanging around Lucy's house whispering and giggling with Anna. It was Anna who got my father to go to Lundstrum's dance school. Technically speaking, these evenings were not dances. Mixed dancing was banned in Catholic schools for children eighth grade and under. These were dancing lessons and practice. By the spring of eighth grade, my father's shyness was behind him as he and Ceci swiveled around the floor in a slow waltz or bopped their legs off in a Charleston. They wouldn't have put it that way, but one of those evening dance lessons must have been their first date.

About that time, the Saturday Night Show started. The idea was to revive those evenings of entertainment on the O'Brien's farm in North Dakota. Lucy played the piano. There would always be an *étude* or *polonaise* from Chopin to give the night a touch of class. The Frankmans came over. The Garrity brothers were usually there. The Kolb girl was always there. She was Eileen's friend and had a crush on Jim. Nick brought out the bourbon. On Lucy's piano the classics gave way to Broadway. With bobbed dark hair, dark eyes, and a straight line dress, Anna had a face as cute as Betty Boop and was about as close to being a flapper as a Catholic girl in Minneapolis could be. On any given evening, she might do the Jitterbug first on her own, then coax a shy brother into showing his stuff. After awhile she had at least one of the Garritys dancing on the rug. Eileen and the Kolb girl mostly giggled and sang a bit. By the time my father and Ceci Frankman did the Charleston, things had gotten far, far out of Archbishop Dowling's hands. The highlights were captured on Jim's brownie and cut and pasted into the monthly family newspaper he hammered out on his Remington—*Le Cheval du Nord.*

Things were too good. Something had to go wrong. It was my father's height that got him in trouble. By eighth grade, he was pushing the red crop of hair on top of his head to nearly six feet, and stood a head above almost all the other guys his age in the neighborhood. It was the combination of the presumed dominance bequeathed by his height and the vulnerability betrayed by the thinness of his frame that invited challengers. His red hair was also a problem. It and the bright splotches of freckles drew more than a few heckles on Ascension's playground. Swappach was his rival on the basketball team. They were both guards. Swappach was much shorter but stout, muscular, and tough.

There had been a few words and shoves on the playground, not much but enough to prompt the guys to separate into different circles shooting the bull, passing around smokes, and giving an unspoken allegiance to one or the other. A friend of Jim's—the Lynch kid, a funny little guy—palled up with the Hayes's crowd. One spring afternoon, my father, Uncle Jim, and Lynch were ambling down Bryant towards 16th street. Swappach and a few guys stood midway down the block and faced them as they approached. Swappach opened the conversation by taunting Lynch. Lynch was one syllable into his reply when Swappach drove both fists into his shoulders, sending him stumbling backwards. *Knock it off,* my father yelled, and stepped toward Swappach, whose fists went up as a string of foul remarks about the Frankman girl began to pour from his mouth. In a rage, my father led with a misguided right.

Swappach's fists were all over him, driving him back and then taking him to the ground. His fists were within a few seconds of completing his takeover of the neighborhood when the shout came: *What's this? We got some tough guys here?* It was Dunphy, barreling down the sidewalk like a bowling ball with two arms in the wind and rolling toward a perfect strike.

Swappach jumped up. My father rose from the ground. *Don't give me any of your, He started it's,* Dunphy injected before either boy uttered a word. *You're going to finish this the right way.*

The next night, at the Ascension Club, the rivals donned boxing gloves and head gear for three rounds with Dunphy as ref and judge. Each had a half dozen or so of his guys there for support. Standing in his corner, nervous, my father crossed himself, said a silent Hail Mary, and drew a deep breath. Dunphy called both of them to the center. They touched gloves. Dunphy reminded them that this was the way real men settled arguments. My father was hardly out of his corner when Swappach was all over him, hitting from the inside to take away the advantage of his opponent's long reach. My father backed away throwing up an aimless left. Swappach was on him again in a second and he went down fast and hard. *That's it!* Dunphy yelled. *It's over boys.* Swappach smirked, hopped out of the ring and sauntered out with his buddies.

The loser sat on the mat. Dunphy helped him up and waved his hand at his friends letting them know that they should get out. It started as a stutter and blurted out as *I, ah, ah, I, ah, I did everything. I made the novena, I said a Hail Mary.*

My boy, Mark, Dunphy replied, *that stuff's no good at all, if you don't know how to fight.*

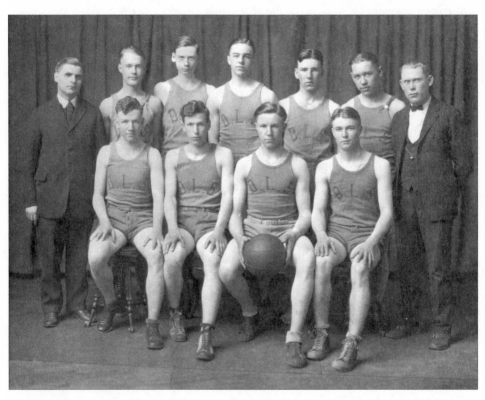

My father, back row, third from left, De La Salle Islanders, 1926

4
"D"

Hayes intercepted a forward pass and, aided by good interference made a great run of forty yards for a touchdown.

– The De La Salle Islander ,1923

The Rock on Nicollet Island

My father attended De La Salle high school; I attended the same school four decades later. For four years, five days a week, I walked underneath his basketball team photo in the main hallway, read the same textbooks which had been passed down from his class to mine, and was haunted by a line from Virgil in our Latin reader. *Optima dies prima fugit—The best days are the first to flee.* I was several sizes too small to measure up to the legend of my father's glory days in high school, yet, I had no choice but to don that legend just as my Uncle Jim had worn his older brother's hand-me-down clothes. Jim never grew into his brother's cast-offs, but he wore them with the humor and irony we all need when we inherit expectations we can never fulfill. In the 1920s, my father had played a lead role in the first act of a show that promised to go on forever. By my time—the 1960s—the high school's best days had fled to that place where old men save memories so they can tell their grandchildren about the way things once were. My class of Catholic baby boomers was the largest in the school's history, yet I knew I was playing a bit part in its last act. My role was to turn out the lights when I left.

In my father's day, the American teenager had not yet been invented. Upon entering high school, students of his day suddenly ceased to be "boys" and "girls" and became young men and young women. Thus, he was spared the god-awful lectures on how to chart his passage through the troubled waters of adolescence. This was especially true for

Catholics, whose fundamental approach to adolescence had changed little since the thirteenth century. The purpose of a Catholic high school education was to prepare young men and women serve as priests, brothers, sisters, or good Catholics in the world. Life's other choices went unmentioned except for the periodic homilies on the sad lives of the "fallen away" Catholics.

The Catholic American rite of passage from child to adult was graduation from eighth grade. My father belonged to the elite of his class, which meant his name appeared in *The Ascension Messenger* on a list of those new grads who were continuing on to a Catholic high school. Other smart kids, whose families could not afford the eighty dollars a year for tuition, went to North High School. The Minneapolis School Board had never welcomed these graduates of the Catholic parish schools into the public high schools. To the mortification of Ascension's Principal, Sr. Aquin, the Protestants who ran the state schools required the graduates of Ascension and other parish schools to take an entrance exam in order to advance to the ninth grade. As for the rest of the class, a lot of them were just proud to have made it through eighth grade. A grade school diploma was good enough to open the doors to jobs waiting for them out there on Broadway. Half the guys setting pins at the local bowling alley, unloading freight, or stacking groceries at Brix's, had never even made it that far.

The summer after eighth grade had little purpose except to give the new grads a better sense of what "Limbo" meant. But there was baseball. The Ascension team took the city championship one more time—a result that was about as much of a surprise as heat and humidity in August. A few transfers on the street car would take my father south to Calhoun Beach on the Chain of Lakes, where he could listen to his sister Anna and her friends talk about the same old boys.

One day that summer Father Dunphy, accompanied by dance instructor Dorothy Lundstrum, loaded the recent grads into the Ascension bus for a picnic at Bass Lake. They brought along a wind-up gramophone. That day a taboo of their grade school years crumbled forever as the young men and women danced under the Bass Lake Pavilion and breathed the air of their first parish "mixed party" under the watchful eyes of their two chaperones. Other than that sweet day, the summer of my father's eighth grade year passed with a boring redundancy not even broken by Anna's place of honor as a Princess in the August North Side Parade down Broadway.

After the parade, there was no point in pretending any longer that life revolved around Ascension, with its intertwined families, priests, nuns, and pecking order that was as obvious as it was inexplicable. The grade school look no longer suited my father. Lucy took him shopping on Broadway for this year's new pair of shoes, a handful of ties, and a suit to replace the knickers that would soon be swallowing up younger brother Jim.

My father didn't go to just any Catholic high school. He went to *D*. Its formal title was St. John Baptiste de la Salle, or De La Salle for short. Its students drew a comparison of the school's placement on an island to a more infamous institution in San Francisco Bay and called it "the Rock." To the outside world, students called their school *D*. Nothing more needed to be said. Only one high school in Minneapolis had the cachet to be known by a one letter name.

D was a working class Catholic's Eton entrusted by the Church to make the young men of second generation European immigrant families into a Catholic middle class. With a gift of $25,000 from local railroad robber baron James J. Hill, Archbishop Ireland in 1900 planted a shovel in the ground of Nicollet Island, situated just above St. Anthony Falls on the Mississippi River in the heart of Minneapolis. With that act the archbishop struck a blow for Catholicism in the very heart of Protestant Minneapolis. Let every Protestant know that there was a new covenant of the One, Holy, Catholic and Apostolic Church with the Mill City, and that on this rock of an island Ireland would build the city's first Catholic high school.

The school was a gift of the Diocese of St. Paul, His Grace said, generously given with only one condition. It must be run by the Brothers of the Christian Schools, or, as the order was known to most Catholics, the Christian Brothers. The Brothers, like the Sisters of St. Joseph of Crandolet who provided the teachers for the grade schools of the diocese, traced their origins to France but had come to America by way of Ireland.

Archbishop Ireland's choice of the Christian Brothers also reflected his dislike of the Jesuit order, which had done little to ease the suffering of common people during the Great Hunger. By contrast, the Christian

71

Brothers, whose vows stopped short of ordination to the priesthood, had rolled up their sleeves and tackled the tougher job of teaching the hard-scrabble Irish in the cities. Ireland never doubted that he could work well with the Christian Brothers whose lack of pretense was better suited to his flock.

Within months of the ground-breaking the building was ready and the Brothers had arrived from Chicago. Some found it odd that the new school was named after the order's eighteenth-century French founder, St. John Baptiste de la Salle, who was not a popular saint among the Irish, German, and Polish Catholics of the region. The choice also left the school forever with a sense that it was an inferior copy of the legendary Christian Brothers high school with the same name on Chicago's South Side. But at least it was a better name than Cretin, the Brother's school in St. Paul, which was named after a former bishop whom few had even heard of, and provided boundless opportunities for schoolyard insults.

D started out modestly. In 1900 three Brothers made up the teaching staff for the fifty young men who attended. The education concentrated on the teachings of the Church, the basics, and business. It worked. All seven members of *D*'s first graduating class in 1903 had job offers in hand "from respectable Minneapolis businesses" before graduation day. Before long the student body has risen to 350 and it was necessary to add a third floor to the building.

But from the first *D* carried a chip on its shoulder. The Christian Brothers stood low on the ladder of Catholic status; they weren't even priests, let alone Jesuits. And those Catholics who could afford to often sent their children to St. Thomas Academy or Cretin High School, both of which were across the river in St. Paul. In an effort to elevate the school's cachet, the *D* student newspaper, *The Islander,* carried ads from Rothschild's Clothing in downtown Minneapolis catering to "young fellows who want style" and promising to give *D* men "the identical style they're wearing at the big Eastern prep schools." To add a further touch of class, the archbishop pressured his friend James J. Hill to coax Minneapolis lumber baron William King into giving the Brothers his palatial old home near the school on Nicollet Island. The mansion had misplaced associations with the underground highway of the antebellum period, and this aura later rubbed off on the Brothers' image, allowing their students to think they had something to do with the end of slavery.

King was a notorious recluse who loved only the company of his horses. He could often be seen charging out of his carriage house holding the reins of his two champion stallions. He would cross the river and head up Hennepin to his farms south of Lake Street—a route now memorialized by "King's Highway" on the east side of Lake Harriet.

The old lumber baron had actually given the Brothers more of a plumbing problem than a home, and in 1950 the Brothers gave up on the structure, building a new residence adjacent to the "C" Building that would never earn a mention in anybody's architectural history of the city, and replacing the legendary mansion and livery stable with a parking lot. Old Man King had never thought much of Archbishop Ireland anyway, and years later he bequeathed his mansion on Lake Harriet to the Jesuits. (An ironic footnote: the Jesuits couldn't pay for the upkeep of that structure and sold it to a millennial Christian sect who, in turn, left it in a shambles when they gave up on the predicted Second Coming and moved to Montana, perhaps confirming Archbishop Ireland's belief that things go to hell in a hand basket when you let the Jesuits in.)

After the First World War, pressure from the parents in the parishes to enroll more students and to add maybe just a touch more class to the schooling brought changes at *D*. The parents wanted a modern building and they wanted "college prep." Ascension took the lead in a fundraising drive that pulled in $200,000 from the parishes across Minneapolis for construction of the "New" Building in 1923. The old three story original building thereafter became known as the "C" Building or "Commercial" Building where those judged not to be college material concentrated on "mechanical arts," typing, and accounting. It lived on for generations like a neglected elderly relative, beloved but hopelessly impractical, until a fire in the 1970s left it in ashes.

At *D,* the Brothers delivered Catholic education with attitude. They pounded into young heads a hard education that added Latin, muscular Catholicism, and middle class airs to the street smarts the boys brought with them from the North Side. Each class hour began with the recitation of a Hail Mary and a chant that came out as a cheer, *St. John Baptiste de la Salle, pray for us!* If the prayers weren't enough to keep the boys in line, as was often the case, the Brothers didn't hesitate to whack them with rulers, paddles, and even bare knuckles to keep them on track. On rare occasions outside re-enforcements were required. My father recalled a morning in his senior year when two policemen appeared in the doorway. *Sorry, Brother, but we have to speak to Dahmon.* Dahmon jumped out of his seat, cut across a row of desks, and made it through the first floor window.

Gender at *D* referred to the rules of declension and agreement in Latin grammar. *D* was no place for women. Beyond eighth grade, Catholic schools kept boys and girls far apart. A mixing of the sexes was one of the occasions of sin that lay in wait for those who had to go to North High and was likely to turn them into something less than "good Catholics." The women went to St. Margaret's on the other end of Hennepin, close to the protective eyes of the Basilica of St. Mary. The only women inside the walls of *D* cooked and served the lunch in the cafeteria. This changed somewhat in my father's second year. The Brothers hired a Miss Thelma Slattery to teach speech. The school newspaper noted the she was "well known in the Twin Cities and is considered very good in this line of work." That fall, "a larger number than ever before" registered for speech.

Miss Slattery earned her place in *D* history by daring to mix the sexes, organizing and chaperoning *D*'s first "mixed party." My father was in his senior year. For one night, the women of St. Margaret's and the men of *D* socialized on the gym floor where they were free to dance or, in a nod to the awkwardness of the men, play cards. My father's crowd shunned the event for the most part by caucusing in the hallway, assuming an immobile posture at the card tables, or altogether stiffing the event in favor of one more Saturday night of shooting buckets at the Ascension Club. Not so my father. Let his friends say only fruitcakes danced. He had learned a few things in Dorothy Lundstrum's dance class and the young women of St. Margaret's were going to reap the benefits.

My father was college material, which meant he knew nothing of the business classes over in the "C" Building, but continued with Latin to take a third and fourth year beyond the required first two. History courses charted the rise of civilization to its glory in the 12th and 13th centuries and then bemoaned its decline into heresy and atheism. The textbook on the modern era began with the phrase "That viper, Martin Luther" and went on to expose in minute detail the fallacies of every Protestant sect. It was easier to find common ground with modern science than with the Protestants. On the second floor of the New Building, state-of-the-art chemistry and biology labs let the boys conduct chemistry experiments and dissect frogs under the watchful eyes of Louis Pasteur and Father Gregor Mendel, whose portraits hung on the wall.

A proper appreciation of the arts and literature rounded out my father's education. Private piano lessons could be arranged after school with Miss E. Annette Smith, but the spotlight on the arts fell on Mr. Elmer Bohling's 23-piece orchestra. Novels still belonged to the vulgar genres of literature—at *D* the emphasis was on drama and poetry. Shakespeare took the form of a detailed reading of *Macbeth* and a very narrow selection of the Bard's sonnets. The boys went on from there to read and memorize the classics of modern English poetry starting with Milton and focusing at length on the lyricists of the nineteenth century.

Brother John noticed that my father was memorizing poems by James Whitcomb Riley, and encouraged him to take a look at the new poems of Edna St. Vincent Millay. He found and checked out the four volumes of her work from the *D* library shelves. In my senior year at *D* more than four decades later, I took it into my head to impress a girlfriend by memorizing some poems by the same author, and as I pulled her volumes off the same library shelf I found my father's signature, the only one on the check-out card other than Bother John's, and discovered my father's secret affair with the poetry of a woman.

Everyone at *D* took four years of religion, regardless of career path, and this curriculum was largely devoted to battling medieval heresies. During my father's first year at *D*, for example, an essay contest was held to celebrate the sixteenth centenary of the defeat of the Arian heresy. The theme, of course, was the Divinity of Christ with special reference to the First Council of the Church and the formation of the Nicene Creed. Otherwise the religion courses continued to drill in the laws of the Church and mysteries of the sacraments. References to Scripture were few and indirect with the exception of the frequent repetition of Matthew 17: 18. It's the singular, boys, the Brothers would say, Our Lord said he would build his *Church*, not *churches*. It was a useful verse to know by heart in the event you were confronted with having to defend the faith against the Protestants.

In the senior year of a religion class, students were given the opportunity to tame their tumescent hormones by exploring a passionless textbook called *The Ring*, in which vexing issues of sexuality were reduced to minor detail in the discussion of the sacrament of marriage. It featured a classic diagram of the fallopian tubes and vas deferens and explained their functions within an Aristotelian model of cause and effect, the end result being the fulfillment of God's desire to produce more Catholic children within the sanctimony of Holy Matrimony. The acts of fornication, adultery and self-abuse were thus obviously both irrational and sinful. Not every issue had an Aristotelian explanation, however. During the annual Lenten retreat, for example, many a young man would ask the priest, *Then, what about "nocturnal emissions," Father, are they sinful?* Only if they took pleasure in them, the priest would reply, implying that the authority of the Church extended even into the realm of the unconscious.

D had its own way of keeping the Aristotelian balance of mind and body—physical education. In the era before the New Building, Phys. Ed and sports were pretty much limited to calisthenics in crouched positions beneath the eight-foot-high ceiling of the basement. The gymnasium of the New Building opened the way for a new era. It comprised about half the cubic feet of the New Building and could accommodate a full basketball court with bleachers on the side. It rose to two stories, with interior balconies on each side and also a rear balcony for seating. Facing the gym stood the elevated Garrick Theater stage from where the Drama Club performed Shakespeare, light comedies, and the annual Lenten Passion Play.

Monday through Friday, the daily regimen of Phys. Ed classes occupied the gym floor. At any given hour, third and fourth year students moving along the second floor corridors could see their classmates doing jumping jacks, walking duck squats, sit-ups, and fifty push-ups. The weakling who fell short of the required mark could often be seen holding a stationary push-up position with his feet raised against a bleacher and his arms holding him upright until he cried, collapsed, received mercy from Coach Roberts, or a simultaneous mixture of all three.

The new gym borrowed a tradition from the Ascension Club. It had a boxing ring where the boys learned how to take care of themselves and settle disputes in a gentlemanly way. Boxing was required in Phys. Ed. There were also rare and dramatic moments when the Brothers would bring two boys whose disagreements came to the edge of violence to settle the issue with gloves, a referee, and three rounds in the ring. That ring was the start of a career for more than a few Golden Gloves champions.

D did not have a "toilet" or a "washroom." Rather, it had "the Lavatory." In class, you were to ask politely, "Brother, may I be excused to go to the lavatory?" The Latinized noun both gave it more of a Catholic sound and obscured what went on there. It stood in the lower level of the New Building, corresponding to the lowly position of the bodily functions that were relieved there.

The Lavatory's stalls and urinal were made from the dark stone of Minnesota's Cold Spring Granite. The granite spoke to the young men of the absence of color. The fact that the stone's paisley splotches somewhat varied the somber tones of maroon only re-enforced the monochrome effect and drove home the point that to seek sensory stimulation in the basics of human body functions was as futile as seeking color in Midwestern rock. The stalls had no doors. One year, during the retreat for the seniors, Br. Louis spoke obliquely to the temptation that lurked in those stalls. He was speaking of the life of St. John Neri. He was once tempted by the Devil to touch himself while seated and doing his business. *St. John Neri is called the laughing saint and had quite sense of humor,* the Brother said with a smile. *And he said to the Devil, my mind goes up to God; what goes down goes to you.* For some of these guys, nothing worked. The publicity of the open walls had no effect on Barney McGowan. He couldn't wait to get down to the Lavatory after Miss Slattery's class. Barney thought self-abuse was a competitive sport and never noticed that he was in a league of his own. Then, there was Larry Revak. Larry had a different way of looking at things. "Hey, sometimes, have you ever thought that if you were a girl," he wondered out loud, "then you could feel yourself up?" Larry never made it as a *D* man. He joined the navy in his sophomore year.

A Real *D* Man

There were those who just went to *D* and then there were "the Real *D* men." *The Islander* wrote stories about these "regular fellows." Unlike the students at St. Thomas and Cretin who wore military uniforms,

D men kept to a standard middle class uniform. Like the heroes of "Gasoline Alley," they came to school in suits purchased in Minneapolis' garment district on First Avenue North at clothiers who would have scoffed at the notion of a designer logo, and tore out the labels from the clothes that had them. In winter, *D* men topped off the look with an overcoat and fedora.

Real *D* men were friends of Coach Roberts. He ran the stuff that counted at *D*. Coach Roberts taught history and Phys. Ed. , but that was the small change. He ruled the four corners of the earth that really mattered at *D* as coach of the football, basketball, hockey, and baseball teams. Coach Roberts checked out the eighth graders at the Ascension and had his eye on my father, "Red" Hayes, before he arrived. (With his red hair and smattering of freckles, the guys called my father either "Red" or, among the more literate, "Huck.")

Thus, my father's move from old Ascension to *D* was easy. It was as easy as the walk he and his best friend, Garrity, made every weekday morning on their way to school, down Broadway and then the railroad tracks to the Great Northern Depot and across the railroad bridge to Nicollet Island. Being from Ascension put him a step above the kids from smaller and less powerful parishes, and his height and agility gave him another lift.

But his father, Nick, wasn't sold on sports. The whole point of spending eighty bucks to send his son to *D* was to get him into "college prep" and complete the college dream that Nick himself had left unfinished back in Toronto. Basketball was alright. As for football, Nick had a Canadian's skepticism about that American pastime, and mused that his son would probably end up with a broken leg if he played it. Nick didn't know that in his son's first year at *D* he went out not only for basketball and swimming, but also made varsity in football. In his second year, he was the starting right half and off to glory. *The Islander* documents my father's taste of gridiron glory. The team was trailing St. Cloud Cathedral in the final quarter 7 to 12, when "Hayes intercepted a forward pass and, aided by good interference, made a great run of forty yards for a touchdown."

But in the very next game, an easy match-up against Marshall High, my father fractured his arm above the elbow, mangling it enough to end his football career. To hide the cause of the mishap from his father, my father and his siblings concocted a story that he had broken his arm trying to crank the Model T. Year after year the dramatic details of the Model T episode multiplied, until it soon contained far more humorous digressions and side jokes than could fit within the simple truth of an arm broken in a football game.

It turned out that football didn't matter so much. Tall and thin, my father was a natural on the basketball court, and the name Mark Hayes was written on the opening pages of *D's* greatest story, when for two generations it dominated basketball in Minnesota. A right guard, he was a starter from his sophomore through his senior year. Rarely a game went by in which *The Islander* failed to cite his tenacity at defense and the crisp, cool buckets he tossed through the net as the standing guard far outside the circle. At the end of each year, at the annual June awards banquet, he received not only his letter for basketball but also the special "Silver Basketball" given by Coach Roberts as "emblematic of special proficiency and the keeping of training rules throughout the long season." Every year the Islanders rolled over their opposition in the private high school league, though these victories meant less than its victories over the giant of the Minneapolis public schools—and the non-Catholic rival of the North Side—North High School.

The Islander kept its eye on Hayes going into his senior season (1925-26) and praised him at the start as a "hard but clean player with lots of pep and dash." It was not an ordinary season. The retrospective on the senior class in the '26 yearbook began, "The Basketball Team took on the appearance of a wrecking crew smashing everything that came in its way." For the first time in its history, *D* earned a spot at the National Parochial Title Championship in Chicago. It fell to *D* in the words of *The Islander* to "uphold the prestige of the Northwest."

The prestige of it all was lost on my grandparents. Nick was on the road and Lucy never saw the point nor paid much attention to her son's athletic achievements. By that late date in the season he had worn his tennis shoes to shreds, but Coach Roberts insisted that the players all had to have new shoes for the tournament in Chicago. Lucy wasn't about to waste sixteen bucks on a pair of tennis shoes that her son didn't need in the first place. This hurt. A few days before the team was to depart for Chicago, he spoke to Brother Eugene, the athletic director, at first fumbling and stuttering some vague excuses about not being able to go and finally blurting out that his Mom said they didn't have the money for the shoes. A telephone call from Brother Eugene to Lucy offering to pay for the new shoes ended with Lucy's informing him that her family didn't need help from anyone. After a few minutes, there was a second call, this time from Father Dunphy. When Lucy put down the receiver, she told her son to call Br. Eugene. There would be a new pair of shoes waiting for him at the last practice the night before the tournament. The next morning, the team boarded the Hiawatha 400 and headed to Chicago, eager to put Minneapolis's *D* on the map of American Catholicism.

The Islanders came in as underdogs against Aquinas of Rochester, New York. In the seconds before the game, Coach Roberts brought calm to the boys' nerves by leading them in the usual Hail Mary. Then they took a deep breath and, with the cry of *St. John Baptiste de la Salle, pray for us,* they raced on to the floor.

Their held their own during the first quarter, but in the second quarter, Aquinas "went on a rampage while holding the Islanders scoreless." *The Chicago Tribune* and *The Minneapolis Star* praised the Islanders in their defeat. My father's picture was in the paper. The *Star* had few good words for Aquinas and implied that the boys from New York would do well to learn a bit about the sportsmanship from the *D* men.

On the train back to Minneapolis, Br. Eugene told the boys that they had gone where no *D* men had gone before, and in a rare reference to the Bible, told them that they were something like Moses on a mountain unable to make it to the promised-land, but showing the way to future Islanders. Five years later, in 1931, the Islanders entered that land by bringing back a trophy for a National Parochial Title.

With the passage of time, the stories of the 1926 game became intertwined with that later success in the Hayes family lore. Eventually the details of that 1931 triumph victory made their way back to 1926, adding the luster of my father's basketball career, while the game with Aquinas Rochester and the humiliation over a pair of shoes slipped into oblivion.

My father and *D* came of age together. Everything was going right for *D*. It had at last stepped out of the shadow of the Cretin and St. Thomas in St. Paul. The drama club's production of a romantic melodrama about college life—*The Toastmaster*—played to standing room only crowds and rave reviews in *The Minneapolis Star.* It was said that the play at *D* was even better than the shows downtown at the old vaudeville theaters, the Astor and the Academy. Not bad if you consider that Archbishop Dowling forbade *D* from having women in the cast. The role of the lead heroine and heart throb Cynthia Reed went to senior George Bedard in drag. The guys did find this a bit awkward. Some thought, though no one ever said, that Bedard wasn't quite a real *D* man. In the spring, even Mr. Bohling's Orchestra went big time. 'CCO Radio broadcast a live concert by the *D* orchestra.

"College prep" worked out for my father. His grades were good. In his senior year, he won the annual science competition for an essay on the chemistry of petroleum. He took charge of the art work for the school yearbook. His ink drawings and a few cartoon sketches left his imprint on the yearbook—*The Athanasian.* It was the first yearbook ever at *D*. Archbishop Dowling had banned the idea of yearbooks for the high schools in his diocese, exhibiting that instinctive reflex of the Catholic hierarchy against autonomous lay activities or publications without an imprimatur. In 1926, *The Athanasian* caught the Bishop unawares and appeared with only my father's ink sketch on the theme of "Ex Libris" —not *imprimatur*—on the inside front page. Someone from Cretin told Archbishop Dowling, who immediately put a stop to this. *D* did not have another yearbook until Archbishop Murray inaugurated a new and more progressive era.

Though the 1931 team won the national title, for decades to come the group photo of the 1926 team hung beside the one from 1931 in the place of honor in the main hallway. Brother Eugene left both team photos to hang together, as if to say that those who opened the door to new dreams deserve no less praise than those who realize those dreams.

My father laughed off a chance to go pro in basketball. Well, kind of pro. After the national championship tournament in Chicago, he got an offer to play for a newly formed pro team. It was the New York Generals, a dive team doomed to eternal defeat at the hands of the all-Negro Harlem Globetrotters. My father was going to amount to something more than a fall guy for the likes of Meadowlark Lemon. He was going to college.

Back row: Nick, Jim, Mark, Front row: Dave, John; February, 1932

5

Six to Five Against

I came to the conclusion long ago
that all life is six to five against

— Damon Runyon

RICHARD GILL

The undertaker's son went to *D* with my father. From one generation to the next, from my father's youth on the North Side to his
sons' childhood on the South Side, Gill Brothers Funeral Home would
not let us forget its ties to the family. It was manifest in unusual ways.
Take our baseball uniforms for Christ the King School, for example. The
other teams in our league came out on the field in uniforms with their
undaunted sponsors on the back. Old can-do Settergren's Hardware
covered the back of the Armitage School uniforms. An advertisement
for Hove's, the uppity grocery in Edina, on the Fulton School team
uniforms conjured up images of money and blonde Norwegians. As one
Christ the King batter after another failed to beat out the throw to first
base, he carried an advertisement for Gill Brothers Funeral Homes on
his back, reminding us all that our glory was elsewhere.

My father reminded us it could have been worse. When he was a
kid Northwestern Casket Co. sponsored a team. In any case, the sight
of our uniforms gave him an excuse to re-tell stories from the old days
about the Gill family.

He used to say that Gill was a hard man to like. After Nick's death
in 1932, Richard Gill, the undertaker's son, came to call every now and
then on Sundays. While no time was appropriate for his visits, some
times were more inappropriate than others. The trick was to arrive at
a comfortable interval after the Sunday breakfast and well before the

Sunday dinner. He would never be invited to stay for dinner. Why add to the awkwardness by cutting his visit too close to the time when the place settings were coming out on the dining room table? Most families had their breakfasts after "the 10"—the ten o'clock Mass. On Sundays, the family dinner was not at the mandatory Minnesota 6: 00 p.m. Every family had dinner a bit earlier on Sundays. But, each had a different time. The Hayeses moved dinner ahead about an hour to 5:00 p.m. The rationale for the earlier Sunday dinner was that by condensing the time between breakfast and dinner mothers like Lucy had more time to enjoy their Sundays. Gill took pride in how he knew just what time would be best for each family on his Sunday itinerary.

Before calling on the Hayeses, Gill waited until the creamed cod on toast was finished and the morning dishes were washed. He also knew enough about the Hayeses to arrive before the bourbon and gin came out of the kitchen cupboard and the stream of regular Sunday guests showed up. His conversation had the warmth of granite. There would be a few polite questions about how the Hayeses were doing. Some thoughts were shared about someone in the neighborhood who had passed on. For some, it was a shame that they had gone on before their time. For others, it was a blessing; they had suffered so. When Gill had exhausted this avenue of conversation, he cleared his throat to make sure his voice had the proper tone to bring up the next subject. *Ah, Nick, it was a fitting tribute.* He had the discretion to wait until Lucy was in the kitchen before addressing her oldest son. (The other boys were hiding upstairs.) A dollar, maybe two or even three, came out of the oldest brother's wallet to drop down the dry well that was the debt they still owed years later on Nick's funeral.

For an insurance man, Nick could have arranged things better. Like the cobbler who sends his children to school without shoes, Nick left his family without the life insurance to cover the cost of his own funeral. His final plans went no further than the purchase of a family plot at St. Mary's Cemetery. It was his way of saying he wished he had gone into real estate instead of insurance.

My father learned from his father's mistake. He bought life from Louis Schaller, the neighborhood insurance man. Louis also came to visit once in a while on Sundays. He knew money was scarce in those days and accepted whatever my father could afford as enough for the premium. His visits were different from Gill's. The moment he stepped in the living room he was offered a drink. The other Hayes boys didn't run upstairs at the sound of Louis's knock on the door. Cigarettes were lit, glasses clinked, and a few jokes went around at Richard Gill's expense. *But you got to admit,* Louis would say, *Gill Brothers does give you one hell of a send off.*

STILL LIFE WITH WINE

My father graduated from D full of expectations that were destined to remain unfulfilled. The promise of a basketball scholarship to the College of St. Thomas was later trimmed to reduced tuition and a job on the grounds crew to make up for the additional costs of books, room and board. Nick said no. Anna worked as a secretary and was already helping to pay the bills. Another child, Dave had been born two years earlier. They were now a family of eight. It wouldn't hurt his oldest son to work and help out for a while. Lucy's response was predictable. She would rather her son not go to St. Thomas at all than go there to mow the priests' lawns.

For the next year, Mark worked the same odd jobs in the neighborhood that he had done every summer throughout his high school years. Pick-up jobs were a dime a dozen along Broadway Ave. He stocked the shelves at Brix's Grocery, unloaded box cars at the railroad warehouses, and bottled fruit juices at the Grain Belt Brewery while its German owners prayed for God to lift the curse of the Eighteenth Amendment from the land. For a few extra bucks he even swallowed his pride and suited up with teams that were invariably trounced by the Harlem Globetrotters in their annual game at the Ascension Club.

He also started saving for college tuition, and in the fall of 1927 he took two classes in the night school. That winter he enrolled fulltime at the "U." In Minnesota, "the U" meant the University of Minnesota in Minneapolis. The title was never given to other universities in the Twin Cities or to the two-year normal teacher colleges scattered around the state. For the most part, private higher education in Minnesota brought to mind Lutheran Bible schools or Catholic catechism colleges. There was something faintly suspicious or unreal about the lone exception, Carleton College.

By the time my father arrived, the University had long since abandoned its original site at Chute Square overlooking St. Anthony Falls and begun to fill a much larger area a mile downstream with quaintly Romanesque, Victorian, and Beaux Arts buildings. Northrop Auditorium, the seat of the orchestra and the arts, looked out to a newer complex that stood on the higher ground overlooking the Mississippi. This new acropolis of Minneapolis—Northrop Mall—formed a quadrangle of massive neo-classical buildings that appeared to stand at attention to the right and left of Northrop, and each new building—Morrill, Smith, Tate, and Walter—was a colossus of over-statement. On the strength of the buildings' faux-Ionic columns rested the gravitas of the arts and sciences. Let the children of inherited wealth—the Crosbys, Pillsburys, Daytons, and such—turn their backs on the Mississippi to play their university games at ivy-clad institutions back East. The architectural ensemble of the new U promised a new generation of middle-class Minnesotans a no-nonsense education that overwhelmed eastern colleges and universities in scale.

The U's new buildings were intimidating to many prairie folk. When my father first stepped into the University's solemn halls, he fought back an urge to glance over his shoulder in case a doorman had suddenly come on the scene to shoo him out. His gift for drawing and painting led him to the College of Engineering and Architecture where the U housed the fine arts. At Minnesota, art was a practical matter that led to good jobs as designers and illustrators and kept the art for art's sake crowd out of the picture. The program in architecture was a mixture of Beaux Arts design, mathematics, physics, and engineering. He gambled that a strong hand in art would make up for a weak hand in math and sciences. There were times when his bluff was called. In his second year, a string of D's in algebra, analytical geometry, calculus and physics put him on probation. In his upper class years, a shift of emphasis in his coursework to drawing, painting, and architectural design brought on the long run of better grades that carried him through.

During the five years it took to finish his degree, my father continued to live with the family on Dupont, though his days and nights belonged to his new friends and their way of life at the U. But he still found time to see some of the guys from the old crowd at Ascension, at least on Fourth of July, when they got together for some baseball, a picnic, and lots of beer. The jokes were never new, and the stories had been told before. Meeting with the old friends was like your old high school basketball uniform that you put on just to show that you still could.

New friends at the U, many of them Protestants, were taking him far away from Ascension and D. There was Jerry Jyring, a Finnish guy from the Range whom my father met in design classes. There were the guys in engineering and building construction—Lyle Halvorson, Ray Nelson, and Doug Dunchee.

My father was in his last year when he met Vic Gilbertson. Vic was from Velva, North Dakota, not far from Lucy's childhood home in Olga. For his first year, Vic had gone to Luther College in Decorah, Iowa, to please his Lutheran mother. As an upper classman, Mark picked up immediately that this second year transfer student had an eye for design and a hand for watercolors. Better yet, Vic had a sense of humor, something rare for a Norwegian. Housing was tight, and Vic took my father up on the offer to stay with the Hayes household on Dupont, where he soon blended in like an adopted brother.

In those days doors that had previously been closed to a young Irishman at the U were beginning to open. In 1931, A *Minnesota Daily* survey revealed that 46 percent of campus coeds would not date a Catholic, suggesting that the core conservative Protestant base of the student body was no longer in the majority. And more than half of the women polled expected their date to dance well. To judge by the Camel ads in the *Minnesota Daily*, attractive women preferred smokers. The back page ad featured some doll giving you a "come hither" look while she smoked a Camel, inviting you to "taste the difference ... as you drown in that fragrant, mild, cool smoke, redolent with the joy of the choicest Turkish and mellow Domestic tobacco."

Prohibition made the problem of underage drinking irrelevant. Having a few at the U was a step up from the old days of sneaking in a shot in the backrooms of the drugstore speakeasies on the North Side. Down on the flats by the river just below the Washington Avenue Bridge, my father's crowd were regulars in the houseboats that lowered their planks to the river banks adjacent to the tennis courts on Saturday nights. A bit garish in their furnishings, these "bungalows on the river," as the newspaper liked to call them, were three- to four-room affairs with fully stocked bars and upright pianos bringing the tunes of

W.C. Handy, Jelly Roll Morton, and Fats Waller up the river. It didn't matter that much that the "Drys" busted the joints every now and then. One time, Lyle Halvorson told the agents when they arrived that he was going fishing and took a dive into the river. When my father found Halvorson on the river bank, he asked, if he caught anything. *Just a beer*, Halvorson said, holding up one of the hundreds of beers the "Drys" had dumped in the river. The agents showed up with a conspicuous lack of zeal every spring when some jerk from the Rev. Riley's Youth for Christ made campus drinking an issue. Nobody was ever prosecuted. Most Saturday nights, my father sipped martinis without fear and showed off his mastery of the Charleston. It was worth an occasional citation for appearing "wobbly" in public. Besides (although he never knew it) it gave his younger brothers Jim and John a laugh late on Saturday nights when he came home in the Model T and took a leak on the front yard before coming into the house.

Nights at the houseboats made for great stories. Every woman who responded to the *Minnesota Daily* survey on dating strongly preferred to date "a young man who can converse intelligently," and a "sense of humor" finished a close second. Even if there were reservations about Catholics and drinkers, the odds were moving in my father's favor. Dates came easy. Light up a camel. Persuade her to try a martini. Get her laughing at the story of Halvorson jumping in the river. Ask her if she likes to dance. The *Daily* said, above all else, its study showed the Minnesota women felt "intelligence and old-fashioned manners, with petting not necessary, made-up the perfect man." That being the case, then with his dancing skills, gift for conversation, and repressed Irish libido, Mark Hayes was their kind of man.

THE MINNEAPOLIS OF MY father's college days was a Babbitt's paradise, pandering to minor league dreams of playing big league games, as one new downtown office tower after another sprang up. The booming city offered something more than just a future with good money in front of my father's generation. It promised a chance to make something new, something modern, and something unmistakably *his* in the new Minneapolis. At times, it made him look like a fool.

In his second year, the faculty and students of architecture found themselves worshipping at the feet of Minneapolis's Tower of

Babbitt—the Foshay Tower. Everyone bought into the hype, which went something like this. A real estate tycoon, Wilbur Foshay, packaged his plan for a new skyscraper as an architectural feat unparalleled west of the Mississippi and also as a noble tribute to the city's most venerable architect, Leroy Buffington. Buffington had had his hand in virtually every experiment in modernism in Minneapolis since the 1880s. The old U campus was his architectural autobiography, wandering stylistically from the Romanesque edifices of Eddy Hall and Pillsbury Hall to the Beaux Arts decoration of Burton Hall. In 1888, Buffington had patented a design for a "cloud scraper." The concept was simple—a bigger and taller Washington Monument made of concrete and re-enforced steel. He claimed to have invented the sky-scraper and spent much of his life losing the law suits he brought against other builders and architects for stealing his design.

In 1928, Wilbur Foshay went ahead with a skyscraper in the Buffington image. There was something in the Foshay Tower for everybody. At a height of 447', it would stand as the tallest building west of Chicago. The tower's architects, Magney and Tusler, declared it would put the city in the center of the map of American modernism. At the U, it was the talk of every class in architecture that year, with Dean Ora Leland and the college's senior professors more rapturous than anyone.

One day was not enough to contain the hype for the tower's official opening. In August 1929, Wilbur Foshay spent $119,000 on a three day event. He commissioned a special march by John Phillip Sousa which the composer called "The Foshay Tower Washington Memorial." The architect Magney's son was a friend and classmate of my father, and they got passes to the grand opening where my father stood beside big shots in business and architecture. This was a big deal. He had been right not to have pushed a lawn mower through four years at the College of St. Thomas. Foshay even looked in his direction when the realtor's speech hit its high notes about how his tower pointed the way for the next generation to touch the sky. Not bad for a kid from Williston, North Dakota.

Foshay's check for $20, 000 to Sousa bounced. He vowed he would never play the march again until the check cleared, and he didn't. Not only did Foshay not pay any royalties to Buffington, the flimflam realtor had secretly filed his own application for two patents on the design.

Black Monday came a month after the grand opening of the Foshay Tower, and within three months, Wilbur Foshay's wealth on paper was worthless. He was under investigation for securities fraud. His name was inscribed in large letters at the top of each of the four sides of the tower, and at night they were illuminated, shining out in all directions across the Mill City. Alas, Wilbur himself couldn't see them from his prison cell at Leavenworth. By the time he got out three years later, all the bulbs had burned out.

After the Crash of 1929 a more sober mood settled in at the College of Engineering and Architecture, and the skyline of downtown Minneapolis didn't change much for a long time. Lacking the finances for grandiose statements of bricks and mortar, architects increasingly turned their attention to interiors and the comfort found in the details of design. Students nodded their head in agreement when a professor in class said the lesson of the Foshay fiasco was that architects, not businessmen and engineers, should be in charge in the construction of buildings. A new professor from the Chicago School of Art drew my father's eye to the gift of simplicity in a home by Frank Lloyd Wright, a chair by Peit Mondrian, or a church by Eliel Saarinen.

MY FATHER RETREATED into to his watercolors. In the winter of 1930, his "Still Life with Wine" went on display in the fine arts department's annual exhibition. At first glance, the still life was conventional. On a corner table, there was a cloth, fruit on a tray, a pitcher of water, and a decanter of wine. The earth tones in the watercolors carry a hint of sepia that invite a second look to see time as well as space, and their transparency suggests a fleeting moment as shadows cast by the pale light of late afternoon darken. A few pieces of fruit have rolled from the tray and will soon disappear altogether. These are fruits my father has never seen. A decanter of a wine he had never tasted. The objects levitate away from the corner table on which they are placed. A green cloth runs underneath and up the wall. What was familiar is not familiar. What was in place is not in place or is in too many places at once.

"Still Life with Wine" would hang on the living room wall at Dupont for decades, where, as I looked at it again and again, I saw that my father was drawn to the beauty of details and the details of his heart were somewhere else and in some other time.

Wanted Minnesota Men Who Are Willing to Work

In my father's last year at the University, *Minnesota Daily* ran an ad:

WANTED: SEVERAL MINNESOTA MEN
Who need employment and who are willing to work

His graduation ceremony on the evening of June 6, 1932, came to a close with the chairman of the music department, Earle Killeen, calling on the class of '32 to stand and sing. As he did at every commencement, Killeen conducted the class through an off-key version of his own composition, *Goodbye, Minnesota*. My father lip-synced his way through the song with a heart looking backward. It was not the nostalgia of Killeen's lyrics that turned his thoughts to the past. There is a thing called nostalgia for the future.

His father, Nick, had died from a kidney infection on February 16, 1932. In the two years before his death, his job with Hartford Insurance had come down to closing out policies after the foreclosure of a client's farm or small business and casting a skeptical eye on claims filed in the plague of fires that was striking bankrupt businesses. In these last years, Nick was rarely on the road anymore. His stocky frame became stout and puffy. His spoke in prickly fragments, hectoring his son with incomplete questions like *Just a "C" in Mechanical Engineering?* or *More, watercolors?*

There was only one pleasant memory from this time. One day in early February a blizzard shut down the city. In the morning, my father dressed for the U—a suit and tie, overcoat, and hat—but the street cars weren't going anywhere that day. There were drifts as high as the first floor windows on the house at Dupont. For a long time, Nick had said little around the house. That morning his voice was wistful. The snows were deeper when he was a boy on the farm in Ontario, he remembered aloud. The snows would keep them on the farm and unable to get to town for a week or longer. Big Jim would organize Nick and his four brothers in teams to shovel paths to make sure cows were milked, horses walked, and water drawn from the well.

Such reminiscing was unusual. Nick never said a thing to his sons about his childhood on the farm. After a pause, he said it was time to get going. They had shoveling to do. Each took a shovel and went to work. When the job was done, sensing the day was already a memory, Nick had Anna take a photograph of the five Hayes men: Nick and Mark in suits, ties, overcoats and gentlemen's hats, Jim in a jacket and Irish cap, John in a kid's parka, and young Dave in a snow suit. They stand, shovels in hand, surrounded by snow, and immobile as a still scene about to fade out before the roll of the credits.

On February 16, my father called Father Dunphy for Nick's last rites and Richard Gill for the final arrangements. Nick's sisters, three aunts in black, came by train from Toronto for the funeral and for an unspecified period of mourning. For the week after the funeral, the three aunts in their long black dresses hovered around the house at Dupont mumbling the rosary and complaining that their brother should have been buried at the family plot in Barrie, Ontario. The priest of the family, Parnell, deferred until later their invitation to lead them in the Sorrowful Mysteries of the Rosary. He slipped into the den by himself to sip his bourbon while an ancient aunt's soulful voice intoned, *Our Lord's Agony in the Garden.*

Lucy had enough on her mind already. Her house was at once full and empty—full with the family and guests and empty with the absence of Nick. The rosary helped get her out of there. At night alone in her bed, her fingers moved from one bead to another until they were holding a pen in her hand and she was writing another letter to Nick as she had done every Sunday evening thirty years earlier, in the time of their courtship, from her Langdon home. When she woke in the morning, she sought comfort in established routine. Now, she prepared the morning breakfast for her six children, brother Parnell, and the three aunts, and made it out the back door, down the alley and into Ascension a few minutes later than usual for the 7: 00 a.m. Mass. A few days into the week of mourning, this ritual ended with a twist. After the breakfast, as she did every morning, she grabbed the garbage, tossed it in the garbage pail as she flew out the door, crossed herself at the garage, and sailed down the alley and into the Ascension Church. Taking her customary place on the St. Joseph side of the altar, she raised her right arm to open her missal. In her hand, she found she had carried the garbage to church. She had tossed her *Saint Joseph Daily Missal* into the trash at home. The three aunts were driving her up a tree. She sent them home to Toronto and never heard from them again. She also gave one of them a reason decades later for ignoring my telephone call bearing the news that a grand-nephew would be visiting in Toronto.

Money was always tight, and now, Lucy owed Gill Brothers for the funeral. Anna brought in a little from her job as a secretary in a law office. At the end of the winter quarter at the U, my father dropped out of the regular day program and considered himself lucky to pick-up hard-scrabble jobs here and there along Broadway. He finished his degree requirements in his last spring quarter by taking five classes in the night school. The groceries were on credit at Brix's. After a week of knocking on old doors, my father answered the ad in the *Daily* for "several Minnesota men . . . who are willing to work."

It turned out that Northern States Power was behind the ad for Minnesota men. The promising young architect, my father, took the job of stripping, by hand, the bark off the trunks of long pine trees and trimming them into telephone poles.

Back at Dupont, he joked that at least he was working in design.

When June came, no jobs were waiting for the Class of '32. He stripped tree trunks for the rest of the summer while his friends from the U searched for jobs that didn't exist. Later he moved up in the design field. In the fall, he and his friend Lyle launched their first business venture—Hayes and Halvorson. It was capitalized with a couple of buckets and paint brushes. For the next year, they painted murals on office walls, theater lobbies, and restaurants. Their masterpiece was the mural on the walls of the new Hasty-Tasty Restaurant at Lyndale and Lake in south Minneapolis. As the customers of the Hasty-Tasty dined, the brush strokes of Hayes and Halvorson carried them away in their imagination to tour a few Aegean islands or enjoy a drink on the veranda of a villa under the blush of a pastel Mediterranean sunset.

PLAYING ALL THE ANGLES

Guys who grew up on the North Side associated newspaper boys with criminal activity.

When my father bought his dream house on Forest Dale in 1954, his neighbor across the street was another kid from the North Side who had also made it. He had started out as a newspaper boy. Kid Cann (Isadore Blumenfield) had grown up down in the Jewish neighborhood that clustered around Fourth Street N. and extended northward into Ascension. As a boy, Kid Cann hawked newspapers on Fourth Street. He muscled out a few kids and organized a few others to make "Newspaper Row" along Fourth Street into his first racket.

There never were enough Sicilians in Minneapolis to put together a half-way decent mob. That task fell to the Jews on the Near North Side with the Irish placing a weak second. Kid Cann had kept the peace with Minneapolis's Irish gangsters by dividing up control of the North Side. With a hand shake, Kid Cann let Tommy Banks, Minneapolis's Irish mobster, keep control of the Broadway neighborhood. By the late 1920s, Kid Cann controlled the core of Minneapolis's gambling, speakeasy, and prostitution rackets. His old neighborhood was the vice capital of the Upper Midwest. He covered his tracks by donating to every charity on the North Side. When a reporter noted that his money went to synagogues, Catholic churches, Lutheran ministries, and Baptist revivals, Kid Cann shrugged his shoulders and said, *Why not? I like to play all the angles.*

Kidd Cann was right. During the 1930s you had to play every angle. The lesson taught by the times was, in Damon Runyon's inimitable words, *All life is six to five against.* My father, Big shot Joe College, didn't look so smart playing the college angle when employers preferred to fill the only jobs out there with high school drop-outs. My father's career as an architect survived in the form of a few books on a shelf at Dupont and a drafting table that he had thrown together with a piece of plywood and saw horses. Career choices were limited. When he wasn't out working on telephone poles or murals, my father sat day after day at his make-shift desk in shirt and tie, drawing, and trying to keep his pride intact.

It didn't help his ego when, after Nick died, Uncle Parnell started showing up regularly on weekends from Des Moines, arriving Friday night and staying until the milk train left Sunday night. He had an arrangement with his monastery in Des Moines. He would conduct a mission and a vocation drive on behalf of the Passionists every Sunday at one of the local parishes. At Dupont, the priest took over Nick's place in the armchair for drinks with guests on Saturdays and Sundays. Sipping on a bourbon and water, Parnell always opened up the conversation by telling whatever new guest was on hand that Lucy needed a hand keeping an eye on things. "Things" included his nieces' boyfriends. Lucy had been too easily taken in by the new Packard Anna's boyfriend drove. Young Eileen spent too much time with that Jewish furrier's son.

Parnell also had ideas for how my father could get ahead. The career counseling, however, always involved Saturday afternoon visits with another priest. In the rectory library, the drinks came out. De La Salle, the priest would say, a good start. Although jobs were few and far between, Parnell's nephew needed to know there's work out there for the right sort. Then again, with all the goings-on—communist agitators and the Teamsters making such a ruckus—there was a feeling out there about guys from the North Side. It would also be a bit more helpful if Father Dunphy could be more discrete in his enthusiasm for left-leaning Governor Floyd B. Olson.

Parnell felt his nephew's lack of interest in the Holy Name Society and the Knights of Columbus was hurting his prospects. This observation was about as close as the priests came to practical advice. After a while, it was fine if the young man had something else to do and needed to leave. After most of these Saturday sessions and much later in the night, the bartender at the Leamington Hotel downtown would call Dupont. The pattern was so frequent that the bartender had come to know my father and his brothers by name. He would tell whoever answered the phone that they had better come down. Their uncle was in no shape to make it home on his own.

Meanwhile, Hayes and Halvorson, Inc. had set up their corporate headquarters in my father's bed room at Dupont. A movie theater lobby, here, a dentist office there, a few jobs came their way. My father picked up some temp work as a draftsman for engineering firms. The first turned out to be a bit more temporary than he had planned after he felt obliged to tell the boss that he was not just a draftsman, but an architect. After that, he kept his mouth shut about his degree in architecture.

For the first year after college, you could laugh about it. The money from his odd jobs together with Anna's wages as a secretary in a downtown law office brought home the groceries and spared them from

Richard Brix's generous offer of credit. Some bills got paid on time. By the second year, the joke was getting old. His flannel suits came out only for Mass on Sundays. Monday through Friday, the suits stayed in the closet, waiting for a cue call in a play that never opened.

THESE WERE THE YEARS WHEN North Minneapolis was the nation's by-line for labor troubles. In 1932, when one of the North Side's own, Floyd B. Olson, made it to the governor's mansion in St. Paul on a mixture of the Farmer-Labor Party, populism, and socialism, Ascension parish was the engine of his get-out-the-vote drive. Out of the basement of the Ascension Club came an army of door knockers and a fleet of kids on bicycles fanning out across the North Side to spread Olson's Farmer-Labor message. My uncle, little brother Dave, was at the head of the pack of kids on bikes. Dave played a special role in the operation. In a prescient sign that Dave would be the Mr. Wizard of the family, he broke new technological ground by adapting a small engine to his bike and turning it into the North Side's first motorbike.

Never one to preoccupy himself with all the pettifoggery about the separation of church and state, Dunphy's Sunday sermons that fall were a litany in praise of Floyd B. Olson. My father's vote for Olson meant only that he was from the North Side, not that he was committed to the Norwegian's politics. He enjoyed the Olson governorship because Olson's name came up a lot in conversation, which was the cue for my father to tell the stories about Dave and his amazing motorbike.

By 1934, the city's labor battles threw the streets of the North Side up against City Hall. City leaders in Minneapolis were striving to promote its image as a city apart, less a real city than an urban theme park, and they became downright churlish when labor organizers on the North Side put Minneapolis above the fold in the nation's newspapers, right up there with headlines about violent clashes between labor and police in Toledo and San Francisco. City Hall turned for help to its allies behind the scenes in the form of the Citizen's Alliance. Posing as civic boosters, the Citizen's Alliance was really a bunch of Walter Mittys gone sour. They led a not-so-secret life as vigilantes in cahoots with the Minneapolis Police Department (MPD), which had done little to clean up its reputation for corruption since Lincoln Steffens published *The Shame of Minneapolis* in 1903. Their tactics stopped just short of public lynchings in the campaigns to keep blacks in their place, restrict Jews to a few residential pockets in the city, and bust the heads of labor that dared to preach the gospel of the CIO.

The troubles started in the winter of 1934 with the takeover of Teamsters Local 574. Until then, the local had been a sleepy crafts union made up of guys who were ushers at Mass on Sundays. Monday through Friday, they never let out a peep of dissent against the downtown boys who touted Minneapolis as a national shrine dedicated to the "open shop." Behind the takeover of Teamsters Local 574 were a few guys from Detroit and Chicago who were, in fact, guilty as charged. They did carry CIO literature and pamphlets by Trotsky across state lines. The leadership and rank and file, however, remained local. Old neighborhood guys, the Dunne brothers—Ray, Miles, and Grant—Farrell Dobbs, Carl Skoglund and the rest, should have known better than to quote Trotsky. Almost nobody in Minneapolis had ever heard of the guy in the first place. He had name recognition only among the city's anti-Semites who never missed an opportunity to launch a pogrom.

In February, a strike shut down the creamery on lower Broadway, bringing on a season of social sullenness at Ascension. The strike divided the parish among a few shop stewards ousted for towing the company line, many more guys way down on their luck, tempted but not daring to cross the picket lines, and a score more of men who got back from the Teamsters a swagger they had lost somewhere in their first jobs after high school.

Life in the national limelight might have made Teamsters Local 574 a bit too cocky. When strikers in Ohio and California raised the ante with calls for a general strike, Local 574 did the same. Why not call when the city bluffed with armed police and the governor betrayed his own by mobilizing the National Guard? The downtown boys saw Bolsheviks plotting a communist revolution. My father saw the familiar faces of guys from the North Side among the truckers, some of them dumb, some damn smart, and some just there for the hell of it. It was hard for him to take this labor stuff seriously when he had known many of the key players since he was a kid. The strike's organizer, Farrell Dobbs, was one of the old gang who had hung around North Commons Park. A nice enough guy, Dobbs would probably come up short a few letters if asked to recite the alphabet. There wasn't a guy among them who could even spell Bolshevik.

But it turned out the city bosses weren't bluffing. The Auto-Lite Strike had its "Battle of Toledo" in May. San Francisco's Waterfront Strike had its "Bloody Thursday" on July 5. Minneapolis's turn came on Friday, July 20. A push and shove between strikers and the police, shots fired at unarmed picketers, tear-gassing strike headquarters, a few strikers dead on the streets and many more wounded—the pattern in the three cities was the same, except that in Minneapolis Floyd B. Olson played both sides, mobilizing the Minnesota National Guard but keeping it out of the fight.

It had nothing to do with the Hayeses, though the faint whiff of tear gas did drift on the wind from the warehouse district to Dupont. All the same, this was personal. The MPD and the several hundred overly eager volunteers it deputized from the Citizen's Alliance opened fire on unarmed strikers in the warehouse district killing two, injuring more than 50, and not even bothering to cover up that many had been shot in the back. My father may have had his university degree and big shot ideas, but in many ways he was still just one more guy on the North Side trying to make a buck. Roots trumped education. The MPD and the Citizen's Alliance wanted to send a message on "Bloody Friday" to the North Side guys about just who ran the town. The message my father received was about not trusting those new Republican friends, about sticking up for your own, and about emotions erupting suddenly, seeming to appear out of nowhere when the police came down on Dunne, O'Brien, and countless others whose names could have been lifted from the rosters of old Ascension baseball teams.

It was getting harder to keep up appearances back at Dupont. After eighth grade graduation at Ascension, Eileen had been offered a scholarship to St. Margaret's that would have required her to work in the school cafeteria. To no one's surprise, Lucy declared that her daughter wasn't going to wash dishes for anyone. Instead, Eileen went to North. When parish ladies commented, *Did you know Eileen Hayes is going to North*, the remark was code for saying money was tight in the Hayes household. Her brothers' education, however, obscured the point. The in-house editor of *Le Cheval du Nord*, Jim had gone to North. The family line had been that he wanted to write for the school newspaper at North. Later, Jim scrapped up enough money to put himself through the

U where he studied in the J-School. Among my father's three brothers, only John followed his oldest brother's footsteps and went to *D*. There were embarrassments. After John showed up too many times without a uniform at meetings of his Boy Scout Troop, the Scoutmaster discreetly bought him a uniform. But these things weren't talked about.

The year 1934 made '32 and '33 look like boom years for Hayes and Halvorson, and my father took a second look at an offer he had turned down eight years earlier when he graduated from *D*. On Saturday nights and the occasional weekend tournament, he picked up about five to ten bucks playing right guard for the semi-pro team, the House of David. If God gave you a good jump shot, he must have meant for you to use it.

There was also a little money to be made in the boxing ring at Ascension. The sports promoters were always Jewish guys who convinced no one that they weren't fronts for Kid Cann's gambling rackets. They arranged prize fights that let the better man—the fighter from the Phyllis Wheatly House or the fighter from the Ascension Club—win for the prize of a few bucks on the side. There was better money to be made in the fights at Noonan's on Broadway.

With the repeal of Prohibition, things had changed at Noonan's. The café on the first floor now served 3.2. The third floor, where, as home to the Railway Workers Fraternal Association, the gentlemen of Ascension throughout the Prohibition years enjoyed their drinks comfortably and at ease from any fear of a visit by the Drys, was transformed, alternating from one Saturday night to the next between boxing and wrestling matches with a prize of eight bucks to the winner. My father thought he just might give it a try. With time on his hands, he took to working out in the Ascension Club's training room. Over a punching bag, he could imagine himself playing Jimmy Braddock to some would-be Max Baer on the North Side. Not likely. Six to five, he would go down in the first to an emerging Joe Louis from Phyllis Wheatly.

Ask a man without a job. You don't have to be in jail to do time. Especially when a day of long and empty hours turned to night, my father let his imagination fill up the time with fantasies of other lives. Dreams spun around in his head as if they had come alive out of the detective magazines he hid in his room upstairs where Lucy could not see the covers. Paperback dreams were a ticket to elsewhere. Clean-up after the fight. Joke with the reporters. Then, catch the late show at the

Nicollet Hotel ballroom. A cold, slow sip of the martini. A long drag of the Camel. The doll at his side not half bad. Would she care to? Why yes. *You know, for a fighter, you dance well.*

The next day he was back in his room at the drawing table. It was another slow day at Hayes and Halvorson. His watercolors had given way to black and white, pen and ink. A sketch of the stable and carriage house that had become the garage at Dupont, the old mill at the river by the Lowry Bridge, a pre-Civil War farm house across the street on 16th—these were things to hold on to, and better done with the permanence of India ink than with the impressionability of watercolors.

Downstairs Parnell thought he was being helpful by calling up to his nephew the jobs he found in the newspaper's want-ads.

As 1935 drew to a close, a sense of humor and a gift for drawing was all that was left in the bank. My father made his own greeting card for the New Year, showing him seated at his drawing table, pen in hand and busily sketching. His Joe College look was getting a bit old. The slacks had turned to knee patches for help and even those were frayed at the edges. The elbow patches on his Golden Gopher cardigan were sprouting a bouquet of loose threads. Never willing to sketch his own face, he had cut and pasted a photo that betrayed how his signature red hair had taken on the gray tones of cigarette smoke and worry. On the wall behind him, he posted a resume of his work—sketches of an office building, a church, a neo-classical facade, a house, and an outhouse, which underscored his willingness to take *any* job. Two items suggested time on his hands—a nude in water and a game of tick-tack-toe. Two beer steins and a mug rested on top of a small bookcase, which also held his design books. A scroll in the upper right corner of the card bore tidings for the coming year: "In this Year of Our Lord 1936, Mark Hayes Extends His Greetings."

He answered a newspaper ad placed by the St. Louis firm Maguolo & Quick, and received the reply that went a little further than the standard regrets and best wishes for his success. Maguolo & Quick had already filled its opening for an architect, but informed him that new offices would be opening in Chicago and Rochester in the coming year. In the meantime, Mr. Hayes was invited to apply for a position as a draftsman with the St. Louis office. Six to five against, he held a weak hand. He took the job. Vic put in his two cents worth with a reminder

New Years Card, 1936

that Frank Lloyd Wright had first gone to Chicago to be a draftsman.

A job, a ticket to Union Station, a downtown hotel reservation, the Cardinals, and a song by W. C. Handy pretty much summed up what my father knew about St. Louis when he left Minneapolis in January 1936. He soon learned why he had been invited to St. Louis. After World War I, Maguolo & Quick had established itself as go-to architects for the Catholic building boom that roared through the 1920s, and the "New Building" at DeLaSalle high school had been among their projects. They knew their new hire was over-qualified for the draftsman work but anticipated that his gifts in design, drawing, and painting would pay off when Catholics started building again. To show off their new hire's gifts for drawing and painting, the firm first sent him to do the architect's renditions for plum sub-contracting jobs with Frank Lloyd Wright's firm in Chicago and with Eliel Saarinen at Cranbrook near Detroit. In his first year with Maguolo & Quick, home was a suitcase of soft tan leather with the initials MNH. Nights were downtown hotel rooms or Pullman cars. A future Frank Lloyd Wright by day, Damon Runyon by night, the disparate parts of his dreams had come together. Life was working out.

To ADD TO HIS REVERSAL of fortune, the Catholics were starting to build again, and my father returned to Minnesota to work on the expansion of St. Mary's Hospital in Rochester. He got on well with the Sisters of St. Francis. The work on the hospital was pedestrian with the exception of a few flares of design that he put into the chapel. He had not been on the Rochester job long when Maguolo & Quick decided that he just might be able to pull off a long shot job bid for the new cathedral being built by the Diocese of Duluth.

The detail of an Irish cross distracted Duluth's Bishop Welsh for an instant. As the bishop looked on, my father shuffled through his drawings of the interior of the cathedral. The Bishop's nod of approval for the small bit of old Ireland that survived in the design set off a chain of reflex gestures. His Excellency was nodding, pointing, and uttering exclamations of agreement so automatically and enthusiastically that the adjutant at his side felt obliged to praise Bishop Welsh's creative genius as if the design was the prelate's, not the architect's. *Your Excellency*, my father said in his closing remarks, *you would agree, would you not, that*

Duluth does not have to imitate St. Paul in everything it does? The closing rhetoric had the desired effect. The bids from other architects with
their predictable designs for small replicas of the Cathedral of St. Paul
were consigned sight unseen by His Excellency into the wastebasket of
Duluth's architectural history.

Later that evening, Bishop Welsh invited the adjutant to join him
for dinner. His Excellency told the younger priest how they would take
Duluth out of the Dark Ages and into modern times. It was time to rid
the Church's House of Worship of all those gargoyles, domes, and spires.
Didn't the assistant agree that you could almost see God's grace in subtle
pastel light radiating from the stained glass windows? Somehow, the
bishop could not explain why, the light tones of the bleached red-oak
woodworking made him think of the purity of the Blessed Virgin. The
adjutant wholeheartedly agreed with His Excellency's observations on
the theology of the design. Don't get His Excellency wrong. He was not
criticizing His Grace in St. Paul. Yet, perhaps the archbishop needed to
remember that Our Dear Lord's Sermon on the Mount taught us how
we could say more by saying less.

It did not matter to my father that his ideas went without attribu-
tion. Six years after graduation, he was at last a practicing architect.
And, it would never occur to His Excellency that his new Cathedral
was a composite of concepts my father had taken from the Lutheran
Saarinen, the hedonist Frank Lloyd Wright, and Bauhaus communists
in Europe.

It had been a long time coming. My father was pushing 30, but
finally he had some money in his pocket and some respect. Maguolo
& Quick gave him a bump in salary even though the firm put off his
promotion from draftsman to architect. He had a free hand in carrying
out the Duluth project. Everything, from the design to the details, from
the selection of building materials to supervision on the job site, from
respectfully ignoring His Excellency's suggestions to bickering with local
chiselers over the pricing of materials, fell on his shoulders. This was
the way he wanted it. The trips back to St. Louis were few. The senior
partners at Maguolo & Quick put in their two cents worth and then
pretty much left him alone. When in Duluth, His Excellency's insights
came to him second hand over cocktails and dinner at the Duluth Hotel
with the adjutant. Good points, my father acknowledged. Looking at

the priest across the table, he gave the appearance of jotting down the bishop's ideas as he sat pen in hand, yellow legal tablet resting on his crossed legs. Appearances were the thing. It did not matter that my father's pencil was sketching a fine looking couple at the table behind the priest. By the time the Cathedral was completed, he had a notebook of drawings that made Duluth's hoi polloi look like Peter Arno's *New Yorkers* out on the town, except for one detail. The image of the hotel's stuffed black bear in the background let you know that this was Duluth, not Manhattan.

My father spiffed up his wardrobe. A guy needed to look sharp when he stepped up to the bar at the Duluth Hotel. He also bought a '38 Pontiac Roadster. People took note that there was a new guy on Highway 61 in the summer of 1938. A flair of a roadster on the highway, a dapper architect in a fedora hat at the wheel, his left hand draped over the rolled down window, flicking the ashes of a Camel, and a greeting – *Welcome back, Mr. Hayes, how was the drive up* – at the reception desk of the Duluth Hotel. It all added up to meaning he was somebody. He bought a dog. It was a statement. The black cocker spaniel seated beside him in the front seat added the final touch to the bachelor image.

ANNA

Back at Dupont, there were problems with the men in his sisters' lives. His little sister Eileen had her heart broken. Parnell convinced Lucy that she had to put an end to her daughter's romance with the wealthy Jewish furrier's son. Parnell wasn't blaming Eileen. The problem would never have occurred had she gone to the Catholic St. Margaret's Academy for Girls. Eileen had met the Ribnick boy at North High School. He was a fine young man. He came around to join the family for Sunday breakfast. He always joked it was the only place where he could eat bacon. He never took his eyes off Eileen. These things lead to only one end, Parnell told Lucy. They didn't want a mixed marriage in the Hayes family.

Meanwhile, Anna had become quite the gal about town. All her friends seemed to be Republican. Just maybe, she was doing a bit too well. It wasn't too much of a shock when she announced she was going to work for the gubernatorial campaign of a Republican lawyer named Harold Stassen. She was also serious about Al, a guy with money who drove a Packard. Parnell had his doubts about the guy but understood he was not to meddle in the social lives of the two older children, Anna and Mark. So he said not a word. In fact, he stopped mentioning Anna's name at all when, in the spring of 1939, she and her boyfriend Al went on a cruise. The cruise was not mentioned in the house. Anna was never the same again after she returned. Al stopped coming around the house, and his name disappeared from conversation. Anna's brothers and sister didn't even mention the word Packard anymore.

Anna Hayes

Lucy could not understand why, after all these years, Anna had decided she should have an operation to remove a concentration of varicose veins in her legs that she'd had since adolescence. And why, she wondered, wasn't she having the procedure at the Catholic hospital, St. Mary's? It was a simple surgical procedure. My father took a couple of days off work to be there for his big sister.

The night before the surgery, a wistful nostalgia came over my father. He and Anna had outgrown their lives at Dupont. His big sister was all grown up now, with grown up problems. He stared at an old photo of Anna and himself taken in 1911, two country kids from Williston, North Dakota. They're holding hands. Anna's cropped hair is crowned with an enormous bow that begs the camera to focus on it. She wears her Sunday best dress and pinafore with rickrack edging cut out and hand sewn by Lucy. Her brother is in denim overalls. The folds and high cuffs at the bottoms let you know that he'll be wearing these overalls for a few more years. His broad brimmed straw hat is there to protect his red hair and fair skin from the sun of the North Dakota summers. He and his big sister, they had been together in this thing for a long time, starting out in Williston, moving to Minneapolis, going from one city neighborhood to the next, and making the family name count for something from Broadway to Hennepin.

In a blink of the eye all those years vanish. My father laughed at the thought. He and Anna would have to go out for drinks, lunch, and a good talk after the operation.

In the morning, he drove Anna to the hospital. While Anna was being prepared for surgery, the surgeon, Dr. Jones came out to talk with my father in the waiting room. Jones offered him a Pall Mall. The procedure would be fairly short. His sister would stay overnight for routine observation. He could check her out of the hospital the next morning. Later in the evening, the surgeon called. The hemorrhaging had been completely unexpected.

My father called Richard Gill.

6
If He Didn't Care

Stories about my father's bachelor days always left something out. His old flames had never really burned. The Charleston contests he had won and the fine times at the Nicollet Hotel Ballroom were re-told as solo performances where he danced and dined alone. The girlfriends remained rumors alluded to in incomplete sentences, coming to life obliquely when a second or third martini let down the guard of one of my aunts, uncles, or my father's friends from the old days. An innuendo in the *D* yearbook, *The Athanasian,* that he had danced his way into the hearts of a few St. Margaret's girls, went no further than a bookshelf at the house on Dupont. For decades it discretely shared its secret with the poetry volumes of James Whitcomb Riley on the shelf and was careful not to be overheard by the snooping twelve volumes of the *Catholic Encyclopedia* on the shelf above. My Aunt Eileen once or twice hinted about a North Side girl with a broken heart who never married and cried at my father's funeral.

My mother occasionally let on that she knew something. She would begin by saying she wasn't born yesterday and then recount how she put a stop to her husband's partying with old friends and all those women who wanted to sit on his lap. The presence of one woman in particular was told in bits and pieces over so many years that the parts of her story never made up a whole. A sculptor, she and my father had met during their university days. Later, she did some artwork for his churches. There was always a bit of irritation in my mother's voice when she recalled how the woman would call my father at home. The calls annoyed my father, my mother said, bringing the anecdote to an end and preempting the next question. The woman was nothing more than an inappropriate telephone call interrupting the family dinner. Her letters to my father meant nothing more than something he had forgotten in a drawer and had meant to throw away or, so at least, my mother decided when she sorted through his things after he died. She was in her nineties when she told me about the letters.

A BLIND DATE WITH AN OLD MAN

If I didn't care,
Honey child, more than words can say,
If I didn't care,
Would I feel this way?
Darling, if this isn't love,
Then why do I thrill so much
And what is it
That makes my head go round and round
While my heart just stands still so much,
If I didn't care for you.

— *"If I Didn't Care,"* The Inkspots

My father was working on location at St. Mary's Hospital in Rochester in 1940 when an Ingrid Bergman of a nurse arrived from Winnipeg and turned his head. By then, Vic Gilbertson had joined him at Maguolo & Quick, and Vic was equally smitten. They knew the guy who was dating a friend of this newcomer, and put him up to the idea of arranging a blind date for St. Patrick's Day. They flipped a coin while they were having a few. The winner got the date. The loser paid for the drinks.

Over and over again, my mother has told the story of when she first saw her white-haired blind date at her doorstep. She thought he looked like an old man. *Oh well*, she thought, *too late to get out of it*. This would be a mercy date for an old Irish guy on St. Patrick's Day.

The foursome started out with drinks at Rochester's in-spot, the Hollywood Bar. My father led the group into the bar. The awkward moves of a first date gave way to the polished moves of a repeat act. There was an exchange of first name hellos with Mike the owner. Yes, they agreed, it was a great day for the Irish and, of course, my father would have the usual, a table by the bar and, in case Mike wanted to know, my father's unusual new guest was named Vivian. What would

Above: My mother, Vivian Armstrong, Winnipeg, 1939; Right: My father, 1940

she like to drink? My father answered by telling his date the Hollywood fixed a great martini. She wasn't going to tell him that she had never heard of the cocktail. When she choked on her first sip, she pretended it was just a slight cough that had been nagging her and rasped out a few more for credibility's sake. But an olive gave her away. Pointing to her glass, she asked, *What do you do with this? With what?* My father replied. *The green thing in the glass,* she continued. *This,* he replied as he picked his up by its toothpick and popped it into his mouth. He added that he loved them stuffed with anchovies. The gaps in her vocabulary were already exposed. She didn't ask about anchovies. A quick swallow and a hard blink of her eyes was all she had to say about her first taste of an olive.

They moved on to a roadhouse outside of town which featured a Minnesota version of the big band sound. His stories began to come out—about clubs in St. Louis and Chicago, night life in Minneapolis, and speakeasies on the river back in his university days.

ON THE DETAILS OF HER own biography, my mother was not quite so forthcoming. She was from a small town in Manitoba and had come to Winnipeg for nurses training. In an effort to establish a bit of common Canadian ground, my father interjected that his father was Canadian—

from Toronto, to be precise. He could not have known that with this remark he was moving his family's history away from, not closer to his date's family. So what if she didn't want to talk about Canada? A little reticence works well on a first date. There were plenty of other things to talk about and to do. They danced. Later that night when she was back in her room, she reminisced. The way he moved and held her, he danced so smoothly. She had been fooled. His white hair had fooled her, leaving her unprepared and vulnerable to the sea blue eyes, the curve of a smile, and the features of a handsome face.

On the following Monday, he called her at work to ask her out for dinner that night. She insisted they go Dutch. It was a declaration of sorts meant to let him know that she was a nurse with a good salary and that she valued her independence. You didn't kick up your heels on a Monday date. They went to a local diner where he said they made a great Swiss steak. They each washed down the steaks with bottle cokes poured into glasses over ice that fizzed while the steaks steamed with hot gravy and mashed potatoes. He poured Durkee's Sauce on his. No, he was neither the first Catholic nor even the first Irishman she had dated. There was something about the Catholics that attracted her. The nuns at St. Boniface before and now at St. Mary's were so good to her. She even went to the Catholic Mass at the Chapel in St. Mary's on some Sundays. As she played the Catholic card, her mind's eye brought up the image of her Grandma Larson on the farm at Otter's Lake in northern Manitoba. Every evening after dinner, Grandma Larson—who never spoke a word of English—read the Bible out loud in Swedish while she and her grand-daughter sat by the fire underneath a photograph of Grandma's father, a Lutheran Bishop far away in a village in Sweden. If he had asked, *Do you she speak Swedish?*, he would have learned it was her first language. She might have taught him the Swedish words for their dinner entrees. He never asked.

The next Saturday night they took a long drive in the Pontiac Road-ster to a steakhouse in the country. On the way back, my father tuned in a Chicago station broadcasting a show live from a club. The Inkspots were his favorites, he said, nodding toward her and pointing at the car radio. *If I didn't care*, he chimed in, *would I act this way*. He was adding his half-singing, half-talking voice to the high tenor's talking-chorus. The hum of the Pontiac on the road at night, the lights from the dash-

My father and his Pontiac Roadster, Rochester, MN, 1940

board and radio, the mellifluous Negro voices from Chicago, his voicing of the songs—something happened. She was even starting to catch on to some of his jokes. Yes, honey child, would he act this way if he didn't care for her?

The following Monday morning he called her again at work. Was she seeing anyone else? If so, she would have to break it off if she wanted to continue going out him. She admitted that there was another guy but he was not important. She omitted details. My father never knew the other guy was Irish from St. Paul or that his father owned several Catholic gift stores, and that he had even brought her home for a weekend to meet his family. She also did not mention or drop the slightest hint about a young doctor left on the hook back in Manitoba. Catch and release, she let him go, but not before he had mailed her an engagement ring. She wrote him that she couldn't accept it, but he wrote back, telling her to keep it anyway. The ring went to her younger sister Eva back in Erickson who wore it for the rest of her life.

My father's phone call had changed things. No longer just a date, they became quite the item on the Rochester scene. They were fixtures at Mike's Hollywood Bar and the clubs outside of town. While her friend Germane switched boyfriends every few weeks, and Mark's friends seemed to be tackling the task of dating the entire roster of eligible local nurses, a few weeks of going out together gave Mark and Vivian an aura of immutability. His closest friend Vic filled her in with so many stories about my father's younger days and the Hayeses back at Dupont that he struck her as a member of the family rather than just a friend.

All this while, little came up about her life in Canada. It wasn't because he was not curious. She was embarrassed to tell him. Once he commented on the obvious. The name Armstrong didn't sound Swedish. No, she replied, her father's family had changed their name from Sjogren to Armstrong, and without a pause she changed the subject, neglecting to add that the name change had been inspired by her grandfather's success in a hammering contest at a local fair.

In fact her grandpa and uncles had changed their names back and forth from Sjogren to Armstrong more than once, depending on where they were looking for work. But she didn't tell him these things. When you're dating a guy from the city, you don't talk about a childhood in a three-room wooden frame house in Erickson, Manitoba, that had neither running water nor electricity. She and her sister Eva would walk half a mile from their home every day to a well, buckets in hand, even in the depths of winter. They traveled back and forth from their home in Erickson to Grandma Larson's farm in a buggy in summers and a sleigh in winters, with her Uncle Axel at the reins of the family's two draw horses, Rusty and Dan, whom she knew so well they were like cousins. Their winter food came from the vegetables her mother Elsie had canned and the huge stocks of venison from deer her father Herman had hunted and then hung as carcasses in the smokehouse. She only knew clothes hand made by her mother until Grandma Larson bought her the uniform for nurse's training. In the winter, she and her sister Eva wore mukluks made by the Cree who lived outside the town.

Her father had taught her how to make traps in the winter for rabbits. A furrier from Winnipeg would pay 25 cents apiece for the skins. Would her date care if he heard how her father had to borrow a car to drive her to nurse's training in Winnipeg? At the door to her dormitory, he gave her five dollars, saying it was all he had. He wished he could give her more. It was the only time she had ever seen anything that resembled a tear in his eye. Entering the lavatory in the dormitory was the first time she had ever seen a water faucet. She hesitated and watched what the other girls did. Then, cautiously and slowly, she went to the sink and for the first time in her life turned on running water.

Why bring all of this up? Her mother Elsie called it dumb Swedish stuff. Her date probably thought all Swedes wore helmets with horns on their heads and dressed in animal hides. Then again, he had been a boy in Williston, North Dakota. He must have known the secrets of the coldest nights of those long winters of the northern prairie. He must have heard the same music in the shimmering of the northern lights and seen how their aura came down so close to the earth that the family on the next farm over could touch the light.

She did tell him how the Blessed Virgin appeared to her in the barn, an aura of blue light in the hay loft on Grandma Larson's farm. It was part of her explanation for her interest in the Catholics. Don't all Catholics have apparitions?

In May, things got serious. He asked her to come up to Minneapolis for a weekend to meet his mother and family. It was late Saturday afternoon when they arrived. The dog Ginger rushed the door, curled up at my mother's feet, and rolled over on her back. She welcomed this. It was easier for a Manitoba girl to greet a dog than to meet the Hayes family. Her future in-laws, Lucy, Jim and John, lay in wait at the kitchen table. The first round of bourbon and water was out. A plate of buttered saltines with slices of longhorn cheese was on the table. This was a long way away from Grandma Larson's farm. *Mom, I want you to meet Viv,* was the extent of her introduction. The ritual of names and handshakes went around the kitchen table. *Dave!* Lucy called. It went unanswered. The youngest of the Hayes brothers, Dave reserved his right to stay in his room with his door shut. *What would you like to drink, Viv?* Jim offered, assuming the role of host.

An interruption gave her a few moments to think over her answer to this, the first test question: Eileen had made her way into the kitchen. Seeing Eileen, my mother's first thought was that it was no wonder Vic was always talking about her. He was in love with her. Every guy who had ever set foot in the house on Dupont was in love with Eileen.

Their first meeting was not Eileen's finest moment. Her anxiety about a first date that evening was aggravated by the disappearance of her favorite white blouse. She fluttered about the first floor opening and closing drawers and closets in a cacophony of squeaking and slamming wood. *Where is it?* She cried repeatedly in a voice that was more accusatory than interrogative. She finally located the blouse among the un-ironed laundry, curled up in a ball about the size of a handkerchief. *It has to be ironed!* The young daughter demanded of her mother.

Lucy, who was enjoying her Saturday afternoon bourbon and water, was in no mood to iron. Besides, she had a responsibility as the hostess at the kitchen table. *Oh, I'll iron it for her, I can iron a blouse,* my mother innocently intervened. My mother went to the ironing board while Eileen watched sheepishly. My father fixed the first pitcher of martinis. *Oh, thaaa-nks sooo much, Vivian,* Eileen said when she was finished, over-emphasizing her gratitude. Gad, did Mark's girl make me look like a jerk, she thought as she retreated to her bedroom to complete the finishing touches on her look for the night.

The crowd in the kitchen grew. The arrival of the couple in the Roadster was the cue for the Frankmans, who had been waiting in the wings in their apartment across the alley, to come over. Then Betty Kolb appeared at the door. Jim ushered her into the kitchen a bit self-consciously saying, *Viv, this is Eileen's friend, Betty.* She sure has her eyes on Jim, my mother thought. Parnell arrived a little later. In anticipation of meeting him, my mother had been practicing her line, *Pleased to meet you, Father Michael.* She was thrown off-guard by the arrival of this John Barrymore in cloth, whom Lucy introduced to her with, *Viv, this is my brother Parnell.* What a waste for that man to be a priest, my mother thought, and then chastised herself immediately. His immediate gesture of an out-stretched hand and a warm welcoming, *You must be Viv* relieved her from the confusion over what to call him. Parnell's suit coat came off, his Roman collar was loosened, and his right hand quickly found a bourbon and water. *To Miss Vivian Armstrong,* Parnell said, raising his glass and giving it a tilt in my mother's direction. As the glasses went up around the table and the drinks came down, she pretended to sip her martini. *And let us not forget the lessons of our Lord at the Wedding Feast of Canaan,* Parnell added with a raised glass. *To the Wedding Feast of Canaan,* all the Hayeses responded and clinked glasses. My mother thought the homage to the Wedding Feast of Canaan was some kind of Catholic blessing.

Time was allowed for Parnell's customary two bourbon and waters before drinks were carried from the kitchen to the dining room in a seamless transition from the cocktail hour to dinner. When my mother offered to help serve the dinner, the Frankmans said, *No, no, you just sit down and enjoy yourself. We're here to help Lucy.* That "we" apparently included Betty Kolb, because my mother found herself suddenly the lone woman surrounded by four men at the dining room table. Parnell asked if this was her first time in Minneapolis. Not exactly, I have been to St. Paul, she replied. The look on the faces at the kitchen table suggested she had a made a mistake. Correcting herself, she hastened to add, *St. Paul, I guess that's not the same.* My father decided not to ask his date for more details about her trip to St. Paul.

My mother may have been the odd Lutheran out at the cocktail hour in the kitchen, but ever a daughter of the Canadian prairie, she knew what to expect as dinner came out. The heavy, ancient walnut table groaned under its load of mashed potatoes, roast beef, vegetables re-invented into casseroles with cream and cheese, baskets of bread, and huge bricks of butter. A relish tray was passed from person to person as a symbolic gesture in recognition of the existence of lighter fare. Boats of gravy were navigated from place to place around the table. When Parnell, sitting at the head of the table, clasped his hands to his chest, there was a moment of silence at the table. *Bless us, O Lord, for these Thy gifts,* he began, *which we are about to receive.* As he continued, my mother shot a quick glance around the table and concluded that she could get by with a good Lutheran bow of the head and the placing together of her hands in prayer... *Through Christ Our Lord, Amen*, Parnell said with finality. The Sign of the Cross was rendered so quickly that mother thoughts the priest was cooling his face with a wave of his hands rather than crossing himself.

Though it was customary to linger over drinks in the kitchen, at the dining room table Lucy's charge to eat while the food was hot was taken seriously. Within a few moments, heavy entrees had vanished from plates. Lucy took a perfunctory view of her cooking and the dinner. She cooked well enough but would have been taken aback or even annoyed by excessive and unnecessary praise for her cooking. Dinner was something that had to be done. The emphasis fell on ample quantities of familiar foods with a predictable taste and flavor, to provide the comfort of a ritual without distracting from the lively conversation. No one was ever so dull as to turn the conversation to how a particular entrée was prepared or where a recipe had been discovered. There were compliments to Lucy. When someone interjected the customary- *Everything's so good*, a chorus around the table nodded their heads and added a verbal *ah-huh* in agreement. A higher level of praise came buried in compliments about the vendors involved. The statements that Brix's had excellent roast beef or Reuben Silverman's Great Northern Market is the only store where you can buy good fish were meant as compliments to Lucy. It was she, after all, who had the good sense to shop at these stores and knew how to pick the best cuts of meat and fish.

Jim cleaned his plate, paused and said, *Them's powerfully good vittles, Ma.* Everyone laughed but not my mother. She came from a family that never took for granted its knowledge of correct English and had been the butt of jokes about Swedish accents. Confused for an instant, she smiled nervously as the laughter went round the table. It was Jim's version of one of Lucy favorite parodies of the locals' table talk back in her old North Dakota days.

More, Viv—came the challenge from Lucy. My mother knew this was not a question. *Thank you, yes please,* she replied, keeping to herself a recollection of the hands back on Grandma Larson's farm stuffing themselves at dinner during threshing time.

As the dinner plates were cleared away, Lucy's next comment—*peanut cake*—was merely a courtesy for a new guest unfamiliar with her standard dessert. She was already slicing through the heavily sugared peanut frosting and apportioning evenly cut pieces for everyone at the table. Then the after-dinner brandy came out. It was served in stemmed miniature liqueur glasses. With a cigarette lighter, Jim went round the table and lit each glass. The flaming brandy added an ethereal touch, a symbol of lighter states of being, while the weight of the heavy dinner settled in. The flames were puffed out. The brandies went down. Parnell excused himself, saying he had promised to visit Dunphy at the rectory after dinner.

The main event came next. The dishes were cleared from the table and stacked in the kitchen. Lucy opened the show on the piano with a few chords of Chopin not yet lost to arthritis in her fingers. Eileen had returned by this time with her date, curious about the woman her brother had brought home. She had a role to play. The night belonged to Marlene Dietrich's songs, with a emphasis on the humorous repertoire from *Destry Rides Again* rather than the uncomfortably erotic songs from *The Blue Angel*. Eileen played the piano while the role of the German *femme fatale* went to John, the best voice in the family. John kept to the more light-hearted songs, though the classic *Falling in Love Again* could not be avoided.

The climax of the evening was a raucous rendition of *The Boys in the Backroom*, with all the Hayeses and their friends dancing together in a chorus line across the living room floor while Mrs. Frankman and Lucy sat on the davenport laughing and sipping bourbon and water. The singing did not stop with the finale. Solo voices singing, *Yes, what will the boys in the backroom have?* faded into the corners of the house late into the night.

The following week my father made the news in Rochester. After work, he and his friends had gone out for a few, and the police stopped him on his way home. Following the advice of an old friend from his Ascension days, he would not say whether he had been drinking and refused to get out of the car to walk the white line. The policeman finally relented and let him go, but back at the station, a reporter on the night beat weaseled the story out of him. The next morning, a slow news day, my father's story was on the front page of the newspaper.

As she started her shift that morning at the hospital, my mother noticed that the other nurses were taking an unusual interest in the morning paper.

LOVE AND MARRIAGE

Photography is a trick we play on time. My father tried it in the spring of 1940. He must have sensed that time was not on the side of the playful, childishly happy couple of that spring because he preserved so much from their dates in photographs, as if he wanted us someday to see our parents the way they once were. There are photos on strips of her sitting on his lap in the photo booth. There are photographs of a day in the country. My mother sits on the railing of a wood fence with legs crossed and skirt hem properly just below the knee. She wears a giggling smile that seems to say, *Oh, Mark don't be so silly.* My father's pose looks rehearsed. One foot on the bumper of the Pontiac Roadster, a Camel in his right hand, left hand in his pocket, white cotton windbreaker unzipped to show a tie and white shirt. There's a hint of angst in the look. You would have expected him in the next moment to shake his head and say of all the joints in the world she had to walk into his.

The heart, newly in love, gets nervous over small things. Like when your girl unexpectedly goes away for a week. It was in June when my mother disappeared for a weekend in Hibbing, leaving my father with an address where she could be reached. This called for an air mail, special delivery letter sent from Rochester on June 27 and delivered to Miss Vivian Armstrong in Hibbing, Minnesota, on June 28. Most of my father's letter described how much he missed her. He wrote that he would call her on Saturday after 7 p.m. Or, better yet, he could drive up on Saturday to Hibbing and stay overnight. He provided much too much information on where and when he could be reached, and his line about promising *to ditch that babe in the laundry* probably did not amuse my mother. *Won't it be swell*, he wrote, *when after the revolution it isn't so difficult to see each other?*

My father was not a Marxist. Marriage was the revolution he had in mind. The week my mother returned from Hibbing, he asked the question. No engagement ring in hand on bended knee at the Hollywood Bar. Instead, he proposed over the telephone, when she was working the night shift. (The conversation needed more privacy than was possible on the floor in the day shift.) He had two questions, and she answered both in the affirmative. Yes, she was going to take lessons from the Franciscan priest who was the Catholic chaplin at St. Mary's Hospital and become a Catholic. Yes, she would marry him. In reply, all he said was, *That's good*, and told her he would call his mother and let her know. They set the date for mid-September. She wrote two letters back to family in Manitoba. Grandma Larson cried when she read the letter written in Swedish to her. Elsie did not answer her letter.

The name Mark was popular among the Ukrainian families that had settled near Erickson, Manitoba. At St. Mary's Hospital in Rochester, there was another woman from Erickson. Although they had been in school together, the two were never friends. The woman wrote her mother saying that Vivian Armstrong was dating a drunken Polack, was pregnant, and had to get married. Word spread quickly around Erickson. Elsie wrote my mother to say she was no longer her daughter. She had disgraced the family. The Armstrongs would never speak to her again. A telephone call did not help. Elsie refused to believe that her daughter was not pregnant. My mother admitted that her fiancée enjoyed his drinks but he did not have a drinking problem. He was Catholic but Irish, not Polish. Elsie ended the conversation forcefully, telling my mother to stop lying, that she would never hear from Elsie again, and Elsie was not stupid. She knew Mark was a Polish name.

Lucy's background check went better. Parnell took it upon himself to drive from Iowa to Rochester and pay a call on the priest instructing his nephew's fiancée in the faith. With these Franciscans, Parnell informed Lucy, you never really know what they're thinking, but it looked like they would soon have a convert in the family that they could be proud of. Parnell decided not to share with his sister the story the Franciscan passed on about how Our Lady appeared to my mother in a barn in Manitoba. The Franciscan talked about her as if she was the new St. Bernadette who had a vision of Our Lady of Manitoba. Converts often try too hard to please. Taking care of things, Parnell arranged for the Banns of Marriage for Mark Hayes and Vivian Armstrong to be read at Sunday Masses in the summer in the chapel of the Passionist Monastery of St. Gabriel in Iowa. He was certain none of the monks in attendance had cause to raise impediments to his nephew's marriage.

Almost exactly six months to the day after they had first met, they were married on an early September Saturday morning in the chapel of Parnell's home monastery in Iowa. The ceremony was exceptional in its simplicity. Parnell, now in the presence of the Passionist Fathers, was Father Michael and celebrated the sacrament of Holy Matrimony. His confreres were the co-celebrants. In their white vestments, they formed a secondary wall of monks along the chapel walls and in an arch through the sanctuary. Illuminated by the pastel morning light through the stained glass windows, the monks sang ancient Latin hymns in honor of Holy Matrimony. The solemnity of the monastery endowed the wedding with a medieval beauty and the awe of tradition that trumped any sniping about some customs that were ignored.

There was no bridal gown in white. The bride wore a beige suit and hat. Its black lace veil discretely covered her eyes and passed for her wedding veil. The groom wore a three piece suit. The only concessions to the convention of wedding attire appeared in the form of an orchid corsage on the bride and a carnation on the groom's lapel. She walked down the aisle alone. At the altar, Eileen stood beside my mother as maid of honor and Jim stood beside my father as the best man. As they approached and stood at the altar, John sang the *Ave Maria*. The marriage band was represented by a single gold ring which the groom placed on the bride's finger. There was no wedding ring for him. He told Parnell it was the custom on his father's side. Parnell just shrugged his shoulders and muttered something under his breath about those Waterford Hayeses.

The monks outnumbered the guests. There was the Hayes family and a handful of Mark's friends. Lucy and her youngest child, Dave, sat on the bride's side of the aisle. Just before the wedding, in the bride's dressing room, Lucy told Vivian that it was not too late. She really didn't have to go through with it if she didn't want to. My mother misunderstood and took Lucy's remark personally. But Lucy had only said what she wished her own mother had said to her before *her* wedding. Vivian had hoped that her sister Eva would be her maid of honor, but none of the Armstrongs were in attendance. After the wedding, she called home but her mother wouldn't talk to her, saying only that she should never call again before hanging up.

The ceremony was followed by brunch at a local hotel. Because it was still before noon, Bloody Marys were called for. It took numerous pitchers of Bloody Marys to handle the rounds of toasts to the bride and groom. The couple soon bid the assembled guests goodbye, driving off in the Roadster for a weekend honeymoon in Chicago.

Ready for Chicago? My father said as he helped his bride into the car. *The City of Big Shoulders*, she parried back. *You know Carl Sandburg?* Her rather stunned husband replied. Yes, she said but did not add she had memorized the poem *Chicago* in high school as a fine example of the Swedish immigrant's contribution to culture. *City of Big Shoulders* had seemed to her a better metaphor from the poem than *Hog Butcher* to describe the city of her honeymoon.

Sandburg's poem pretty much covered what she knew of the city. When they arrived at the Palmer House, Mark nonchalantly tossed the Roadster's keys to the parking valet, opened the door for Vivian as she looked over her shoulder suspiciously at the valet, and whisked her into the art deco lobby as if he owned the place. He hurried them through the check-in and a bit of tidying up in their suite. Palmer House afternoons were best spent over martinis in the lobby. She didn't mind, even rather enjoyed (or at least smiled through) his lecture on the history of art deco. With the evening came dinner in the Empire Room—T-bone steaks medium rare, potatoes au gratin, asparagus in hollandaise sauce and champagne chilled in a silver bucket. Then dancing to the big band sound of an orchestra she pretended to know. How about a nightcap at a jazz club he knew south of downtown on Michigan? Just married and in love, that night the girl from Erickson, Manitoba, could not bring herself to tell him she had been terrified. They were the only whites among a crowd of blacks who simply refused to sit quietly and enjoy the music. The next morning, she did have the self-confidence to make a joke on herself at breakfast. OK, she asked, it's not green and it's way too big to be an olive. What is it? *Grapefruit,* he answered with a smile. *You eat it with a special type of spoon. Let me teach you.*

Revere Ware

Their wedding chest fit into the Roadster. In my father's bachelor days, moving involved hauling a suitcase from one place to another. Home or "the house" in his mind had always meant the house on Dupont. His nights after work in St. Louis, Chicago, or Rochester were spent in hotel rooms or apartments suitably furnished to feed his imagined life as a detective in the potboilers he read before bed. When it came to the basic stuff of everyday domestic life, his attitude that his home was elsewhere translated the concept of furniture into the old chesterfield and stuffed chairs of the living room on Dupont or imagined a future where he sat in the Reitveld chairs facing Bauhaus windows he had seen only in his university textbook on modern design. It was no wonder that his office desk had only photos of the black cocker spaniel and the Roadster. Who would bother to take a snapshot of his apartment? He didn't even hang his ink drawings and paintings there. They were all left back at the house on Dupont.

My mother's luggage made a bolder statement. She had bought a complete set of luggage in navy with white leather trim and also a steamer trunk to go overseas with the Canadian armed forces. That dream got no further than Rochester, Minnesota, where it remained in the drawer of the steamer trunk that also doubled as their first dresser drawer.

They had next to nothing for setting up house. Their wedding presents weren't much help either. There wasn't a lot of money to go around at Dupont. For a wedding gift, Lucy and Jim had given them a crucifix designed for Extreme Unction. Fashioned in light Danish wood, the side that held the dying Christ opened to reveal a secret inner box which held anointing oils and a candle of pure beeswax to be lit on the day the priest came to see you for the last time. It seemed odd that they had only just started to enjoy the Sacrament of Holy Matrimony when Lucy was already getting them ready for the Last Rites. But Lucy knew different. She had already seen these crucifixes opened for a husband, a daughter, her father, and a brother. Besides, it was Parnell's idea and his monastery's gift shop gave them a discount on the price. Jim knew his brother's tastes. He had picked out a crucifix not made from the dark walnut woods that hung in North Dakota or at Dupont, but from the bleached Scandinavian woods that matched the imaginary furniture my father placed in the interiors of his architectural drawings.

THEY QUICKLY LEARNED HOW unkind the 1940s housing market could be to a newly married couple even if the guy had a good job. They settled for a cramped apartment that was part of a six-plex of adjoining flats. Each had a living room with a Murphy bed, a kitchen, and little else besides a few chipped dishes and an odd assortment of pots and pans.

In 1940, there were no married nurses at St. Mary's. Once married, my mother had to give up her nursing career, but she wouldn't give up her independence. She insisted her husband teach her how to drive. He picked a Sunday afternoon when the traffic was light. He drove the Roadster a few miles along a main route that led from their neighborhood to the outskirts of town. He brought the car to a stop. His voice changed from the discursive storyteller to strict teacher. The functions of the clutch, the three gears of the transmission, the key, and the brake were described with an engineer's outmost respect for the rational sequence of cause and effect. His teacher's tone shifted to that of an athlete as he went on to demonstrate how the clutch went in, the key turned, the car started, the gas pedal was slowly pushed to the floor, and the car moved forward. He went on to show her how the gears slid from first to second and to third, and how, with a synchronized movement of the clutch and brake, the Roadster could be brought to a smooth stop.

Now, it was my mother's turn. She took the driver's seat. It was the first time my father had ever been a passenger in his car. This alone was enough to make him uncomfortable. He lit up a second Camel from the burning ash of his first. She turned the key. The Roadster hopped forward in a convulsive jerk, and the jolt threw both of them toward the dash. The Camel that had been dangling out the window from Mark's hand fell from his fingers. *The clutch*, he reminded her, *you first have to push down the clutch*. He lit another Camel. The next time she started the car easily and shifted to first. With a slight touch of the gas pedal, she became the first woman in her family to sit behind the wheel of a moving car.

In the history of technology and innovation, there are many examples of major historic breakthroughs that were brief and incomplete in their first try. My mother's first moment behind the wheel was one such example. She needed to ease the clutch out and back while shifting, but my father had neglected to emphasize that she also needed to push and release the clutch with each gear shift. As she grinded into second, the screech of gears elicited an uncensored yell- *God damn it, the clutch!* His expletive drove her to slam down the brake. The Roadster abruptly halted while the transmission jerked the car and its passengers mercilessly back and forth.

It's the clutch, damn it, he said, this time in a restrained whisper that failed to conceal the anger in his voice. She said he could keep his clutch and the car, got out and started to make her way home on foot. After a moment or two, he realized she was serious. He pulled up beside her. He was sorry. She should just get in the car. They could try another driving lesson another day. No response. Her pace picked up. The Roadster inched alongside her again. No, she wasn't getting back into the car. After a block or so, he changed his approach. Trawling slowly beside her, he started to whistle. *Hey doll, you all alone? Need a ride? How about a little spin with me, honey?* Only recently married, she did not yet fully appreciate that marriage brought her into a world where the gods of humor were stronger than the gods of anger. Would he dare continue this all the way home? People might think she was a prostitute.

Ok, it was kind of funny. They were almost home when she gave in. As she opened the passenger door, she was half-laughing when she asked if he hadn't realized what people must have thought. A guy in a Pontiac Roadster was trying to pick up a street walker. *A good looking woman, they probably were thinking and, the line worked, didn't it?*—was all he had to say.

The next day, Monday, she insisted that she ride to work with him in the morning. When they parked outside the offices of Maguolo & Quick, she announced she was going to drive the car home. She would teach herself how to drive. There was not an argument that would change her mind. She could wreck the car. She didn't have even a temporary permit. She would be arrested. As he handed her the keys, a vision of car wreck in his mind was shrugged off with the thought that it was probably time for him to buy a new car, one more appropriate for a married man than a Roadster. And besides, maybe the vision Vivian had seen in the barn was for real. Our Lady of Manitoba was looking after her.

On that day my mother learned how to drive.

AT FIRST, LIVING OUT of suitcases in a barely furnished one-room apartment fed the romantic, bohemian flair of my parents' marriage. Romanticism, however, was no match for the pull of the middle class that soon drew my mother to newspaper ads for furnishings and house wares. My father informed her in a patronizing tone that they would shop for such things in Minneapolis, not Rochester.

They spent their first Christmas on their own in Rochester, and drove the next day back to the house on Dupont. My father had an agenda. He wanted to impress my mother with what Minneapolis could do for Christmas. Vivian's retail horizons had been formed by Dolmer's General Store in Erickson, Manitoba, and she felt she had walked onto the set of a holiday movie when Mark brought her to an intersection in downtown Minneapolis where the cornucopia of three department stores—Dayton's, Donaldson's, and Power's—faced off with windows so over-stuffed that their trove of holiday gifts seemed about to pour out onto the sidewalks. From the Dayton Company, my parents bought starched white bed-sheets, terrycloth towels, two goose down pillows, and two Hudson Bay's Blankets. But my mother's prize purchase was a complete set of Power's stainless-steel-and-copper Revere Ware pots and pans. The wood stove in the one-room house where she'd been raised had only a single iron skillet and a few tin pots to heat up the morning oatmeal and the nightly concoctions of venison, pike, or game. When my father, for one last Christmas gift, threw in the *Good Housekeeping Cookbook*, she didn't think to ask why he thought she needed a cookbook.

Two years later, when Vivian's sister Eva married, my parents bought the same set as a wedding gift for her and her husband, Keith. With no children, she had more time and kept her set polished so the copper shone while my mother's copper faded to darker and darker shades.

When Vivian's third child, my brother Tom was born, Eva said that she should take Tom because "Vivian already had too many babies." Just look at her tarnished Revere Ware, she added, Vivian's doesn't even have the time to polish the copper on the pans. But never mind the tarnished bottoms. For me, these pots and pans offered endless entertainment on a kitchen floor, where I sat taking off the tops and then putting them back on again. Eva didn't know and never would know that there was a lot to be said for pots and pans that doubled as toys.

A Pram by Lake Calhoun

It was only a matter of time before life took a tilt and rolled my father like a marble back to Minneapolis. My mother was six months pregnant when they returned to the city in the summer of 1941.

The move to Minneapolis came on impulse. At Maguolo & Quick, the flair that had come with the first assignment to the Duluth Cathedral proved to be a onetime thing. My father was back to the tedium of being the draftsman for another architect's designs for boring hospital interiors. In the spring of 1941, an older and well-established partner of a Rochester-based firm dangled an idea before my father and Vic. Jim Hills of O'Meara and Hills suggested they quit wasting their talents designing hospital bathrooms and move to Minneapolis where O'Meara and Hills has picked up some sub-contracting work with the War Department. The work would tide them over a few months. O'Meara was about to retire. Hills would work his connections to land big government contracts that were coming with all the talk about war.

The move was a gamble. For the bachelor Vic, the stakes were less. Telling his friend he would see him in January, Vic left Rochester with a ticket to an adventure that fit my father's dreams like a glove. Vic had applied for an artist's fellowship. His proposal worked. It gave him a small stipend and the cost of expenses to travel and paint in the few surviving corners of the Mediterranean where a citizen of the neutral U.S. could still travel. Sketchbook, easel and water colors in hand, Vic left for Spain in June.

The life of an itinerant artist in the Mediterranean was not in the cards for a married man like my father. The wife was expecting. The only choice was Hills's War Department project in Minneapolis. While Vic was doing watercolors and dodging a war by skipping from one of the last few pockets of tranquility in the Mediterranean to another, my father did drudge work at a building at the Minnesota State Fair grounds.

It was the Hippodrome. The building had been converted from an arena for horse shows to a massive office space. Where horses once had gone on parade, men were now seated in row upon row of desks pushed tightly together. The scene might have been mistaken for a WPA piece about Americans answering President Roosevelt's call to build prepared-ness for war. You could almost hear the voice on the newsreel describing the scene, "Wanting peace, these Americans prepare for war." When someone walked by or moved in their desk chair, projectiles of dirt and dust shot up through the floor cracks and joined with the cigarette smoke and heat to prey upon the helpless asthmatic who might have signed on for one of the jobs. Two large fans moved the air around just enough to put a limp ripple in the American flag and let everyone share equally in the dust and heat. The time at the Hippodrome was my father's purga-tory as he paid the price for the vanity of a young architect's presump-tion, spending his days correcting blueprints for military supply depots and waiting for Hills to call.

Great changes in the social history of a city happen one change of address at a time. When my father returned to Minneapolis, he abandoned the old neighborhood along West Broadway and rented a one bedroom apartment in the Uptown neighborhood of Minneapo-lis's South Side. Uptown had won its race with the North Side's West Broadway to become the Minneapolis midtown, and the intersection of Hennepin and Lake was now a vibrant hub of shops, restaurants, and movie theaters. On the avenues to the east of Hennepin, small two- and three-story apartment buildings made the neighborhood one of the rare places in Minneapolis with the feel of high-density big city housing.

Street cars took the residents to work downtown by day. By night, it was a short walk to entertainment. Bars and restaurants thrived in the last neighborhood on the South Side where Minneapolitans could enjoy a drink. The city prohibited bars or liquor stores from 38th Street South to the still-undeveloped southern boundary of Minneapolis thirty blocks to the south. As if to drive home the point of just where the fun stopped, the Uptown neighborhood ended abruptly at 36th St. where it came face to face with Lakewood Cemetery. To the west, two- and three-story middle class dwellings stretched for several blocks until Lake Calhoun Boulevard gave the rich mansions a view for their money. When his family and old friends chided him for giving up on the North Side, he dismissed them, saying only that he wanted to be able to walk with Viv to the Hasty Tasty Restaurant and show off his art work.

He picked an apartment on Emerson Avenue just a half block north of the cemetery. With the exception of its fake Alhambra façade, the apartment building was the standard two -story, six-apartments-to-a-floor, rectangular affair that dominated the neighborhood.

THE LOCATION WAS PERFECT for a new mother. Young Mark was born in August. In the weeks preceding the birth, my father had channeled his preparations for the baby into the purchase of the perfect pram. It fit into place fixed in the center of his image of a new life in Minneapolis. He imagined it silhouetted by the late afternoon sun over the western side of the lake, as he and the proud mother strolled pushing the baby along one of the chain of lakes. Within a month after my brother's birth, my mother, the dog, and her baby in the pram were indeed fixtures of the daytime scene at Lake Calhoun. Every evening, my father came home to the apartment, washed the Hippodrome dust from his face and pushed the pram a few blocks down 36th Street and to the lake. As they moved along the east side of the lake, his imagination stepped back for perspective and sketched the scene in pen and ink. It was an image that could not be improved upon, and that he would return to in his mind night after night during the war.

Lt. Cpt. USNR Mark N. Hayes

7

That Man

THE ARSENAL OF DEMOCRACY IN THE MIDDLE EAST

> *Still hopelessly stalled in Freetown harbor, the ship filled with*
> *rumor, dissension and above all dissatisfaction ... What a damned fool*
> *I was to come on this ill-fated expedition. "Time is the essence" seems*
> *to be a great slogan of our politicians – so here we sit, about 1200 or*
> *1300 men who are to construct the keystone of the allied effort to halt*
> *the encroachments of the axis to the Middle East until sometime in July.*
> *I scarcely think Germany and Japan will politely sit by and give us an*
> *indefinite time to construct the so-called "Arsenal of the Middle East."*
>
> - Diary of Mark Hayes, April 13, 1942

In war, as in love, my father acted on impulse. Dunphy's first sermon after Pearl Harbor carried a clear message: He began his sermon saying unequivocally that if this war was going to be won, it was going to take some men from Ascension to get the job done and he ended with a short prayer popular among Catholics at the time—*Our Lady of Victory, Pray for Us!*. The next day my father started a new routine. On a few evenings a week he returned to the Ascension Club and went through the old drill—jumping jacks, duck squats, a hundred sit-ups, fifty push-ups, jumping rope and whacking the punching bag.

Meanwhile, Mark's younger brother John joined the Marines. A cousin showed up at Dupont in a sailor's uniform. In January, his old friend Vic, recently returned from his artist's fellowship in the Mediterranean, signed up for officer's training with the Army.

A month after Pearl Harbor, a Minneapolis-based engineering

firm, Johnson Drake & Piper, landed a major overseas contract with the Army Corps of Engineers. Two of my father's friends signed on. Although the exact location of the project was classified, the contractor let it be known that it was somewhere in Africa. The deal smacked of intrigue and adventure. The pay was good. It was patriotic. They would help FDR build "America's Arsenal of Democracy." My father remembered a high school geography lesson about Chinese Gordon. He said to himself, *Why not?*

By mid-March, he was on a slow boat to Africa. He packed as if he was to be the artist in residence on a geography expedition, bringing along his Brownie, a tripod, portfolio with brushes, sketchbook, watercolors, easel, and a leather-bound diary for keeping notes. Inside the duffel he had a khaki twill jacket, slacks, shirt and tie, and a white linen Palm Beach suit and black and white oxfords, as if he were going to audition for a bit part in *Casablanca*.

The army had commissioned an armada of antique freighters for the project that might well have been of greater value to the war effort as scrap iron, and the trans-Atlantic crossing was made more interesting still by the German U-boats that were picking off transport ships right and left.

The adventure started off well, with a Pullman car trip to New York and a stop-over at the Hotel Pennsylvania. He caught the fights at Madison Garden and ended the evening with drinks across the street at Roundy's Bar. The next morning he departed for Charleston.

Upon arriving at the port in Charleston, however, *things commenced to be gloriously mismanaged*, as he noted in his journal. At noon, he joined a crowd of 1,400 men standing on a concrete pier with no place to sit down, no lunch, and no explanation from the Army as to why they could not board the ship. At around 4:30 in the afternoon, the men were given salted peanuts and a glass of milk. It was not until 4:30 a.m. the following morning that he finally boarded the *Agwileon*. *A rat hole of a ship*, he wrote in his diary that day. It was to be home for the next two months.

The *Agwileon* was on its fourth life. None of its previous lives showed any distinction. It had been christened the *S. S. Havana* in 1906 and used to run freight between New York and Cuba. During WWI, it became an army hospital ship, the *USS Comfort*, whose main achievement was to transport the flu virus back from the war in Europe to the United States. Grounded in the 1930s, it sailed again as the freighter *S. S. Yucatan* in 1935 until it ignominiously capsized at harbor in New York six years later.

The destruction wrought by the Japanese at Pearl Harbor turned what had been a capsized piece of scrap into a saleable troop transport which the army bought and re-christened *U. S. Army Transport Agwileon*. My father was among the roughly 1,400 men on board when it went to sea again on March 19, 1942.

The passengers were a mix of Army men and civilian contract employees. No one knew the exact number on board, but rumor put it at five times the number the ship had been designed to hold. On the first day at sea, the word spread that one German sub had been sunk and two others driven off in the Charleston harbor shortly before they had set sail. *If that news had been made known,* my father wrote on March 20, *half the gents on board, including myself, would have jumped and tried to swim back to Charleston.*

After a brief stop in San Juan, the *Agwileon* lumbered eastward under the escort of a light cruiser, three destroyers, and a plane carrier fashioned out of a former freighter. The itinerary was provided by rumor. Some said they were heading for Liberia; others said Natal. My father set his hopes on Cape Town, a town that would appreciate his Palm Beach suit. One week out, the captain announced that two months earlier all but one of a convoy of twelve ships had been lost along the same route they were taking. *I guess he was thinking that some of us were sleeping too well at night or sumpin',* was my father's dry afterthought. On several nights, alarms went off and the men rushed to positions by the life boats while the Southern Cross on a distant horizon competed with flares and gunfire for my father's attention.

Mark had the foresight never to have seen *Mutiny on the Bounty*. It might have motivated him to do something rash. By day, heat and filth were everywhere; a hundred men shared the one lavatory with its three broken toilets, and fresh water was limited to three cups a day. Baths were salt water only. Meals were mostly slop, served after a three hour wait in line and were eaten standing up. Pig's knuckles were the chef's blue plate special.

Morale was not helped by the revelation that the *Agwileon's* Puerto

Rican and African-Caribbean crew had no prior experience working on a ship. Their true talents were plainly to be seen: managing the black market in food, alcohol, and drinking water. Complaints to the ship's purser got a shrug of the shoulders and a gesture of up-turned palms indicated that the crew was out of his control. When Mark tried to discuss the service on board with one of the crew members, he was asked in reply if he would like a knife through his shoulder blades.

Soon jaundice had yellowed the faces of many on board. In addition to the visible evidence of hepatitis, there were more than fifty confirmed cases of yellow fever, and also a few confirmed cases of diphtheria that put my father in a state of constant fear. Dehydration gave him excruciating back pain that neither he nor the ship's doctor correctly diagnosed as kidney stones. The *Agwileon* was healthy only for the flies that infested the ship and increased exponentially with the increasing heat. For such service, the Army had paid $685 per passenger on the *Agwileon*. The price was slightly more than the equivalent price of a first class ticket on a trans-Atlantic passenger liner at the time, and enough to raise my father's doubts about the honesty of Johnson, Drake & Piper.

Back home, the family was growing. My mother had not told Mark when he left that she might be pregnant. Life became more complicated still when Vivian caught the building's caretaker in the basement laundry room gazing at her intimate wear on the clothes line. She looked straight at him. He said, *I need to find a place to store some tires.* The irrelevance of the remark was probably as good of a defense as any, but the next day Mark's brother Jim moved her and young Mark to the house on Dupont. For the next eleven months, my mother, young Mark and, as of September 30, new baby Brian, made the best of a life lived under her mother-in-law's roof.

She moved into the "machine shop." It was the nickname Jim had given to his youngest brother Dave's bedroom. It was an honor of sorts. Dave did not grant entry into his room to just anybody. The bedroom stood on the first floor by the dining room. Dave had installed a padlock on the door to keep his siblings and mother out. The "machine shop" got its name from the gadgets, gizmos, and piles of electrical wizardry that covered every available flat surface in sight. Vivian told Lucy that the room would do nicely and moved in, spending the next eleven months wondering just why her husband had to go to Africa.

There were times when Mark wondered the same thing. When the *Agwileon* reached Freetown harbor on April 3, 1942, the captain announced that due to an outbreak of cholera in the city, there would be no shore leave. Next, he announced that the *Agwileon* had not been deemed sea-worthy, and another ship was on the way. Two weeks later he reported that the rescue ship had been sunk.

For a month, my father and his fellow passengers were prisoners of the *Agwileon* in Freetown harbor, where the heat was extreme, and the relief of an occasional breeze was accompanied by a dose of septic air from the scent of raw sewage floating in the harbor waters. That same water was their only source of bathing water. There were two reprieves. Once it rained, and the men took a rare freshwater shower in the downpour and wrung their clothes in buckets of rain water. And each of the men was granted one trip to a clean beach, with groups of 100 taken ashore at a time.

From the day the *Agwileon* anchored in the harbor, local boys paddled out in dugouts to hawk coconuts and oranges to those aboard the ship. The ship's marksman, one of the army men on board, took it upon himself to fire warning shots sending the boys into flight. Some keeled the dugout around and paddled quickly back to the shore, while others dove into the water and swam away. A cold stare from my father prompted the marksman to reply, *niggers might be German spies.* Or, as my father's lingering stare implied, they might be desperately poor kids risking their lives to make a few pennies.

One day four of the boys paddled up to the side of the *Agwileon* in a makeshift boat. The marksman fired over their heads. Terrified, the boys dove into the water. One of them could not swim, and his companions abandoned him. The boy floundered and flapped his helpless arms in the water while a swift tide drew him further out into deeper water. My father and a few others tossed life preservers which fell far short of the boy, joining the flotsam that drifted with the tide—and the boy—further out to sea. Two men from the *Agwileon* dove in the water to save the boy only to be taught a lesson about the strength of the African tides. A life boat was dispatched. It caught up with the men about a quarter of a mile away from the ship. The boy was never found.

Every time my father looked out on the harbor waters the boy's ghost appeared in his mind, flapping his arms and disappearing beneath a swirl of water. He re-appeared to trouble the pages of my father's diary, reminding him that Africa did not play by his rules. A few weeks later, MPs came on board the *Agwileon* and took the marksman away.

One day it was announced that the captain was ill and had been taken ashore for treatment. The news prompted my father to recall that in 1930 the captain of the famous luxury liner, the *SS Morro Castle,* had taken sick the night before the ship burst into flames and sunk. The captain's departure removed the last bar between any semblance of discipline and the reality of anarchy. A pushing and shoving match between passengers and crew turned into a riot. It also increased the availability of warm beer, candy, and much-prized tins of spam. The ship remained afloat and the captain returned, but took no action. The brigs were already full. He merely harangued the men over the loudspeaker and ended by reminding them that the *Agwileon* was a transport ship, not a floating reform school. *Who said it floats?* My father replied. The loudspeaker was not taking questions.

A few days later Mark was among a group of men invited to the captain's quarters. *The big shot,* he later wrote, *didn't know enough about engineering to ask intelligent questions.* But it was best to play dumb, he figured. Otherwise, he might find himself working as the captain's man on the repairs to the *Agwileon.* Some of Mark's friends had not been so shy about impressing the captain with their drafting skills. A few days later they were part of a group of twenty men taken ashore and rushed by air from West Africa to Ethiopia, and Mark, watching them leave, gave himself a few hard kicks in the behind for having disguised his talents.

But his friends put in a word on Mark's behalf, and within days my father's name was on a second list of men to be taken ashore and flown to Eritrea. His attire was touchingly hopeful. He disembarked in Freetown all decked out in his Palm Beach suit, a matching silk tie with wide navy and yellow stripes, a clean shirt, black and white Florsheim oxfords on his feet, and a straw Panama fedora.

The trip from West to East Africa took a week. It involved short flights from Freetown to Maiduguri, then on to Kano, Legos, Khartoum, and Asmara. Mark took the convoluted route as his first lesson in the ways of the African continent. Things do not rush in a linear path from A to B. On his pre-dawn flight from Freeport, a leopard challenged the plane for rights to the runway and gave my father a long stare through the airplane window that brought to mind lines from a William Blake poem memorized in high school. He marveled at the crocodiles, rhinoceros, elephants, and leopards that could frequently be spotted running riot across the countryside beneath the plane. Maiduguri and Kano appeared to him as the keeper's of ancient bible stories written in adobe, and he admired the mostly naked women whose dignity and lack of inhibition had not been repressed by the preaching of the missionaries or the vices of the white colonialists. If his shipboard diary told a story of unremitting hell, once in Africa his notes took on the tone of a gentleman geographer in the mode of Sir Richard Burton. Included among such ethnographic observations were a few rough sketches and notes for paintings that my father would someday like to do, for example, of women unapologetically squatting to relieve themselves in the sand without upsetting the large urns of water balanced on their heads.

In Maiduguri, immediately and without solicitation, Mark acquired an entourage of male personal assistants who sat on their haunches and anticipated his every move. A step toward the latrine prompted one to run ahead, bow and point the way with gently up-turned palms. My father had no idea why another stood behind him and then offered a straw broom when he stood up. Another, squatting on the sand, suddenly jumped up and caught a large snake that was slithering in a nearby bush; he killed it with a knife, removed its fangs and offered it to my father as if in tribute to a new master.

On an overnight in Legos, his British host took it upon himself to teach Mark a few things. He expounded at length about the poor quality of American beer, though that didn't keep him from drinking the better part of a case of Pabst Blue Ribbon. A gourmand, the Brit rated American bacon as the world's worst. My father only confused him by noting that he was eating Spam, not bacon. He felt obliged to show my father the way to treat the natives, tasking his "boy," a silent young man, with utterly needless requests. At one point, the Brit went into a rage, cursing and beating the young man. His crime was having failed to anticipate the need to kill a roaming housefly that later annoyed the drunk. Finally, the Brit announced that it was time for a white man to do his part in support of "the main industry in Legos." When my father

On location, Massawa, November 1942

declined to join him, the Brit slurred back something about how, as usual, the British would have to go it alone.

In Khartoum, his group was put up in an excellent hotel where at last he felt at home in his Palm Beach suit. He was enjoying a long slow scotch with no ice—telling his diary that the connoisseur prefers his scotch without ice—when word arrived that he was to catch a 3:00 a.m. flight for Asmara. It was also revealed to him for the first time that Massawa, the Eritrean port on the Red Sea, was the secret destination for the Johnson, Drake & Piper project.

One of the World's Less Promising Deserts

For fourteen months, Africa was a stage that gave my father some of the best roles of his life, and he never tired of re-telling stories of that period. There was a routine to his African monologue. He would take a long sip of an extra dry martini, savor it on his tongue for a few extra seconds, let it roll back and away, and then, in a raspy martini voice, dry as the winds of Eritrea, he would begin, *Now, this was the deal in Africa.* To hear his version of things, you would have thought he was the hero of a new series by Lowell Thomas—"Mark of Eritrea."

The first thing you learned about Massawa was that it was hot. Second. Dress like a Brit. A pith helmet replaced the Panama, and the Palm Beach suit went to the closet, to be replaced by an outfit of khaki shorts, a short-sleeved shirt and tie, knee high socks, and engineering boots. The third thing you learned was never to forget that the contractors were crooks.

The big shots who ran the show for Johnson, Drake & Piper took good care of themselves. They settled in Asmara where they appropriated the lifestyle the Italian colonialists had left behind when they abandoned Mussolini's imperial dreams and fled the advancing British troops. There, in the cool mountain air of 7, 000 feet, they enjoyed a gentlemen's life in the colonial mansions and cafes along Asmara's Corso del Re. They ignored the annoying harping of Captain Edward Ellsberg, the naval commander down in the harbor of Massawa, which they had been hired to rebuild, but when my father's group showed up in Asmara on the morning of May 7, 1942, Johnson, Drake & Piper processed their paperwork, issued them Army IDs, and sent them on to Massawa without delay, hoping to shut the captain up with a busload of men primed for the task at hand.

When my father's group first stepped off the bus in Massawa, Ellsberg greeted them sardonically, *Welcome to one of the world's less promising deserts.* He had assembled Italian POWs and local Eritreans, Sudanese and Ethiopians, but the bus load from Asmara represented the first Americans Ellsberg had on the job. He gave off an air of a sardonic and understated self-confidence, but the job itself was daunting—to salvage and re-build the port which the Axis powers had abandoned during the East Africa Campaign. For starters, they would have to raise a sunken dry dock and a once-floating crane to the surface, then remove the seven ships that the Italians had sunk themselves to block the harbor as they were departing, then build a new navy pier and a series of warehouses. And, all the while, they would need to be mindful of the underwater mines and booby traps scattered here and there.

Under normal conditions, such an undertaking would require about one year. Captain Ellsworth and his crew had at best two months to get it done. So, as my father would say, *that was the deal in Africa.* Either get the job done before Rommel threw the British in Egypt into retreat eastward, or they would all end up in a Nazi concentration camp.

Ellsberg was short and to the point on the work to be done. He was long and rambling when he began to dilate on the climate and the locals. He might begin by telling his men what they already knew—you could hardly inhale the Red Sea air, which was blasted with heat and thickened with humidity, salt, and microscopic particles of dust. A normal day's work in the prickly heat brought on dehydration, fatigue, and festering boils. The men were advised to take ten salt tablets a day for the heat and quinine for malaria, and were on the alert for the symptoms of diphtheria. The locals comprised, Ellsberg paused for emphasis, *the worst labor in the world.* An American could do in an hour what six Eritreans did in a day. Sudanese and Ethiopians weren't much better. The Italian POWs were the best. But don't count on the swarthy southern Italians. Try to hire only blond north Italians.

Mark soon found himself in drill every morning, Monday through Friday, with an Italian carbine on his shoulders, pacing through forward marches, about-faces, and at-eases. These "Massawa Volunteers" were probably the most ludicrous boots the Allies put on the ground in WWII. You would not have been surprised to find Laurel and Hardy marching with the occasional skip and hop among the Massawa volunteer regiment. Mark had been authorized to wear side arms on the job, but he declined. If they really had nothing to worry about, why let the Italian POWs know they were nervous?

His letters home dropped the Lowell Thomas tone in favor of something akin to Fred Allen doing a skit about an explorer in Africa. These letters arrived at Dupont in envelopes crammed with photos and souvenir postcards. Though there was a certain *gravitas* to the photos and the sketches of his various building projects in Massawa, there was also a steady stream of self-deprecating remarks and poses. On the back of each letter, he wrote one-liners that served as comic sidebars to the more matter-of-fact narration inside.

My father took an avid interest in the postcards left behind by the Italians featuring air-brushed black and whites of a *Ragazza bilena, Abissina or Araba* with little or no attire and a distinctly "come hither smile" on their faces. In so doing, he continued a long standing tradition of white guys in Africa who shuffled such photos among scenes of villages, tribal rituals, and street life to disguise a bunch of African girlie photos under the cover of ethnology.

In one letter home, he included one such postcard with the inscription, *This is the babe I've been taking out Sat. nites lately – kind of cute, huh?* Though she pretended to laugh when the others did, his wife was not amused. Lucy told her boys to put those photos away but even she laughed a bit and didn't raise the ante of her objections as her sons continued to pass them around, conjuring exotic fantasies about Nubian slave girls and Arabian nights in the silence of their repressed Catholic libidos.

In the late fall of 1942, the big shots at Johnson, Drake & Piper came down from the mountains of Asmara to set themselves up in Massawa. They seemed oblivious to the fact that Rommel's defeat at El Alamein and Eisenhower's landing in North Africa had made their plans for an expanded facility in Massawa irrelevant. Its key military assets—machinery, ships, cranes and a floating dry dock—had already been shipped westward to support the campaign in North Africa. Ellsberg was packing his bags for the new front when the contractor arrived. My father took legitimate pride in knowing that he had been on the job when the real heavy lifting had to be done.

For the next six months, the contractor devoted itself to the task of building a compound in the desert where gentlemen could work, live, and relax in comfort. It ignored Ellsberg's suggestion to build portable iron structures that could be moved where needed on the next front. Johnson, Drake & Piper went ahead and poured mortar into buildings that might outlive the pyramids and house about the same number of residents. It built spacious residences, office buildings, and even a gentlemen's club complete with dining room and lounge, game tables and outdoor athletic courts. Stories about sores from prickly heat became tall tales of the past among the new men on the scene who lived and worked in comfortably air-conditioned buildings.

The grand opening of the men's club in March coincided with the first anniversary of the transatlantic voyage on the *S. S. Agwileon*. Formal invitations were printed and sent. The Palm Beach suit hidden in the deep recesses of my father's duffel came out once again for the event. My father declined the offer to move on with Johnson, Drake & Piper to new projects in Palestine and the Arabian Peninsula. The contractor left behind in Massawa a world class facility that the Allies never used.

IN EARLY APRIL, AS my father prepared to leave, two things remained undone. The first had to do with the bulky 9" x 14" portfolio that always travelled apart from his luggage, tied shut with ribbons. It held a few unfinished watercolors, quick studies of scenes that deserved greater attention. As the job demands for Johnson, Drake & Piper slacked- off, Mark found the time to paint.

He painted a Baobab tree under the relentless sun in the desert with a yellow the color of a fire you had never seen before. He put this yellow into the massive rock which seemed to have rested for eons in that place. He gave the rest of the landscape a color that suggested the absence of color, so that the yellow rock, the green Baobab tree and a landscape the color of nothing, taken together, seemed to say something about the mysterious origins and sustenance of life, and implied that the rock and tree just might be eternal.

Mark also painted a café on a street in Massawa—his homage to the art of wasting time. An overhead awning, sewn from hides, ripped open here and there to suggest its surrender to the power of the Eritrean sun, did what little it could to shelter the guests. Two men stand while others sit on benches at tables. There is no movement, only a mood that suggests. Don't bother, stay forever fixed in your beloved state of inertia.

Beyond the unfinished watercolors, Mark also faced a second uncompleted task. He had someone to take care of. Every white man on the job had been given a local boy as a servant. Mark's servant, Haile, was only ten years old. His parents had been killed during the war's first phase when the British defeated the Italians. He adapted well to the Americans, and had been at my father's side for more than a year, running countless errands, often without even a hint of request. He introduced my father to the magical and mysteri-

Haile

ous world of the local Coptic Christians. He would watch intensely whenever my father drew or painted. Step by step, my father taught him the gift of creating an image of life out of a few lines drawn in pencil, and of inventing new colors by mixing paints.

My father knew that things would not go well for Haile when the Americans left. Thoughts of another boy drowned in Freetown harbor returned when he looked at his young servant and he also remembered the sadistic Brit in Legos who beat his boy over the presence of a fly. He thought of the character played by Spencer Tracy in the movie *Boys Town*. You take care of orphans. He wrote home to my mother that he had decided to adopt Haile. The paperwork was in order when her telegram arrived. He already had two sons, one of whom he hadn't met yet. He needed to take care of his own.

The uncompleted watercolors and the unfinished business with Haile were my father's way of convincing himself that he had a place in Massawa, a job to do, and that he would return. He believed this when he said something of the sort to Haile before boarding the plane that would take him back to the U.S. Within minutes, as he took his place and stared out the plane's window, a mood of sadness tinged with guilt overcame him. None of it was true.

The return from Africa took 32 days. The homecoming was muted. My parents were not ones to make a display of emotion in front of the family. Young Mark hid under Lucy's kitchen table. Brian was a bit bolder. He stood sideways, clutching his mother's knee, and cast an occasional glance over his shoulder at the tall, talkative man that everyone was making such a fuss over. In the morning an alarm went off beside my parents' bed in the "machine shop." My father's arm was still in Africa. It clumsily reached over to shut-off the travel alarm on his Massawa bed stand and instead hit a switch that turned on one of Dave's inventions, which began to emit an annoying whirling noise. *Oh, shit* were the words with which my father started a new life back in Minneapolis.

They were appropriate. Mark had come home to find himself an outsider in wartime Minneapolis. He grumbled to old friends that every landlord rejected him for the crime of having children. At the bottom of his housing list was a duplex in a hellish part of town. The Jewish owner, Mr. Brill, had given a flat "No thanks" to my father's offer of several months' rent in advance, but his wife convinced him to take pity on my mother with her two children.

The outlook for jobs was similarly bleak. The architect with St. Louis, Rochester, and Eritrea on his resume had to settle for an underpaid job as a mechanical draftsman with a local war contractor. He sent his resumé to several big time war contractors in California and then declined their offers, reluctant to leave Minneapolis. A new refrigerator was about the best thing that happened in his new life in his old hometown. Refrigerators were rationed and under price controls. Each month, the dealers unenthusiastically raffled off a few to those on their waiting lists. When luck came his way, hyperbole betrayed my father's pent up humiliation. His mood had to have been low for him to have told with friends without a trace of sarcasm that the Kelvinator was a "dream come true."

On his first Sunday back, Father Dunphy included his name in a sermon extolling the men of Ascension who were laying their lives on the line in defense of their country. Mark knew his days in Africa were not really made of that kind of stuff. Maybe he shouldn't have told Dunphy about the threat of Rommel and the Massawa volunteers. And he had better include those *ragazza* postcards in his next confession. Better to go to the new assistant than to Dunphy. On Sunday morning after his first full week home, he finished the newspaper and made an announcement. *I'm joining the Navy,* he said, *I'm doing this for my sons.*

THE HARBOR PILOT

My father carried the Midwestern gene than drove its men to enlist in the Navy in much higher numbers than men from the coasts. By October 1943, he was on the Navy Reserve's fast track. Officer's training in Tucson made him into one of its "90 day wonders," a man transformed from a land-locked Minnesota guy to a U.S. Navy Reserve Lieutenant Captain commissioned in January 1944.

The morning of his departure was a January day cold enough to prove Dante was right—Hell is made of ice, not fire. My mother Vivian had decided not to tell Mark that she was probably pregnant again. Young Mark cried and dragged his feet while being pulled by the hand, and Brian, then a year and a half old, added his wails in protest to being carried aloft by his mother. Lucy made matters worse by telling the boys not to cry and adding irrelevant remarks about how it was colder in North Dakota. The bitter cold provided an excuse to make the

Somewhere in the Pacific, 1944. My father is second from the right.

good-byes brief. Dressed in his Navy blues, Mark was already a bit of a stranger as he stepped up into the train car that would take him away to New York.

From there, he flew to San Francisco and then sailed to New Guinea. Mark received his assignment as a harbor pilot. The task required strong skills and experience as a mariner. When asked about his experience as a mariner, he joked that he had navigated a few rowboats and even one or two vessels with trawling motors through the rough waters of Minnesota's Bass Lake. In 1944, the U.S. Navy was losing its sense of humor and clearly not picky.

He soon learned that the role of the harbor pilot was the Navy's version of the canary in the coal mine. His first lessons came in the Battle of New Guinea and later off the Georgia Islands, where a mortar barrage blew a gaping hole in the hull, water rushed in, four men out of his crew of eight were lost, and the ship was run aground on a sand bar. At the time, my father did not write my mother about his brush with death. She learned of it years later when he talked in his sleep. This rest was borrowed time that took him into the Battle of the Solomon Islands, the Battle of the Philippines and Iwo Jima.

In August, he landed in Japan. His letters home were vague about his location. Everything was fine, he wrote, except that he was sick of eating mutton.

BACK HOME, VIVIAN FOUND comfort in established routine. Stuffed with new furniture and shielded from want by the presence of a state-of-the-art refrigerator, the duplex had a cozy and protective feel. She was still struggling at the time to get straight the innumerable holy days and saints' feasts of her new Catholic faith, and things weren't made any easier when the landlady, Mrs. Brill, began to introduce her to a whole new calendar of Jewish holidays. In some respects, my mother found the transition from lutefisk to gefilte fish smoother than her leap from the faith of her Swedish grandmother to that of her Irish mother-in-law.

The news that Vivian was pregnant again drew a predictable response from her mother, Elsie. In late spring, my pregnant mother and her two sons drove back to her home in Erickson. Elsie made her stay inside the house the whole visit; she didn't want the neighbors to see that her daughter was pregnant again.

When the new baby, my brother Tom, was born in the summer, 1945, Aunt Eva proposed a solution to the problem that Vivian had too many babies. *She* should take Tom. Eva's husband was in England and she had already moved into the duplex. As summer passed to fall and winter, Vic's wife Carol often joined the two on weekends. The three war widows laughed, sang a bit and developed a taste for wine spritzers, finding in weekend after weekend a measure of time that made sense out of the present and put out of mind the uncertain future.

This went on for an endless year and a half. His occasional letters home committed the sin of omission in their truncated and vague prose. There were a few photos of him and his buddies smiling and shirtless as if to say that all he could say about his location was that the tropical heat and sweat was unbearable and he was somewhere out in

Somewhere in the Pacific, 1944-45.

the Pacific. The photos revealed that his frame was changing from thin to emaciated.

THAT MAN

Whenever the subject of the war or my father's service in the Navy came up, my mother would re-tell the story of his telephone call from San Francisco. He had been overseas for fourteen months at the time. The war had been over for four of them. My mother was bottle-feeding their latest, the third son, Tom, whom Mark had never seen. For weeks, she and her sister Eva had been scouring the newspaper daily for the announcement of ships from the Pacific that had docked in California. Eva spotted the news one morning and exclaimed, *It's there! Mark's in San Francisco.* That same instant the phone rang. My mother was still holding Tom with one arm while the other hand picked up the receiver. Mark was at a hotel in San Francisco. He would be home the day after next.

My father's favorite story about the Navy was not really about the Navy. It was about a hotel in San Francisco and creamed cod for dinner. The Mark Hopkins put up my father's unit for a night on the house. Acknowledging the doorman's welcome with a nod, my father abruptly stopped before plunging his foot into the deep pile of the thick black carpeted stairs. Such luxury can stun a sailor. He paused to be sure of his footing for the next step. An automatic reflex left-over from childhood re-awakened. Take your shoes off before stepping on the carpet. It was a long step up from the clammy hulls of the Third Pacific Fleet to the opulence of the Mark Hopkins. A touch of insecurity prompted him to give a happily obliging bellboy too large a tip for carrying a duffel bag that my father had wanted to handle on his own. Inside his hotel room, the plush furniture brought him to a stop. He gave it a studied stare. He sidestepped around a stuffed chair. Bumping into the armrest, he mumbled *excuse me* as he slid by. He didn't sit down. Opening the door to the bathroom, the sight of its glistening yellow and black Italian marble forced him to pause again. Yes, the ornate toilet, commode, sink and bath were there to perform the customary duties, though it seemed beneath them, somehow. Mark went to the window, which looked out to the bay, and lit up a Camel. The long distance call home was also on the house. *Mark!* His wife said on the other end of the line. *I have to put Tom down.* Tom, the familiar name sounded strange. He had never heard it like this before—*Tom,* spoken as the name of his son whom he had never seen.

At dinner he took up the chef's offer to serve every sailor his favorite dish. If it wasn't on the menu, the chef would prepare it to order. The request for creamed cod on toast caught the waiter off guard. Mark explained that it was the salted cod from the wooden boxes served with cream sauce, hard boiled eggs, and boiled potatoes. Evidently this Irish delicacy had not yet made its way as far west as San Francisco. Even if it had, the doorman would have turned it away at the entrance to the Mark Hopkins. After a conversation in the kitchen, the waiter returned. The hotel had sent someone out to buy a box of the salted cod. My father was invited to enjoy another martini while he waited. It was hard to tell if the creamed cod really was his favorite dish, if he simply needed something to remind him of home, or if the creamed cod was a set up for a story to tell the folks at Dupont when he got back.

The telephone call from San Francisco and the story of the creamed cod were my parents' way of forgetting the war. The full story of what happened the day my father came home from the war went untold until much later when the story could no longer hurt him. Six decades later, after watching the Ken Burns TV documentary *The War*, my mother told me the details that had been left out.

It was December 19, 1945, and Minneapolis was under the grip of an early and hard winter. My mother bundled up young Mark and Brian in their parkas and wound scarves around their faces until little more than their eyes were visible. The baby, Tom, stayed back at the apartment with Eva. As the Empire Builder pulled into the platform at the Great Northern Depot, it hissed steam into the air, and Vivian found herself in a dream, walking through a cold cloud where shadows of people appeared and then vanished into the mist again. *You don't recognize, me,* Mark called out as she walked past him on the platform. Embarrassed, she said she didn't recognize the uniform. She had expected him to be in his navy officer's blues. Instead, he wore the officer's khaki work uniform with its jumper and a dixie-cup hat. There was the hug and the kiss. *Boys, this is your father,* she said. She had to tug the children forward. They resisted, holding their ground behind her back and hiding in the fog of steam on the platform. Thank God they had the cold, unusual even for a Minnesota December, to talk about.

Back at the apartment, things lightened up. It was the first time my father had seen his four-month-old son. A pitcher of martinis appeared on the kitchen table as Vivian and Eva filled Mark in on how the war widows had spent their weekend nights.

The eyes of young Mark and Brian stared in from the other room. *Don't talk to that man,* young Mark told Brian. When their mother said it was their bedtime, young Mark looked hard at her. *Momma, tell that man to go home. That man should go to his home now, Momma. Tell him to go home.*

In the years after the war, he never talked about his time in the Navy and the War in the Pacific. There were no sketches or watercolors. In fact, after he joined the Navy and after his discharge in December 1945, he never painted again. The same was true of his love of drawing and photography. His passion for watercolors, the pen and ink sketches, and the Kodak black and whites never returned from the War in the Pacific.

Sometimes in the middle of the night, nightmares came, and he would shout out names of people my mother didn't know or scream about fires everywhere. Maybe he meant to tell his sons something on Sundays as he watched "Victory at Sea" on television, his leg crossed, seated on a straight backed dining room chair. But he never said a word. The show's longhair music told us that we should be quiet. If we wanted to ask questions about the war, we should ask the officer's uniform in the closet. If we wanted to know his opinion about the navy, he left us his thumb-worn copy of Herman Wouk's *The Caine Mutiny* to read.

Once, someone from the Navy paid us a visit. My mother told my brothers and me to behave ourselves. The guest was a Navy big shot. When she said his name, I thought she was referring to Halsey Hall, the guy who did the broadcasts on 'CCO Radio for the Minneapolis Millers. Two cars pulled up, one, a limousine with flags on the front. Two guards in dress uniform stepped out of the limo. One opened the door; the other stood at attention. Two others stayed by the limousine and the first pair accompanied him to our door. At our door, the man smiled at my father, calling him Hayes, and asked if he was going to give him the martini he had promised they would have together after the war. They sipped martinis and laughed. A short while later the man left. My father watched him from our picture window as he got back into his limo and drove off. *Let me show you, Nickel-plate, where the Philippines are,* he said to me as he spun the globe we kept on an end table in the living room.

III

A Good Death

Ultima in mortis hora,
Filium pro nobis ora!
Bonam mortem impetra,
Virgo Mater Domina!

At our death's last hour,
To your Son pray for us,
A good death ask for us,
You who are Virgin, Mother, and Our Lady.

- Ultima (Traditional Latin Chant)

8

We Liked Ike

Minneapolis seized the post-war years and Eisenhower era as its chance at last to live out its dream as the "modern" city of the prairie and take its place in the front row of America's second rate cities. Developers were given the green light to drain and fill in the wetlands and buy out the old family farms that still operated within the city limits and convert what had been a prairie within the city to sub-divisions of nifty ramblers and cape cods. Declaring that the city's streetcar system stood in the way of progress and the triumph of the automobile in American life, the city fathers sold the streetcars to a business man with suspicious ties to the mobster Kid Cann who bought low and sold high, unloading the cars on the scrap metal market and to buyers in Mexico City. As if to prove that Minneapolis's minor league dreams really had come true, the Minneapolis Millers ruled AAA baseball, winning the Junior World Series three times in the 1950s.

My father bought into this Babbitt's bargain but not without a twinge of buyer's remorse. Although he had long ago moved from the city's North to its South side, he refused to follow his friends to the western suburbs where new money moved in next door to old money and gobbled up every vacant lot along the shores of Lake Minnetonka. An architect is not safe out there, he maintained, reminding his friends that Frank Lloyd Wright was arrested in Minnetonka in 1926 for immoral behavior in violation of the Mann Act. He settled in Minneapolis's far southwestern corner, as if to say that he was not deserting but re-grouping for one last defense of the city.

Among his siblings Mark stood alone in his loyalty to Minneapolis. His brother John moved to Brooklyn Center, the first suburb across the North Side's city line. His sister, Eileen, climbed up the social ladder to reach Edina, where she dared not tell her neighbors that she voted for Adalai Stevenson. His youngest brother, Dave, took his Ph.D. in physics all the way to Texas, where he became a name without a face, the hero of a story about an amazing motor bicycle and a distant voice at the other end of a few rare and unexpected long-distance telephone calls.

Lucy and Uncle Jim sold the house on Dupont, leaving the old manse with its rambling porches, parlors, two stories of bedrooms and secret stairwells for a boxy Cape Cod with two bedrooms, living room, and kitchen in St. Louis Park, an "inner ring" suburb just west of the city. Inside Lucy's new suburban house, the old Victorian bookcases, writing desks and bedroom sets, together with a few American Indian rugs and blankets, came to their last stop in a long journey that had started on the O'Brien farm in Olga, North Dakota.

My father kept one lifeline to the old neighborhood open. He arranged to have Brix's deliver groceries all the way from the old North Side to Lucy's new home in the suburbs and to his own new home on the far southern edge of the city. But in time, the old house that had once ruled the intersection of 16th and Dupont Ave. N died the death of a landlord's thousand cuts. First, it was chopped into a two story duplex, then a four- plex, and then spliced up into claustrophobic "efficiencies." The city of Minneapolis finally condemned it and tore it down. The old stable that the Hayeses had converted into a garage by the alley survived another half century until the police decided it had hosted enough crack cocaine parties and it too was demolished.

In August 1947, my parents and my three brothers moved into a new house on Queen Avenue, adapting to a new neighborhood and new times that would just as soon not bring up the old stories about getting out the vote for Floyd B. Olson and simply wanted to like Ike. I came along that December. But in those days the long hand of the Lutherans extended across Minneapolis from 38th street south to the city limits, and aside from a few bottle clubs, American Legion posts, and 3.2 beer joints that had been grandfathered in, a dry Christianity ruled, forcing more than a few residents to run long and seemingly all but unnecessary errands late in the afternoon.

When all else failed, our neighborhood had a secret oasis in the form of Ready's Dairy, a convenience store. Mr. Ready let the neighborhood men buy cans of 3.2 Hamm's Beer and enjoy them in the conviviality and privacy behind the cooler. On weekend afternoons, Ready set up a TV on a folding chair, fidgeted with the rabbit ears, and let the men watch the game of the week, which, appropriately enough, was sponsored by Hamm's Beer. Ready's Dairy did not survive the lifestyle changes of the 1960s. In its place today stands a wine bar. It caters to the grandchildren of the old Lutherans of Ready's day. They test exotic wines, commenting on the bouquet and the tannins, and have probably never heard of Hamm's Beer.

Our new address at 5809 Queen Avenue stood about as far into Minneapolis's South Side as you could get without crossing over to the suburbs. The house itself was like an architect's model, a miniature that displayed my father's sense of style and ambitions for his next house.

For the exterior, he rejected off-the-shelf paints one after another until he found the perfect pastel green. From there several strands of influence diverged. His watercolors of Africa went up on the living room wall and the handsome portfolio bearing the title *Middle East War Projects 1942*-1943 sat on the coffee table. The robust comfortable chesterfield and arm chairs belied that their owner admired the austere work of Piet Mondrian. Books by Peter Arno and Charles Addams lying here and there exposed a man who subscribed to *The New Yorker* for the cartoons. A biography of John Barrymore, *Good Night, Sweet Prince* lay on the table like a script for a try-out at other roles my father might have played. A Finnish writing desk went up against the dining room wall. Yes, the details of this house set it apart from the other houses on the block that had nothing to say.

After the war, Southwest Minneapolis held the last few square miles of undeveloped land within the city limits—small farms wrapped around ponds, swamps, and creeks. As development got underway, redwing blackbirds, mourning doves, pheasants, and muskrats made a naïve effort to stay on in the neighborhood with the new baby boomer families.

The task for our southwestern corner of the city was to complete Minneapolis's alphabet of avenues. It started a few miles to the east with Aldrich and advanced westward through Bryant, Colfax, Dupont and so on. Our neighborhood completed the exercise by laying out the avenues from Queen through Zenith. Unfortunately the alphabet fell a bit short, and the city found it necessary to add a second alphabet after Zenith stretching from Abbot to France at the southwestern boundary. Beyond lay the posh suburb of Edina with its graceful homes and covenants restricting ownership to members of the Christian faith.

Our landscape was nearly treeless, though an occasional cluster of stately elms remained from the family farms of the previous generation, and the boulevards had been dusted with a smattering of newly planted saplings by the city. Brown sod lay on the ground in long strips, having failed to overcome the heat above or draw sufficient sustenance from the tired soil below that had long forgotten how to grow anything other than corn. The summer heat was triumphant in the absence of shade, and the humidity seemed to rise from the ground, resurrecting in the air the swamps that had been driven underground by bulldozers.

Our neighborhood had been carved out of three farms—the Irwins, Barretts, and the Jacobsons. Two of them—the Irwin and Jacobson farms—lingered on in the new subdivision, surviving as rural prisoners, with the old farm houses surrounded by a pittance of acreage for truck farming. The Barretts, on the other hand, continued the farmer's fight well into the 1950s. Mr. Barrett thought he had gotten the better part of the deal. He had yielded a few acres from the northern edge of his property and kept the bulk of his farm which straddled the line between the Minneapolis city limits and Richfield, which had yet to make its move from a sleepy village into a middle-class suburb. Our neighborhood provided Mr. Barrett with a market for fresh eggs, poultry and vegetables. He tilled the land with his twelve children, an old tractor, a few other odds and ends of obsolete farm machinery, and a wagon for hauling drawn by two draft horses. You might have mistaken the Barrett farm for an Amish community except that Mr. Barrett bought all the machinery he could afford and he liked his drinks. When the time came, he surrendered with dignity. He sold the farm and got his picture in the newspaper alongside a story about the demise of the last working farm within Minneapolis city limits.

Our house was the first to be built south of 58th Street and west of Penn Avenue South. Unlike the small, boxy two bedroom structures that had sprung up a few blocks north a few years earlier, these sleek new dwellings—mostly three bedroom rectangular ramblers and ranch houses had the style of a new era that hinted at a readiness to pack-up and leave Minnesota for California.

The Irwins once raised corn on the land where our house stood. All that was left of their farm was the old farmhouse, a half-acre vegetable garden, another half-acre of swamp and the Irwins themselves. The row of elms that had once been their windbreak became our Sherwood Forest. Around the edges of the swamp, the bulldozers had pushed up hills of sand, dirt and assorted pieces of broken concrete. The city had drained half of the swamp and leveled it into a low-lying sand lot as a promise of a park to come. The ground there never forgot that it had once been a swamp. Every spring, water gurgled up and spread out into large puddles that put an end to hopes for baseball fields there. At the far end stood the newly built Armitage Elementary School.

Uncle Jim, who had documented in black and white photos the lives of the Hayeses on the North Side, now turned his Kodak Brownie to photographing his brother's new life on the South side. One shot summarized it all—though taking it required a special effort. Moving the furniture and getting us kids to line up was the easy part. Setting up the "Quick Set" tripod manufactured by the Whitehall Specialty Co. of Chicago seemed to take forever. The tripod was a miracle of weight-less aluminum. It obliged Jim to tighten screws and twist the steel legs into the three adjustable threads, leaving you with the impression that a pipe-fitter held the patent for this design.

The camera balanced on the tripod and focused on young Mark in the center to underscore that this was a photo of the new genera-tion. On the far left, our father towered above the rest of us lined-up against the wall alongside him: my mother, young Mark, Brian, Tom, and me. The occasion for the photo is Brian's First Holy Communion. An eight-year-old Brian holds his prayer book and poses piously in his white shirt, pants, and tie. The second child, he was cheated again. This photo was not really about his First Holy Communion but about my father, a family man who was having it all in the 1950s. Jim had moved the davenport parallel to the window. The red leather chair was pushed back from where, Socko, my stuffed monkey seated on the cushion, kept an eye on the scene. The polished, hardwood floors were bare and waited for the carpet that the Dayton Company would soon deliver. The tightened belts and rolled up cuffs on young Mark's tweederoys and Tom's jeans showed our parents respected the lessons of the threadbare

My family ca 1950

Depression. Despite much better times, they did not waste money on new clothes every time the boys grew an inch or two. I completed the line-up in short pants. Young Mark knew what to do. He stood straight and smiled. Brian held a missal in his hands and gave an angelic smile worthy of a boy who had only hours earlier received the body of Christ. Tom and I appear to have been given a pass to goof-off for the camera.

Jim had framed and shot this unbalanced composition intentionally to draw attention to the extremes of height. The lack of symmetry also betrays the fault line between our father's sense of a life finally coming together and our mother's edginess, between his self-assurance and the dependence of us—my mother, my brothers and me—on him.

WATERCOLORS IN LIMESTONE

My father's churches from those days—his best days in the 1940s and 1950s—are still around. As I drive through Minneapolis, its suburbs, and the prairie towns, I nod my head in their direction as if greeting old friends. Once on the cutting edge of the new, they are now, a half century later, the senior citizens of modernism in Minnesota. A few have applied for assisted living in the national registry of historic buildings. When I stop by for a visit, they welcome me, the son of an old friend, knowing I'm one of the few left who gets their jokes and wants to hear their stories.

Architecture loves to gossip about the past. A detail in a church tells the story of a pastor's foibles. A name in bronze on a side altar invokes a priest's homily on the sin of presumption and a wealthy donor who never understood the passage in scripture about the rich man and the eye of the needle.

There is a secret history here. The Catholics left behind the immigrant churches that had professed in doleful bricks and mortar an old time European faith. They locked the doors and turned out the lights on old church buildings where the old statues did their best to lead empty pews in the old prayers of the Faithful. The flocks followed their shepherds to modernist churches, seldom pausing to dwell on the irony that their new places of worship had been designed by leftists of the Bauhaus or the apostates of the Prairie School. In this new generation of churches, Frank Lloyd Wright settled his score with the town that had arrested him.

The best of architectural modernism in Minneapolis belonged to this new generation of churches. The hunger of the clergy for reform was fed by the audacity of a handful of local architects. There was a history behind the choice of small, modest churches over the strut of phallic office towers. Visible from every corner of the city, the Foshay Tower stood as a reminder from one generation to the next that the first bright flare of Minneapolis modernism had been a dud. In 1954, the architect Ralph Rapson, a protégé of the Bauhaus legend Walter Gropius, told his mentor that he was taking a job in Minneapolis as the Dean of the School of Architecture at the University of Minnesota. Gropius wryly cautioned his protégé. *In no other city in America is there so much modernism as there is in Minneapolis.* He added, *and, so much of it is so bad.*

The trick for an architect was to be part of the building boom but not part of the mimetic modernism that was creating the Foshay Towers of tomorrow. By the end of the 1940s, the post-war building boom had brought Hills, Gilbertson & Hayes enough work to pay the rent for the offices downtown and to move their families from apartments in the city to new homes—ours on the southwestern edge of the city and Vic's in newly developed wetlands that tapered off east of Lake Minnetonka. A branch office was opened in Fargo from where, my father liked to joke, a guy from Williston and a guy from Velva (he and Vic) directed "the North Dakota Renaissance." The early work with Maguolo & Quick on hospitals in Rochester was also paying off with one new hospital contract after another generating easy money to subsidize the architecture of their hearts.

IN HIS ARCHITECTURE, my father was a convert. He left the gothic Catholicism of his Irish boyhood for the spare modernism of the Scandinavian Lutherans. The result was a quiet reformation of Catholic space. One parish at a time, my father changed the look of Catholicism in the region by convincing Irish priests that the history of architecture did not stop in the thirteenth century and God could speak just as easily through metaphors of light and abstract form as through medieval ornamentation and shadow. The old obsession with neo-gothic overstatement gave away to the subtleties of limestone, pale glass and light wood.

One of the first fruits of my father's new approach could be seen in the simplicity of the rectory he gave a parish priest in Valley City, North Dakota—a dwelling in which Frank Lloyd Wright would have been very much at home. My father's design included an acknowledgement that there were easements by custom to the vows of celibacy. The parish priest, Father Dawson, had a distant connection to the Hayes family. The priest and the architect were honest and discrete with each other. He insisted on providing the priest's housekeeper with a Prairie School house in miniature connected to the rectory by a walk-way enclosed in glass and bathed in light. The walk-way was a discrete answer to the gossip in the parish. It was all that needed to be said.

There was the case of Father Mark Farrell. He and my father went way back to the playgrounds of Ascension and the hallways of *D*. In 1948, Father Farrell approached my father with his dream of a new church on Minneapolis's South Side. The priest's eyes were filled with grey arches, spires, and bell towers. My father persuaded his old friend that the purpose of the design was not to create a place where Quasimodo could hide. The design should be a metaphor of the Church as a ship at sea guided by the light of faith and God's grace. The buff limestone exterior hinted at weightlessness and the sense of being afloat. The interior rose up to beams of blond wood that replaced the image of cathedral beams with the image of the interior ribs of a ship's hull that trained the faithful's eye on the sanctuary. Stained glass windows infused the church with ambient light. The bleached woods from the pews to the railing of the sanctuary completed the sense of a ship sailing secure in the light of faith.

Father Farrell's parish drew from humble working class homes and included some of the few African-American Catholics in the city. They readily accepted the simplicity and humility of its design as a Beatitude in stone that blessed the meek. Appropriately, in view of the implied defiance of Catholic architectural custom, the new church was called St. Joan of Arc, hinting at a confederacy of Catholic insubordinates in south Minneapolis. Father Farrell embraced the new design with the zeal of a convert. For the next decade, he lectured his fellow priests to think modern and embrace the metaphor of a ship with Father at the stern and the sacraments for its compass. Father Farrell skipped the point about Quasimodo. Victor Hugo's novel was on the Index of Forbidden Books.

The idea spread from Minneapolis and St. Paul to the suburbs and beyond to the remote Catholic enclaves of the Protestant prairie to the north. The roots of my father's family had produced a host of distantly related and connected priests and

St. Joan of Arc Church and School, Minneapolis, 1947.

nuns across North and South Dakota. From the northern tier where the continental divide turns the rivers north to Hudson Bay in the towns of Valley City, Harvey, Jamestown, and Cooperstown; to the southern edge of South Dakota where the Missouri bends toward the Mississippi in Mobridge, Aberdeen, Yankton and Sioux City, my father left behind an archipelago of churches, rectories, convents and schools to house prairie priests and nuns. The buildings were more likely to be applauded in the pages of *Architectural Digest* than *Catholic Digest.*

My father's favorite was the Church of St. George in Cooperstown. Designed and built in 1950, St. George's was little more than a chapel tucked away in a family neighborhood where it shyly avoided comparison with the tall, white-washed Lutheran church that dominated the center of the town. The parish priest, Father George Steinert, had wanted a dwarf Cathedral in red brick that honored his patron saint—St. George, the dragon slayer—and also honored the men of North Dakota, who, like him, had served in the war. In my father's design, the homage to St. George and the veterans took the form of abstracts in Swedish steel above the church entrance that hinted of a saint, his sword and evil vanquished. My father's signature was written in the pale shades of stone, wood, and glass that set the Church of St. George to sail as a Catholic vessel in the sea of the Lutheran prairie.

SOME OF MY FATHER'S best work can be seen in a building designed by someone else. A Lutheran pastor had discovered the work of Eliel Saarinen during his wartime travels as a chaplain in Germany and Scandinavia. After the war, he returned to his congregation at Christ Church Lutheran situated in a bungalow and stucco Minneapolis neighborhood. The pastor believed he had received a call to bring the hand of Saarinen to render in a new church a modern and quintessentially Lutheran sacred space. In 1948, Saarinen contacted Hills, Gilbertson & Hayes to serve as the on-location associate architects.

A little more than ten years after his first visit to Cranbrook on behalf of Maguolo & Quick, my father returned. There Saarinen conveyed his ideas for the new church in abstractions and vague generalities which my father rendered into balsa wood models and a watercolor painting. Saarinen visited the construction site and ranted over every detail, throwing out as many of his original ideas as he added new ones. For example, on the exterior, the masons had laid walls of perfectly placed limestone bricks. Saarinen ordered lines of brickwork at random to be pulled out and then re-set unevenly so that some of the bricks pointed out or sidewise. The point, Saarinen explained, was the hand of the mason, like God's hand in creation, deliberately leaving imperfection in place. The masons said they wouldn't be part of such nonsense. They had a reputation to protect and quit, leaving my father to hire new workers less concerned with their pride.

Inside the church, the instructions had been to whitewash the brickwork. As Saarinen took his first glance at the interior walls, he said no, that wasn't what he had in mind. He had my father order the painters to wash and scrub off as much of the paint as possible. Saarinen liked the ambiguity of the washed-out white paint on brick.

Today, the exterior of Christ Church Lutheran strikes you at first as a simple design in the brick box modernism of the late Bauhaus school. Geometry dominates in the form of the rectangular church and its narrow rectangular bell tower. The interior abandons the symmetry of the exterior. The northern wall curves

Christ Church Lutheran, exterior and interior.

The construction site for Church of the Visitation, 1947. My father stands in the center wearing a dark suit and panama fedora.

out of sync with the straight southern wall. It leads the eye through the sanctuary, drawing attention to the pulpit and leading in a final turn behind the altar to the natural light that emanates from the window, almost invisible at the far end of the southern wall at the apex of the nave. The natural light from the rows of low standing windows on the walls and the recessed lighting tucked within the blond wood-working of the ceiling combine with the white-washed brick walls to cast the interior in sheens of wan illumination. The balcony for the choir reaches low and close toward the rear of the congregation. Undulations of sound, sheens of light, and asymmetrical walls guide the eye and ear toward a Lutheran theology that, out of apparent imbalance, reveals a greater balance of the word, the sacrament and sacred song.

At the opening of Christ Church Lutheran in 1949, the ailing Eliel Saarinen asked my father to attend in his place. When the American Institute of Architecture (AIA) posthumously gave Eliel Saarinen the Twentieth Century Award, identifying Christ Church Lutheran as the most brilliant example of modernism in religious architecture in the previous quarter-century, only a few insiders congratulated my father, who had been Saarinen's hands on the job. Eliel's son, Eero, graciously invited him to the award ceremony. The newspaper published my father's picture and explained that Hills, Gilbertson & Hayes had been the local architects on the project. A job offer from Frank Lloyd Wright's firm in Chicago came my father's way. He turned the job down but accepted the implied compliment. He belonged to their club.

But neither compliments nor churches paid the bills. In the summer of 1954, my father put in a bid on behalf of Hills, Gilbertson & Hayes for a major reconstruction of the old St. Mary's Hospital that faced the University of Minnesota from the opposite bank of the Mississippi. A lot rode on this one. The project would bankroll the firm comfortably for the next decade. On the morning of his presentation, he lit one Camel after another from the burning tip of the one before. Suits, ties and shoes went on and came off. Take it easy, calm down, you're meeting a nun, not a fashion designer, he tried to convince himself. Nothing worked. Later, at the hospital, director Sister Rita Claire of the Sisters of St. Joseph brought his ordeal to a quick end. Who else would the sisters turn to? It was only when he returned to his car that he noticed the distinguishing touch of his look for the day. There was a brown oxford on his left foot and a black one on his right.

Mark was soon on the phone with Vivian, Vic, and the old crowd of friends. This was cause for celebration at Harry's. A long day turned into a long night of martinis and shoe jokes. He was just showing off, my father said, that he had two pairs of shoes.

The next morning he experienced a few chest pains. He was certain they had to be heartburn—the aftermath of too many martinis with anchovy-stuffed olives.

The records of Hills, Gilbertson & Hayes contain the secret of how my father had convinced Catholic priests of the old school to buy into churches of the new school. On the right margins of the invoices, beside the line item for the architect's fee he wrote in perfect Palmer's penmanship "gratis." There was no charge when the heart and work came together and when he could pick-up where his African watercolors had left off. From Minneapolis to the North Dakota prairie, these churches were his watercolors in limestone.

MY SISTER CONSUELA

My sister Consuela was born a few weeks after I was.

My own arrival had not been a cause for celebration. When my mother realized she was pregnant for the fourth time, she worried about what she was going to tell her mother *this* time. She thought that as a nurse she should have known better. Of course, if there had to be one more, she hoped at least it would be a girl. On the other hand, my father always said that if they had a girl they would name her Consuela. My mother hated that name.

At least she got a new house out of me. When the news came that they had done it again, my mother insisted they couldn't have four children in the duplex that had housed them during the war years. That's when they moved to the house on Queen Avenue.

I came early. My due date was Christmas. Early in December, my father and Vic were having martinis at Harry's. When my father said the baby was due on Christmas, Vic bet him a fifth of gin that the baby would come on *his* birthday, December 11. On the afternoon of December 11, my mother had just started to clean the oven in her new kitchen when her water broke. She called the family doctor who told her to get to the hospital immediately. She said she had to clean the oven first. My father rushed home and hurried her to St. Mary's. I came within minutes of their arrival at the hospital. When one of the nuns announced, *It's a boy*, my mother felt a moment's relief. She couldn't stand the name Consuela. Then came a second thought. All those diapers. Then, a third. It would be another five years before the new baby was in school. Vic had won his bet and a fifth of gin was his.

Lucy was not happy when she heard I would be called Nicholas, saying the name belonged to *her* family. Father Dawson from North Dakota was there when my mother told her about my name, and he put in his gratuitous two cents worth, observing that Nicholas was a Greek, not an Irish name. Lucy was indifferent when my mother added the second name of Patrick, and never acknowledged the nod to Ireland that came with it.

Custom prescribed a ten-day stay in the hospital. When my mother finally brought me home, she found the unpleasant surprise of a welcoming party. My father had set up his friends in the house and they had already gone through a few pitchers of martinis rehearsing their welcoming toasts in my honor. Vivian told Mark to send them home. Although he protested on my behalf, he surrendered to the tone, not the words, of her response. She said, *I have to clean the stove.*

A few days after my first Christmas, my father announced that they had one more very special Christmas gift. He was uncharacteristically guileless and naïve in the way he broke the news. *Our boys have a baby sister, Consuela,* he proudly declared. His wife gave him a blank stare. A few months earlier, the nuns at the Catholic's home for unwed mothers had approached him several months earlier about a "good" girl who had made one mistake, and was due in December. A few days before Christmas, a baby girl was born. Perfect, he thought. The boys need a sister. My mother had always wanted a girl. It would be like having twins, Nickey and Consuela.

This Christmas surprise did not go over well. They were supposed to pick-up baby Consuela the next day. Before he had finished the story, Vivian was muttering, *Over my dead body.*

SATURDAYS AT THE OFFICE

Week-days, my father was a top coat and hat who sailed out of the kitchen door in the mornings and returned at the day's end. Saturdays, he was an Eisenhower jacket with beef roll penny loafers who took his sons along for half-days at the office.

Hills, Gilbertson & Hayes had opened in 1946 on the second floor of a small office building overlooking Loring Park. Nestled around a small pond, Loring Park stood at the southern edge of the downtown district. The streets around the park were lined with offices, three story walk-up apartment buildings, the genteel Minneapolis Women's Club, and the sizzle of the newly opened Downtown Chevrolet dealership.

Inside the offices of Hills, Gilbertson & Hayes, the contemporary Scandinavian furniture, watercolors on the walls, and art magazines strewn about almost pulled off the mid-town Manhattan look, except for one stubborn detail. Dr. Raymer Petersen, DDS, shared the second floor with the architects. Dr. Petersen's clients were few on most afternoons, and he had gotten into the habit of lying on the couch in the reception room with the door open, waiting for walk-ins. When not napping, he read deer hunting magazines and shouted the latest details out across the hall to my father, whose familiarity with such activities did not extend much beyond wearing a wool Pendleton shirt on Saturdays.

Bringing his sons to the office was father's way of exposing them to a man's world where he was a player. Back home, he had introduced us into the manly ABCs. A boxing bag and two sets of gloves marked a space in the basement where Father Dunphy's tips on the left jab and the right hook could be passed on to the next generation. He had accumulated enough hand tools at Settergren's Hardware to get us started on the primitive hammer-and-nail school of carpentry. A well-equipped tackle box and four rods and reels made it possible us to bring home miniature perch from nearby Lake Harriet to the restrained delight of my mother, who was expected to praise her sons' manly accomplishments and turn them into dinner. And we also had plenty of access to the footballs, baseball gloves and bats, basketballs, and hockey skates that all kids need to develop their talent at team sports—though he never gave us hands-on lessons, presuming that his sons had a genetic predisposition for these things.

All of this stuff was only the chump change any dad could give his sons. Trips to his office were a big deal. The sense that he had another space, a place outside the home, was re-enforced by his name on the door, by a hint of deference in the greetings of a draftsman or a secretary who might be working on Saturday, or the way he leaned back in his chair and put his feet up on his desk. The message didn't lend itself to words. One time, as he relaxed at his desk, my father made a sweeping gesture with his hand in the direction of the drafting tables and his partners' desks and struggled to find the words to convey to his sons what it all meant. *Boys,* he said with an air of self-congratulation, *this is where the groceries come from.* My brother Brian looked around. *But, Dad,* he said, *there aren't any groceries here.*

Eventually, my brothers outgrew the Saturday ritual, and I had my father to myself. One morning, he tried to show me the basics of an architect's craft. I was fixated on the notion that he was a "boss," as if that, rather than architecture, was his line of work. *Are you a boss,* I asked? When his head nodded, I added, *Did you ever fire someone?* There was irritation in his silence. Ignoring my second question, he walked to one of the board tables and began to unfurl large rolls of papers, flatten out photos, and arrange the architectural models on a desk. My attention went exclusively to the blueprints and tubes. It was clear to me that the grand prize of being an architect came in rolling up of soft blue sheets of paper, inserting them in a tube, and carrying it around like a knight's sword. Soon enough, my father would look at his watch and announce, *Nickel plate, it's time for lunch. How about Harry's?*

Harry's was my father's place. The building stood on 11th street. Better times after the war meant new businesses sprouting up beyond the old limits of downtown at 9th street, leaving behind a cluster of fail-

Harry's Café, 74 S. 11th St., Minneapolis.

ing shops, bars, and hotels at the other end of downtown, around lower Hennepin and Washington Avenue. My father's favorite haunt had once been in that neighborhood—the Nicollet Hotel, which was hanging on like an aging swinger from the Jazz Age keeping its nose up, holding onto a touch of class, and ignoring its new neighbors. The street scene outside the old Nicollet Hotel was now likely to include guys who slept on park benches and drank Petri and Irish Rose

from half gallon bottles. A few blocks away on Hennepin, there was Auggie's, a g-string and tassel joint named for the owner, one of the Jewish guys from the North Side who had been a professional boxer and was on a first name basis with Kid Cann. The 620 Club proclaimed itself as the place "Where Turkey Is King" and drew sports stars and high rollers. Autographed photos of Jack Dempsey were on the wall.

But these places were no longer points of my father's downtown compass. The man who had once won a New Year's Eve Charleston Contest and cruised the Avenue in his Pontiac Roadster now drove home from the other end of downtown in a Ford sedan to a house, wife and kids in south Minneapolis. Harry's was his place, a place where businessmen ordered "sizzling platters" for lunch and had old fashioneds, high balls, or manhattans with friends before going home for dinner with their wives and kids.

But Mark Hayes had no desire to make that next step up the downtown social ladder; he did not aspire to become a member of the Minneapolis Club, where men had names that were the same as department store names or a brand of flour. He didn't like big wheels. *Blessed are those who go around in circles for they shall be called big wheels,* he used to say.

Although mine was a supporting role, I loved my part in my father's act at Harry's. The script began with our entry on the scene. My father never walked the few blocks from the office to Harry's, preferring to drive in style with a suave flip of his keys to the valet at the end of the trip. The restaurant was on the second and third floors. The woman who operated the elevator winked at my father and looked at me saying, *third floor Mr. Hayes?* She let me close the bronze grill door when we entered and then open it when we came to our floor. When we got off the elevator, a man named George greeted us in a tuxedo. George was Greek. I never knew what Greek meant other than that it had something to do with my name and therefore George and I should be friends. The restaurant had tables with white linen table cloths and napkins. In the corner was a little bar where they mixed drinks. My father ordered the steak sandwich. George laughed when he said – *the usual, off the menu for Nickel-plate.* My specially ordered peanut butter sandwich arrived on a large white plate with potato chips. I washed down my sandwich with a kiddie cocktail while our conversation turned to the finer points of how to spin the Lazy Susan.

THE DAY WE WENT TO THE CIRCUS

Every March, when Minneapolis kids were still captive to parkas, mittens and galoshes but the novelty of sliding, skiing and skating had faded, entertainment went indoors as the high school basketball tournament commenced and the Shrine Circus returned once again to the Minneapolis Auditorium. My father had his own way of taking us to the circus. He didn't exactly take us to the circus; he dropped us off at the circus.

The Minneapolis Auditorium stood at the southern edge of downtown a few blocks beyond Harry's, protected on two of its four corners by somber churches—the faux Gothic Central Lutheran Church to the east and red rock Wesley Methodist to the west—as if to caution families on their way into the auditorium not to have too much fun or stray afterwards toward upper Nicollet Avenue's low life district, with its cluster of beer-with-a-bump bars and all-night cafés.

On the day of the circus, the snow started in the morning and delayed the arrival of our Ford at the auditorium. We parked on the street in front of the main entrance. Waving his hands like a football referee calling interference, a policeman rushed toward our car. Our father got out of the car and hurried toward the policeman. We guessed the policeman was just another friend of our father's when they shook hands and smiled. Our father hurriedly shooed us up to the entrance and turnstile where he handed young Mark the tickets and money and gave him directions. He pointed to an exit at the other end of the auditorium. When the circus was over, we were to exit through that door, turn right and walk a few blocks to his office. We couldn't miss it. With a laugh, he said we had enough money to buy hot dogs, peanuts and even hair-cuts afterwards at the nearby Moler Barber College. Then, looking at me, he said, *Get ready to see some elephants.* He was at a loss for a comeback when I asked if I would also get to see Ramah. He didn't watch Saturday morning television and knew nothing about Ramah of the jungle. My brothers went through the turnstile and my father lifted me over it and placed me inside.

We sat high in the bleachers. The auditorium went dark. A search light shone on a man in the center who called us "ladies and gentlemen" even though almost everyone there was under age 12. A door burst open. The circus people came out. We knew that one of the clowns was the famous Emmet Kelly whom we had seen on the Ed Sullivan Show, but we were too far away to see the faces and argued about just which one he was. We also failed to resolve equitably an argument over the equal distribution of money for hot dogs, peanuts and candy floss. When Tom decided to have *two* hot dogs instead of one *and* some candy floss , Brian made a point of slowly savoring his candy floss inches away from Tom's face until he pushed it into Brian's hair.

I thought the jugglers on the *Ed Sullivan Show* were better than those at the circus. The man on the trapeze was too old and fat to be playing on a swing. The elephants were tired and never gave out their loud shrieking hello the way Ramah's did when he called to them on TV. All in all, the circus lasted too long, and I wanted to get to my father's office while I would still have time to play with the blueprints and tubes. Long before the circus ended, I had stopped watching and listened instead to my brothers argue about which door our father had said to take when we left.

Heavy wet flakes of snow fell on the sidewalk and quickly covered our foot prints as we left the auditorium. A four block walk became five, six and then more and more blocks of walking in the snow. My brothers started to argue about directions and came up with three different proposals. Brian pointed left, Tom pointed right, and young Mark pointed straight ahead arguing that all he knew was we had to come to a dead end at Loring Park in front of our father's office. The houses around us seemed small, unlike the four- and five-story buildings around his office. I saw a barber shop and said this must be where we could get haircuts. A man in a car stopped beside us. This is what our mother had warned us about. When he rolled down his window, we ran, just as she had told us to do, cutting through an alley and then circling around another block, until young Mark looked around and declared that the man in the car was gone. We had come to a corner grocery store. Maybe we could go in there and ask the man if he knew where our father's office was. After all, everyone knew him. Tom said we couldn't go in there unless we bought something. Young Mark said we didn't have any money left. I had started to cry and couldn't stop. We decided to stand by the door away from the snow and think of something to do.

Hey, you kids cold? Come on in, the man inside said as he swung open the door. *My name's Morry. What's yours?* Young Mark started to say his name was Mark Hayes and to ask the man if he knew Hills, Gilbertson & Hayes when Brian started to cry. And then, we all started crying. *Hey, hey, try one of these, they'll make you feel better,* Morry said and gave each of us a Holloway Sucker. Our mother had told us to never take candy from strangers, but we knew she meant kidnappers in cars and not men who worked in grocery stores. After young Mark told him some stuff about our father, Morry looked in a book on his counter, picked up in the phone and in a second was laughing and talking. He must have been a friend of our father's, or maybe, I thought, all grownups just knew each other somehow.

The calm of snow on a March afternoon at the office had turned into panic when we had not shown up at the office on Loring. My father searched the streets, traced the four blocks back to the auditorium, tried without success to look inside the locked building, and alerted the police. They told him to go back and wait at his office until they called with any information. A call home only got my father an earful from my mother on the danger of kidnappers, and why in the hell did he have to go to the office every Saturday anyway? Couldn't he for once do something like go with his kids to the circus? By dinner time, the police still had not found a trace of us. Then, Morry called.

We saw our father through the grocery window. He had left the car running and parked illegally on the corner, slipping for a moment on the snow before he reached the door to Morry's Fresh Foods. There were his four boys crying and sucking on Holloways. Mark pulled out his wallet but Morry motioned with his hand saying it wasn't necessary. When we got home, my mother repeated too many times, *For crying out loud, Mark, you and your damned office, they could have been kidnapped.* By then, I had forgotten about why my pants had frozen and was thinking back on our adventure in the city. Someday, I was going to go back, get a haircut and visit our friend, Morry.

But we never went to the circus again.

SUNDAY MASS

Before the war, Minneapolis's Catholics walked to Sunday Mass. After the war, they drove. The type and model of car was a statement of sorts, as in the case of the Hutches who lived only a block away from church and nevertheless drove in their Cadillac Fleetwood. We were a Ford family. It was a statement of a lack of pretense on my father's part that I mistranslated into a sense of superiority over families who drove Chevrolets and watched the *Dinah Shore Show* on TV.

We hadn't always been a Ford family. Our father's '38 Pontiac Roadster lived a second life as a legend of his bachelor days and the honeymoon years of his marriage. Next, before he left for the Navy, he bought a new '44 Pontiac big enough for a family of four. He gave that car to Jim and Lucy when he turned and became a Ford man starting with the black shoebox '49 Ford, then an identical brown '51 shoebox, and a '53 Fairlane.

The last one came with a story. One day young Mark and our mother were in the kitchen when my father came home from work, opened the kitchen door, and said, *Viv, what's that old heap doing in our driveway.* Without a word to my mother, my father had given his old car to Lucy and had come home in this new dust green '53 Fairlane with a sleek design announcing the end of the shoebox era and the beginnings of true 1950s style.

My father took his time on Sunday mornings smoking and reading the Sunday newspaper in the bathroom. My mother said again and again—*Mark come on, we'll be late for the nine-forty*—never understanding that her husband had his own schedule for the time to arrive. When we finally got into the Ford, I sat in between my father at the steering wheel and my mother in the passenger seat. Young Mark, Brian and Tom sat in the back.

Our father dropped us off in front of the church, telling us to go ahead while he parked the car. My mother never understood why. There had been free-thinkers in her Lutheran childhood, men who turned against Lutheranism and never again stepped inside a church. But, there was nothing in the Lutheran Sundays of her childhood that could explain why a man never sat with his family at church, but always stood in the back and darted outside at the priest's first cue that the Mass was about to end. Other men sat with their families. There were the Dorns who lived on Lake Harriet Boulevard. Why, my mother asked over and over, did the Dorns sit in the front pew while her husband persisted in standing with a crowd of men in the back or along the aisle?

In the back of the church and along its aisles, men had negotiated a separate space for themselves. Implicit rules restricted the space. Grade school age boys still sat in the pews with their families. Otherwise, men from high school age up exercised their option of arriving late, avoiding the ritual of the genuflection in the center aisle, and clustering in the back and the sides of the church. If a sanctimonious usher occasionally attempted to make eye contact and indicate an available seat among the pews, he was greeted by mute, blank stares. At the first breath of the priest's *Ite, Missa est-Go ,the Mass is ended,* they whispered the response *Deo gratias – Thanks be to God,* their only verbal participation in the

Mass, and quickly filed out, even though the Mass still had a few more rounds of prayer to go.

Mr. Brandon belonged to the group of men in the back of the church who arrived late and left early. He owned a string of movie theaters downtown and gave us free passes to the best of them, the grand movie houses of old Hennepin Avenue—the Orpheum and the State. Young Mark called him "old man Brandon" or even "old John Brandon" to hint that there was a story here. He was as handsome as he was sad. He dressed like Broderick Crawford in the TV show. The Brandons didn't have children, and after depositing Mrs. Brandon at the church entrance, he would stay in the car a while before shuffling into the back of the church.

Once, all four of us skipped out early from Mass and ran back to our Ford. We were parked behind Mr. Brandon. Young Mark told us to hide. Mr. Brandon walked up to his car and looked around a bit, then opened the trunk and reached in. He took a wary look over at the house across the street, then took a fast gulp from a bottle wrapped in a brown bag and wiped his forehead with a hanky.

My father showed up a few minutes later, smiled and nodded toward Mr. Brandon. He said nothing to us about Mr. Brandon and the brown bag in his hand. They did not know each other well. They were both just part of the crowd of men who had their own separate reasons for standing in the back of church and leaving early. Catholicism on Sundays was a world of few choices, but my father had let us know that we at least had this symbolic right of assembly in the back of the church. Between those in the pews and the unseen damned who had chosen to stay home, there was the crowd of men who choose to stand in the back of the church. You didn't judge another man's choice. My father arrived late, stood in the back, and left Mass early because he could. Besides, he needed to smoke.

We were back home by 11. My mother turned to the task of making breakfast, while my father merely removed his suit coat but stayed in the white shirt and tie with slacks. Sometimes, he changed the suit coat for a vest, which was the final touch of style that placed his Sunday look somewhere between the Monday through Friday suits and the casual Pendleton Saturdays.

Most Sundays, we had our father's favorite dish of creamed cod over toast with hard-boiled eggs and boiled potatoes. The cod came in a wooden box. Its top slid open on grooves that my Canadian grandfather might have carved. One Sunday in April after breakfast, I took the cod box outside. The skies let you know it was April, but the flurries let you know it was Minnesota. The snow reminded me of how the nuns told us that no two snowflakes were the same and that was just one more proof of the existence of God. I went over to the old farm house by the swamp and slid the cod box open, trying to catch as many snowflakes as I could. I wanted a whole box to show the Protestants, not because they didn't believe in God but because I wanted to show them how smart the nuns were. The snow didn't cooperate and vanished inside the agnostic pine box that didn't care much about theology anyway.

COMPANY

On Sundays, we had company. *Boys, we have company,* our mother would announce. It was a cue for us to behave. The word "company" did not apply to the guys who joined my father for martinis on Saturdays. The word "company" signaled us to be prepared to meet guests and oblige their polite questions with answers that showed we came from a good home. We would sit on chairs in the living room and smile at the guests until their disinterest in us matched ours in them and we could slip away to games in the basement or the freedom of the outdoors.

Priests were company. Some had distant family connections like Father Dawson from North Dakota who shared with us some obscure common ancestor out in the prairie. After Parnell's death, Father Pendergast pretended to be family. The Passionist priest reveled in his appropriation of his late confrere's weekend routine at Lucy's house. *Just call me Little Parnell,* he said every time he came to the door. He never seemed to notice that he was the only one laughing at his old joke.

Father Novak was company. He came alone or sometimes with other priests. When I asked him once if he knew Father Driscoll, he replied irritably that he wasn't like Father Driscoll. Pulling rank in the obscure Catholic world that placed the religious orders above the diocesan priests, he said that he was a Redemptionist. *Here,* he said, *I write this* and he showed us a magazine called *The Ligourian.* Young Mark would find lots to read in it. The magazine began with a story called

"Summer Is No Time for a Young Boy to Lose His Vocation." Once, a priest who had something to do with the archbishop in St. Paul came and asked us all kinds of questions about what schools we went to and what we wanted to be when we grew up. Our mother never forgave the priest for his remark to her, as he left the house, *You know, Viv, for a convert you're a pretty good Catholic.*

One day, our father came home from the office with the Catholic newspaper that Father Driscoll left in piles in the church vestibule. You were supposed to buy the newspaper when you left Mass but we never did. On the front page was a picture of the archbishop, the priest who had come on Sunday, and our father. It was the announcement of a new church to be built. Even if the archbishop's priest had been worth a few martinis, our mother didn't want him around the house again. After the priests left, as she made the rounds of the cocktail table and end tables, picking up the empty glasses that had held the various martinis, high balls, low balls, manhattans and a few straight shots, she muttered to herself about those damned priests.

The insurance man, Louis Schaller, moved his old routine from Lucy's house on Dupont to our new house on Queen. Once in a while, he came on Sunday afternoons. Louis wore a blue suit that he kept buttoned even on hot days. My father said Louis never unbuttoned his suit because he didn't want anybody to know there were no labels inside. The two men sat at the kitchen table, and not on the chesterfield or red leather chair where the other guests sat when they visited. Old friends, they smoked their cigarettes, clinked their glasses together, and quickly slipped into a conversation that took them back to the old neighborhood.

The cigarettes had taken their toll on Louis. He coughed too often and his voice sounded to us kids like Froggy the Gremlin on TV. He would take some folded papers out of his pocket, my father would wave his hand indicating that he would look them over some other time and offer Louis another drink.

One of Louis's visits coincided with our production of *Peter Pan*. As we passed through the kitchen on our way downstairs, Louis was telling my father that he was a good provider and did not have to worry. Tom and Brian had already put on their feathers and Minnetonka moccasins to play the Indians. Tom suggested that I play Michael, the youngest of the Darling children. Our dog, Doby, refused to play the role of Nana and stayed upstairs by the kitchen door. Tom and Brian tied me with newspaper twine to the basement pole, and then crumpled up some newspaper into little pieces and arranged them in a little circle around my feet. Tom, who had grabbed some matches from the hiding place by the fireplace, lit the pieces of newspaper, and he and Brian chanted *What Made the Red Man Red, What Made the Red Man*, as they danced around me like real Indians on TV. The newspaper pieces burned and turned to smoke and ash. When my brothers finished the song, they tore up some more newspaper and repeated the performance, this time singing the war chant, *Wu, wu, wu, Wu, wu, wu*. Young Mark kept his distance by pretending to be Captain Hook keeping an eye on his ship.

Viv, do you smell smoke?! Mark yelled from up in the kitchen. Our mother was already down the stairs. *Shit!* He yelled even louder from the top of the stairs. *What the hell are you kids doing?* A pause. *We're playing Indians and Peter Pan.* Our mother had a rolled-up newspaper in her hand and she was hitting the burning pieces until there was only smoke and ashes at my feet. She kept saying, *You kids! Who did this? Tom? Was this your idea? You're going to burn down the house.* Our father would turn his head to say something to Louis and then turn it the other way to yell *Shit* in our direction. Doby went number two on the kitchen floor. Louis was laughing. *Don't worry, Viv, Mark's got fire*, he said.

Grandma Lucy and Uncle Jim were not exactly company. There was no invitation and no special event. They just came to our house every Sunday. Uncle Jim was our favorite. Every Sunday, about two, he and Lucy pulled up in the Pontiac. You didn't hold the door for Lucy. She let herself out of the car as Jim walked around from the driver's side. Uncle Jim twirled his keys on a long chain as he walked up the steps towards the front door. Lucy had presents for young Mark. Brian still expected something and would stand right beside young Mark but she never said anything to him, Tom or me. Brian's feelings were hurt but Tom and I had long before understood that our grandmother bestowed her favors on the first born of each of her children, whose names she pronounced slowly and with affection. She passed over all those other grandchildren, who were left to speculate among themselves whether she knew their names. At our house, she did acknowledge the existence of grandchildren other than young Mark by bringing us a Hills Brothers coffee can filled with peanut cake and sugar cookies, each individually wrapped in wax paper.

As soon as Uncle Jim had entered the house, he greeted me asking —*Heads or tails?* and tossed a coin in the air. I looked at my monkey Socko hoping he could tell me what was heads or what was tails. *Heads! You win!* Jim said slapping the coin to the back of his hand and then putting it between his thumb and big finger. *There, it's yours!* It was a quarter. *And don't trade with your brother*, he added, winking at Tom, who already had a smile on his face that betrayed a plan to see that the quarter would soon be his.

The adults moved into the living room. My father reserved his usual place on the couch by placing his lit Camel in the nearby ashtray and disappeared into the kitchen. When he returned with a pitcher of martinis for him and Jim and a bourbon and water for Lucy, she had taken her place on the couch and Jim, positioned in the red leather easy chair, was ready to get started. *They're switching to French in the state capitol, Mark*, he began.

Uncle Jim had worked as a reporter, copywriter, and editor for the newspaper as well as for WCCO Radio and WCCO-TV. Downtown, every journalist knew our Uncle Jim as Johnny Dare, his alias for a newsletter of his latest jokes, anecdotes and exposes of gaffes of the city's high and mighty. The State of Minnesota should have been more cautious when it tried to show off its French. Johnny Dare was covering the story. Since high school, my Francophile uncle had shown off his French in the weekly newsletter *Le Cheval de Nord* which he wrote and published and which did for us and the old Ascension crowd what Johnny Dare's column did for the downtown boys. In 1950, the State of Minnesota launched a national promotion campaign for tourism using the French slogan on its state seal to add a touch of class. Harkening back to the French fur traders of the eighteenth century who first explored the state's waterways, Minnesota lyrically called itself *L'Etoile du Nord*. Somebody in the governor's office leaned a bit too heavily on his one year of college French and for the sake of a national tourist promotion campaign rendered the slogan, *Le toile de Nord*. Johnny Dare caught the error and pointed out to his readers in the Minneapolis press corps that our state officials were promoting visitors from across the nation to come, see, and enjoy the "towel of the north."

A bit of laughter went out of the newspaper, WCCO Radio, and the nightly television news when Uncle Jim died. That evening, in the winter of 1953, the affable Cedric Adams faced the camera sitting on a stool as he did every night, sipping his mug of coffee, and exhaling for the benefit of the television audience a mixture of words and the caffeinated aroma in the phrase *Ah, Maxwell House coffee, good to the last drop*. He then looked at his notes on the paper he always held in his hand and said, *This is a sad one*. Viewers had come to expect Adams to read another joke or story from Johnny Dare. On this evening, he read the article he had written for the newspaper that day, *The Funniest Man I Ever Knew Died Today*. Adams told the viewers about Uncle Jim's fine work as a journalist and re-told the best of the jokes and stories from Johnny Dare. The article appeared in print the next day.

A weak heart had cast a shadow over Jim's life. Girlfriends came and went. Men with heart trouble did not marry. The need to stay close to home and doctors brought an early end to his jobs as a reporter in Texas and Oregon. Our mother told us sons that Uncle Jim decided to have an operation because he had a girlfriend at WCCO Radio and this time he would not let marriage pass him by. On the Thursday night before the surgery, Jim stayed overnight for observation in the hospital. In the morning, he was found dead in his room.

Jim's wake was the first time I saw death in my father's face. He held me by the hand and led me to the kneeler beside the coffin. The color of my father's face matched the gray of his gabardine suit. I looked at Jim's hands thinking he would be holding the key chain that he always twirled around his fingers as he walked. I turned to ask my father why there was a rosary in Jim's hands and not his key chain. My father's face trembled until his hands covered his eyes. My question went unasked. He kept Cedric Adams' article folded and tucked inside his wallet until, over time, the newsprint faded and Adams' words about Jim's jokes and stories were absorbed into the tanned leather and faded away.

It was a long time later, almost forty years, before I heard Jim's laugh again. It was in the seasoned voice of an older woman who had been on WCCO Radio for as long as anyone could remember. She had heard I would be on the evening talk show and was waiting to meet me in the studio. It was Jim's laugh that was in the back of her mind, like a roll of undeveloped film from Jim's camera, as her tittering voice said, *Your uncle, what a character! I would have married that man.*

YARD WORK

In the summer, the urbanity of late-lunch Saturdays at Harry's gave way to the simple domestic virtue of cocktails on the lawn. But that was after the work was done. In our first summer on Queen Avenue, my father, a child of the prairie who had become an architect, was determined to reconcile these two elements in his background by convert-

Yardwork at Queen Avenue

ing his little parcel of prairie overlain with sod into something more than just another lawn. There was a yeoman's simplicity in the image he cut as he stepped outside on Saturday mornings at dawn, dressed in cavalry twill slacks, a white short sleeve shirt, and U.S. Keds Boosters. Water from the hose loosened the ground; a small spade cut into the sod and opened the earth to accept the dominion of tree saplings, bushes and hedges put there to serve a higher purpose. There was also some posing for the camera.

One Saturday morning he planted a huckleberry hedge on our lawn's eastern edge to protect our privacy from the passenger cars on busy Penn Avenue. By ten in the morning, the hedge was in place and my father had done more than enough for the day. He and my mother rewarded themselves by enjoying a few cool martinis safe, from the prying eyes of Penn Avenue.

In a nod to the Prairie School style, he put in a Western ranch-style fence along half of the northern edge facing Queen. On the other half of that property line he planted a string of spruce trees in homage to the forests of northern Minnesota, shouldering the added expense and effort of planting larger specimens because he wanted to see them standing tall as a wall of evergreens before he died.

Circumscribed by the hedges, fence and spruce, the center of it all was my father's patio. After the war, the concept of a patio entered the vocabulary of Minneapolitans. It symbolized the leisure and modernity that separated the new times from the Depression era. In the 1930s, a man sitting on the lawn outside his home meant he was out of work. In the 1950s, a gentleman in a lawn chair on his patio meant a man with a job good enough to afford him the enjoyment of leisure time. Configured out of tinted bricks, my father's patio was an outdoor summer stage waiting to breathe new life into an old script of cocktails and conversation that had already had a long and successful run in the living room of the house of Dupont.

But Mark's attempt to add to the symbolic connections between the new house on Queen and the old manse on Dupont by planting a clump of birch trees was doomed to failure. Birch trees have shallow roots; they thrive in the dappled shade of taller species. In the blazing sun of a new subdivision, the small leaves on our cluster of birches yellowed. Eventually the frail thin trunks turned to three dead stalks in the ground.

The promise of modern science went unfulfilled when it came to insect control. The problem was not mosquitoes. The city took care of those pesky creatures early in the summer, when large tanker trucks painted a fatigue-green crept along the streets and men in space-age uniforms with hoods and gas masks aimed a sweet smelling fog across the asphalt, and then, lifting their hoses, allowed it to spew up into the air and float down onto our lawns. Sitting on the curb, my brothers and I were wowed when the spray crept toward our feet and circled around us in a magic cloud. Suddenly the mosquitoes were gone—no further need to spray pesticide up and down our arms. The sounds of summer evenings were no longer punctuated by hands swatting and scratching. But along with the mosquitoes we also lost the fireflies that had glowed along the hedges at night and that I never saw again.

And nothing in the city's arsenal of chemicals could eradicate the flies. On Sundays, Lucy refused to eat outside where we had set up a picnic table and small barbeque. It was a carryover from her North Dakota childhood. She never could understand why anyone would want to eat outside when they had a perfectly good dining room and kitchen inside. But she never said it that way. Instead, she complained about the flies.

At school, we were told that flies were the reason the little girl in the March of Dimes ad wore braces on her legs and walked with crutches. Our kindergarten teacher, Sister James Patrice, had also gotten sick from the flies. We were taken once to visit her in a special clinic in the hospital. They called the machine an iron lung. We could only see her small head at the top end of a cylinder that made a wheezing sound and scared us. After that visit, I decided to get rid of the flies in our yard. I stole one of my mother's Ball mason jars. With the lid off, I went around the yard trying to capture a fly in mid-air and swoop it to the ground.

My father had a better idea. One Friday, he came home with a fly-catcher. It was a canister about a foot long with holes in the sides and openings at the top and bottom. You put a piece of fish in it. The flies swarmed to the fish inside where they mysteriously perished. But the device worked too well. Too many came. Swarms of flies from across the neighborhood and as far away as the swamp by Armitage Park made the pilgrimage to my father's flycatcher tucked in the front yard by the patio. There were so many we couldn't go outside. As evening approached my mother finally went out, rolled up the fly-catcher in cloth and threw it in the trash can in the alley. She vomited when she was done. The next morning there were still swarms of flies hovering around the trashcan.

The scene required a dog. Though my father often mocked his brother-in-law, Aunt Eileen's husband John Nevin, the fact that he owned a palatial lake home in northern Minnesota lent more gravitas to his opinions on dogs. The Doberman was Nevin's idea. Our first one was Kurt. He didn't last long. After a few weeks, Kurt bit a neighbor girl in the fanny. My father didn't say a word while the girl's father yelled at him. He simply wrote the man a check. Then, he took the dog away.

The next week, he came home with Doby, a mild reddish-colored Doberman who fawned on children and channeled his police-trained aggression into the noble pursuit of catching muskrats. They were easy prey for him. He would scout one out at the Armitage swamp, corner it, swiftly catch it in a pounce or two, and return to deposit the wounded rodent on the patio bricks.

MY FATHER'S COMMITMENT to the yeoman's spirit didn't run for a full season. By mid-summer, the spade had the weekends off. By that time Mark had put his stamp on his own piece of the Midwestern earth, and felt no need to enter into neighborhood discussions of the relative merits of the Scott versus the Jacobson lawn mower, preferring to devote his remaining summer weekends in an unending tribute to the martini that broke the prairie.

But Mark had allies in the neighborhood, men who appreciated a good martini and a story to go along with it. The old gang still came around—Halvorson, Dunshee, Vic—joined by new faces from across the street. Frank Butler, host of a popular morning radio show on 'CCO, was a regular. And a favorite among the neighbors was a lawyer, Lee Loevinger.

A newspaper story brought Loevinger to my father's attention. Loevinger was defending the strip clubs on the lower end of Hennepin Avenue from city's latest fit of Christian righteousness. My father threw his support behind his neighbor's client, and throughout the summer Loevinger regularly joined my father on the patio to discuss the nuances of the case.

Mark's recipe for martinis has been preserved in innumerable copies written out for friends on cocktail napkins. Vic had a copy from 1947. A generation later, in an age when martini bars had corrupted the genuine article with vodka and flavorings, Vic entrusted his copy of my father's recipe to me to safeguard the secret of the original faith. It reads:

> *Put mixer & glasses in freezer*
> *Put ice in mixer or pitcher*
> *Add 1 part dry vermouth (I use Tribuno)*
> *Add 8 parts gin (I use Fleishman)*
> *Shake to thoroughly cool*
> *Pour into glasses*
> *Squeeze oil from twist of lemon onto drink*
> *Add olive stuffed with anchovies*
> *ENJOY!*

My father's zeal for yard work soon grew weak, and the turf in the yard suffered. My mother's comments on how nice the grass looked in the yard across the street went without comment. One Saturday, she had had enough, and demanded that he mow the grass. He informed her that he and Loevinger were just about to go and do some "field work" on Loevinger's case. The joke fell flat, and pursuing a sudden flash of insight, Mark brought out a new-fangled electric knife sharpener from the kitchen and proceeded to apply this technological innovation to create the sharpest, most effective lawn mower ever known to south Minneapolis. It was an engineering act of genius worthy of his younger brother Dave (though Dave would probably have anticipated that the device would quickly buckle and break when applied to such a task.)

One summer, MY mother's father, Grandpa Herman, came to visit. I had never spoken to either of my grandfathers or even heard them speak. Nick was long dead, and he was mentioned rarely. His few words were passed along, second and third hand, in indirect quotations of mostly incomplete phrases. When my mother's parents visited us that summer, Grandma Elsie talked all the time. Grandpa Herman said nothing.

One hot June afternoon, my grandfather Herman set to work in the yard, exposing my father for the *faux* agrarian and handyman he was. Herman removed his shirt to reveal a type of undershirt I associated with men from Brooklyn on TV. It was not a "T-shirt" with short sleeves. It had thin cotton bands that drooped down from his shoulders and expanded into the undershirt that covered his chest and abdomen. I sat and watched as he silently built me a sandbox. He sawed and fitted the boards for the four sides by hand. With a small jig saw, he cut out curved benches that he set along the upper edges of the sand box. His ponderous silence made me study him more closely and put me more in awe of his massive strength. Not far from where he worked in the yard on my sandbox, my father, his brothers Jim and John, Lucy, my mother and Elsie sat. They sipped cocktails and laughed as Lucy's sons retold old stories and jokes that everyone except Elsie had heard before. Grandpa Herman could have picked the three of those men up in one hand. He finished the sandbox and shook his head when my father invited him to have a drink and relax. I followed Grandpa Herman into the garage where he turned old pieces of scrap lumber into storybook cut-outs for my bedroom wall.

HOLIDAYS

The tribal holiday gatherings of the Hayes family on the North Side did not survive the migration to the other end of town. I have only two fragments from a toddler's memory of those massive holidays. On one Christmas I brought my Pinocchio doll along and insisted that he sit beside me at dinner. And one Easter I refused to give up the palm branches I had taken from behind the crucifix on the wall. I always preferred the story of Palm Sunday to the story of Easter.

At first, we tried to continue the old traditions by cramming into Lucy's new house in the suburb of St. Louis Park, giving palpable proof (if anyone needed it) that the new suburban tract housing wasn't meant for an Irish family with its roots in the pre-war era. With the exception of Uncle Jim, who always stayed with the kids, the grown-ups sat around a kitchen breakfast nook extended with a card table. The grandchildren were organized according to their respective families and seated at card tables in the two bedrooms, the living room, and the basement where my brothers and I usually ended up.

Lucy was her most fun at Easter. During Lent, she gave up her bourbon-and-waters, and throughout Easter day Lucy rewarded her thirst for its perseverance and long commiseration with our Lord's suffering. She laughed so hard one Easter that she fell backward, hit a floor lamp, and knocked the shade in such a way that somehow it ended up on her head. *How do you like my new hat?* she said, and continued on with her fit of laughter.

When we were not consigned to the basement, my brothers and I ate with Jim in his bedroom where a small TV taught us not to take for granted the miracle of broadcast television. The images were mostly blurry. Jim told us he could talk to those people on the screen, and proved it by dialing the phone and then raising his voice to let us know that he was talking to Arthur Godfrey, Cedric Adams or whoever happened to be on the TV screen. *Arthur, yah, this is Jim, you need to sit closer to the camera or adjust the lights,* he would say, *my nephews can't see you.* As the image came into clearer view, he would say, *There, that's better. Yah, thanks, I'll talk to you later.* Uncle Jim's hand on the rabbit ears escaped even young Mark's notice. We believed him in part because he worked at WCCO and must have known these people. Most of all, we believed him because he was Jim, our favorite uncle. Jim didn't even mind when we threw away Lucy's stuffing . The grown-ups talked about how they loved Lucy's sage dressing. Young Mark smelled it and said it was green. We rolled it up in our handkerchiefs and threw it out Jim's bedroom window.

It was pretty obvious that the holiday gatherings in Lucy's new house, like the over-stuffed chairs and davenport she had moved from Dupont to St. Louis Park, just didn't fit. One November, my father announced that this year Thanksgiving would be at our house. His one sentence brought to an end a family discussion that never occurred. However, each time the roll was called at our house on Thanksgiving, Easter, or Christmas, there were fewer voices. My mother was not about to set-up card tables to disperse her ever-growing flock of nieces and nephews to the far corners and basement of our house. Instead, an unspoken system of rotation was established whereby the two most populous branches of the family—Uncle John and Aunt Ardis, or Uncle John and Aunt Eileen—took turns, with one staying through dinner and the other stopping by for cocktails and discretely leaving when the clamor of pots and pans in the kitchen rose an octave or two.

On one Good Friday, as we drove to the drawn-out *Tre Ore* service, my father decided to delay our arrival by slowing down to point out sites of interest along the way. *Look over there, Nickel-plate,* he said, pointing to a small stone garden shed built by the WPA next to Minnehaha creek, *It's Peter Rabbit's house.* I had no reason to doubt him. That Saturday night he devoted himself to daubing bunny tracks across the floor in trails leading to four secret places. The artist in him insisted that the distinction between the front and hind paws be maintained and that the angles of direction change as the Easter Bunny shifted and altered his path. He added a few false paths to give a bit of a challenge to his boys' search for their Easter baskets in the morning. The tracks were so fresh when I came upon them the next morning that I was sure the Easter Bunny was still somewhere in the house. I wanted to follow him back to his house by the creek. Young Mark thought differently. *But there's no snow outside,* he said. *How could a rabbit leave white footprints?*

The Easter Bunny was not the only holiday legend to fail the test of my oldest brother's skepticism. When Santa Claus came to our house one Christmas Eve, young Mark pointed to Santa's wrist and said, that's

Mr. Koval's watch. Why the watch? You would think young Mark would have first picked upon the pillows the skinny Koval stuffed inside his red jacket peeping up like rabbit ears around his collar. A second fake Santa was exposed when young Mark identified an uncle's six o'clock shadow around the edges of Santa's ill-fitting beard.

On my first Christmas Eve, my father arrived home in the early evening. The shops were closed. Hills, Gilbertson and Hayes closed up the office at noon and threw themselves a party at Harry's. A bit of a spat went back and forth between our parents. Our father discovered that there were no toys for me. *We have to have a gift for Nickel-plate*, he argued. Our mother countered with the obvious: I was all of thirteen days old, what difference did it make. Besides, the stores were closed, and it was snowing heavily. The gentle argument turned on ties to the old Broadway neighborhood, the lack of any real resistance on my mother's part, and the force of sentimentality at Christmas time. My father called a friend from the old neighborhood who owned Friedman's Department Store. It was closed, but no problem. The owner met my father, opened the store, and together they decided that a wooden Pinocchio was just the right thing. *You know it's the reverse*, Friedman said to my father as he was leaving. *You're an old man with a real boy but you want a wooden toy Pinocchio.*

After young Mark had exposed the second fake Santa, our father gave up on the ritual of that visitation and inaugurated a new tradition. The next Christmas there was a knocking on the French doors in the dining room. *One of you boys answer the door*, our father feigned enough annoyance to fool us. Though Santa was nowhere in sight, on the step outside the doors a sled held a carefully arranged mound of gifts.

Our favorites were the Howdy Doody string puppet set. Phineas T. Bluster suited young Mark. Brian led the show with a puppet of Buffalo Bob. I was jealous when Tom unwrapped Howdy-Doody, though Tom's carrot top of red hair and face of freckles did give him legitimate claim to that role. Flapadoodle on string was the first pet I claimed to be mine alone.

One Christmas brought two Hopalong Cassidy's to our house. Both Tom and I received the complete outfit—ten gallon white hats, black western shirts and slacks, pointy cowboy boots, and best of all, a belt with two six guns. Tom, who would soon wear jeans sized "husky," pulled off the look. Mine worked as long as I stood still. A few steps brought the gun belt and slacks down to my ankles. My mother said it wasn't funny when my father quipped, *Hey, Hopalong, are you looking for a gun-fight or a toilet?*

On Christmas morning, we explored the out-of-the-ordinary gifts that came our father's way. A tad shy about their presence at a family Christmas, these gifts came from his clients who like the Magi curried his favor. They stood diffidently in the corner of the dining room far from the Christmas tree. A Lazy Susan in Danish wood whirled in a circle and promised to be both a toy and a platter for hors d'oeuvres at the next cocktail hour. A brass barometer and thermostat mounted on sculpted oak and crowned with a brass miniature of a clipper ship on the top made me think some of his friends must be pirates. There were crates of grape-fruit from Florida; table games made of wooden boxes with handles on the side designed to navigate a steel marble through a labyrinth of treacherous holes; illustrated decks of cards in leather boxes for poker games that we didn't know our father played; and, my favorite, a potted kumquat tree that I believed would be planted in our garden in the spring.

Christmas Eve we fasted. Fasting meant creamed cod on toast for dinner. The ample space and formality of the dining room table, the linen table cloth, the china, gold plated flatware, and candlelight imposed a subdued, almost liturgical mood on the dinner until a word from my father signaled that the ritual was over and the bedlam of opening Christmas presents was about to begin.

For dinner Christmas Day, our mother drew upon her childhood on her Grandmother Larson's farm and produced roast duck and geese. At the dining room table sat our family of six, the Nevins' five, Lucy, and Uncle Jim. Uncle John and Aunt Ardis came over in the afternoon. By late afternoon, as the shuffling of the Revere ware pots and pans in the kitchen reached a pitch of G-sharp, Uncle John and Aunt Ardis said it was time for them to go. Uncle John left behind a record album of his choir, "Schola Cantorum"—that was his Christmas gift. It featured renditions of Latin hymns and motets with John himself as the tenor soloist.

For all of my mother's work, it was not her roast ducks and geese that I remember but the flaming brandy plum pudding. To heighten the drama of the presentation, the lights were turned off, and Aunt Eileen snuffed out the candles at the table with her fingers. My mother carried the plum pudding to the place at the far end of table where our father sat with his back to the French doors. He flicked his lighter. The brandy-soaked desert went up in a blue flame. Next he went around the table setting aflame the snifters of brandy at the grown-ups' places at the table.

As our dinner came to an end, our father played the "Schola Cantorum" album, bringing his brother's voice back into the family's conversation, though when John's lyrical tenor voice rang out in a solo, he lifted the turntable's arm and advanced the needle.

As the choir began *Adeste, fideles,* the blue light of flaming brandy cast a glow on my father's face that matched his eyes. From the outside, the Christmas lights that my mother had hung around the doors formed an arch of light around his quivering shadow. We knew the Latin hymn's chorus by heart. *Venite adoremus,* the words of the refrain formed and repeated on our silent lips in an automatic Catholic reflex. In the third verse, Uncle John and another voice, both lyrical tenors, hailed the King of Angels in a duet. *Natum videte,* Uncle John pitched his voice as if lifting the other tenor's voice to reach its higher notes that broke out in *Regem angelorum.* We knew that the other tenor was partially paralyzed from polio and sang from a wheel chair. The strength in Uncle John's voice carried him on his shoulders as the tenor reached to the high notes of a Beniamino Gigli in the final refrain. *Venite adoremus Dominum.* Free of polio, the tenor walked in song leading us toward the manger. *Venite adore-MU-us Do-O-minum*

VACATIONS

My father did not embrace the new 1950s concept of the family vacation. Instead, an older custom prevailed. My parents did the town. Actually, they did a number of towns. You didn't do the town with your kids. There were Saturdays when Lucy would come to stay with us while our parents left for drinks and dinner at Harry's and a night at the Radisson Hotel downtown. Once in a while, they went away for a weekend. Early Friday morning, Mark brought Lucy to the house and then he and Vivian took a cab to the Great Northern Depot to catch the Hiawatha 400 that would have them in Chicago by five. When they returned on Sunday night, my mother would be in a new hat and outfit.

We learned the names of the Palmer House, the Blackhawk, and the Berghof, and ate chocolate mints bought for us at Marshall Field's.

Once, my parents flew to New York. When they returned, they showed us a photo of them having cocktails at Roundy's across from Madison Square Garden. I asked my father if he had seen the Empire State Building. He said no, he wouldn't do that without me along.

There were also the weekends up North. The phase "up North" referred to the northeastern quadrant of Minnesota where the prairie and farmlands gave way to endless lakes, wetlands, and coniferous forests peppered with hunter's shacks, lake cabins, and resorts. Many Minneapolis families went up North in the summer. Some were merely returning to the small towns or farms where they had grown up, or gathering with aunts, uncles and cousins at lake cabins their grandparents had built before the war.

For us up North meant the one weekend every summer when our family of six and the dog Doby packed into the Ford for a visit with Aunt Eileen's family at Lake Vermillion. Eileen had married into the North Dakota gentry. Her husband John ("JD") Nevin brought a lake home to the marriage. It stood on Daisy Bay on the south side of Lake Vermillion where settled Minnesota faced off with the wilderness that started on Lake Vermillion's northern shore and journeyed northward into the depths of Canada. This was a time and place in Minnesota where you could still believe in the existence of a northern frontier where black bears held the upper hand in the competition for territory with hunters and gatherers, lumberjacks and woodsmen.

The Nevins' lake home had the pretense of a manor. Built by John Nevin's father, the home's spacious living room looked out to the lake from a set of French windows. The show-piece was the robust field-stone fireplace. Two bedrooms extended behind it. At the other end was the dining room and kitchen with a small alcove where the maid had once waited dutifully until called. By my time, the maid was long gone, though she played a role in the stories told about JD's father.

A wide staircase ascended to a second floor with more bedrooms and a spacious bath. Outside, a year-round dock led from the stone seawall to a gazebo overlooking the lake. A boathouse on the water had berths for two water-craft. Pulleys elevated and stored the boats on a second level through the long, harsh winters. Separate from the home stood the maid's house. The only connection between the Nevins' lake home and the average Minnesota cabin was the two-seater outhouse on the grounds which acknowledged that modern plumbing had not entirely conquered the long, arctic winters of northern Minnesota.

We didn't need to sit around a campfire and tell made-up ghost stories. The Nevins' place was haunted and its ghosts were not shy. Their dog, a boxer named Gertie, would never enter the bedroom where the grandfather had died, though at night she would often growl in the dark, whine, and pace back and forth on the old pine-plank floor outside that room.

My father was not an up North kind of guy. He read *True Magazine*, not *Sports Afield* or *Field & Stream*. A return to his family's small town roots brought to mind the broken farms and dirt prairie lives the O'Briens left behind in North Dakota. To his mind, Williston was a good place to be from. But on one occasion he did venture off on a fishing trip with his usual gang of friends. Vivian wondered aloud why, when his friends had homes on Lake Minnetonka, they had to go fishing up North. On the Monday after the trip, he put the Red Wing boots he'd purchased expressly for the occasion out in the garage where they waited, good as new, for another fishing trip that never happened.

My father gave in to the weekend trips to Lake Vermillion with the resignation of a hostage in the culture wars of the 1950s. The drive took seven to eight hours, giving him ample time at the wheel to contemplate the difference in style between these trips with a family of six and a dog in a four door Ford and his bachelor journeys solo in the Pontiac Roadster from Rochester to Duluth. North of Minneapolis, place names like Forest Lake, Pine City and Moose Lake signaled we were leaving city life far behind. South of Duluth, we veered northwest toward the Iron Range. Just outside of the mining town of Virginia, the state had given up on investing in asphalt for its highways. From there, a dirt road ambitiously named Highway 1 took us under an arch of cathedral pines until the sign for "Daisy Bay Resort" let us know that the ordeal by car was over. The Nevins' place was just around the next bend.

We kids were not good travelers. You could bet the mortgage that Brian and I would start throwing up somewhere between Pine City and Moose Lake. That was why charges of unfairness entered by young Mark and Tom went without redress. Brian and I always got the seats by the rear windows so we could hang our heads out in the wind in the desperate hope that it would blow the nausea away. I shared the open window with Doby.

These trips did not bring out the best in my father. There was the time my teddy bear was sick and needed fresh air. I held him out the window, and promptly dropped him. My father gruffly muttered something about too much traffic and refused my mother's request to retrieve it.

On another occasion, my cousin Mary Nevin came along with us. She was my age and my favorite cousin. She had been staying with Lucy, and the plan was for us to take her back to Vermillion to meet up with the rest of her family. She had dressed for the journey in a navy-blue sailor's outfit; she was the princess of the family as she sat in her place of honor on her Aunt Vivian's lap in the front passenger's seat. Seeing that we were all sticking our heads out the back windows, Mary decided to follow suit. As she craned her head outside the front passenger window to catch the rush of the oncoming wind, her sailor cap took flight, soaring quickly high above and behind the car as it vanished from view. My father stupefied everyone when he refused to retrieve his favorite niece's cap. She was still whimpering when we arrived at the Nevins'. *You jerk, Mark,* our Aunt Eileen said when Mary's story was told. It was the only time I ever saw my Aunt angry with my father.

At Lake Vermillion, my uncle "JD" assumed the air of a gentleman gone native. He sported the old Abercrombie & Fitch look fashioned from corduroy hunting jackets, felt hats, and leather boots purchased mail-order from the store in New York. In fact, the A & F catalogues themselves lay casually on the end tables and cocktail table.

JD claimed he knew the best fishing spots, and where you could find bears and the occasional moose. Or at least, he convinced his four nephews that he knew such things. *Boys, up here, it's like this,* he would say, taking his pipe from his mouth and giving his voice an authoritative tone. One day he packed the four of us and his twin sons, Mike and John, into a boat and cranked up the old Evinrude 25 HP. The old outboard fought hard to preserve its retirement, but at last it kicked in, and soon we were speeding to those out-of-the-way spots on the lake where bears roamed the shores and muskies and northerns leaped from the water high into the air. We never *saw* the wild animals and caught only croppies and sun-fish…but JD attributed that to our inability to remain silent for more than thirty seconds at a time.

My father invariably stayed behind, preferring to lounge in a neatly pressed Pendleton shirt. On Sundays he headed off to Mass in the nearby town of Tower, and dressed down in the afternoon only so far as to take off his suit coat—the same routine he followed at home. Such behavior may have been a subtle way of distancing himself from JD, but avoiding the fishing trips also gave him a rare opportunity to talk to his sister without her husband around.

My father, Eileen and my mother spent the afternoons on lawn chairs overlooking the seawall or at the end of the wooden dock in the screened-in gazebo. In the gazebo, my father and aunt revisited the days on Dupont, leaving my mother to intervene in the disputes that invariably arose between her boys and their cousins. She struggled in vain to enforce her rule against swimming beyond the dock where in the cold dark waters beyond she saw the shades of Grendels beneath the surface stalking her young Geats. Once, my father took a swim. He quit after a few strokes reminded him of how many cigarettes separated his past on the Ascension Club swim team from the present.

The pressure to take a family vacation mounted with the passing years. My mother made frequent digs about my father's membership in the AAA. What was the point of paying for a membership if we didn't go anywhere? Each month, the AAA monthly newsletter came in the mail with tales of the glory of America's new highways and the family vacations that were paradise on the road. AAA would chart your family trip along the best highways from Minneapolis to the Black Hills, Yellowstone, or even California. The hazards of the highway were no excuse to stay home. AAA was there to save you from the pitfalls of flat tires, car breakdowns, and bad motels. Mt. Rushmore was the vacation of choice for Minnesota families. Its popularity only intensified my father's intransigence. In his mind, Mt. Rushmore was the Golgotha of boredom at the end of the family vacation road.

Eventually my father gave in. But, we didn't go west like everybody else. Our compass pointed northeast, heading first to Duluth and then up Lake Superior's North Shore. We were heading to Ottawa to visit our mother's sister, Aunt Eva, and her husband Keith.

We left early, and upon arriving in Duluth, we drove up the city's hills to see the cathedral our father had designed in the earliest days of his career. He prevailed over our mother's complaints of how long it would take, and we ate lunch at the Duluth Hotel, reliving another chapter from that phase in his career. It might have been a sense of pride at the sight of his early work or the martini that went with his steak sandwich, but as we continued up the North Shore my father regaled us with stories about odd priests and a bishop he had known in Duluth. His humor kept rolling along with the cliffs and hills of Highway 61, even after Brian and I had discharged our lunches out the window.

We entered Canada a bit late and stayed overnight just across the border in Port Arthur. When I asked if the Canadian town was named after a popular Chinese restaurant in Minneapolis, my father said that Nickel-plate was right again. At a gas station, he indulged Brian's wish to buy the window decal of a friendly and waving Royal Canadian Mounty, which he affixed to the front passenger side vent window, telling us that Mounty would keep us safe in Canada.

Once we'd arrived in Ottawa, we took the predictable snapshot of a tourist family in the old stone square where Parliament and Canada's other grand buildings of state stood. Later that same day history was made. As the family picnicked in a park along the Ottawa River, Uncle Keith took out his new Kodak 16 mm movie camera and the Hayes family entered the era of the family home movie.

It turned out that this was not entirely a family vacation, however. One morning our parents departed for a weekend in Quebec City, leaving us behind with Eva and Keith. When they returned late Sunday night, our mother had stories of a city more exciting than Chicago. A room at the Hotel Chateau Frontenac with a fireplace and room service. Sunday Mass at the Shrine of Sainte Anne-de-Beaupre where miracles made cripples walk and their crutches and wheel chairs hung by the thousands on the church walls. Quebec was a Canada she never knew existed in her days in Manitoba. The French speaking Métis who lived outside Erickson or the French nuns who administered her nursing school in St. Boniface were only faint echoes of this other Canada which spoke in its own soft language of miracles and romance.

Early Monday morning, we took off in the Ford heading west for home. By late afternoon, my mother felt obliged to observe that every motel sign read "no vacancy." Late in the day she saw a "vacancy" sign in front of a motel in a town called Blind River and she insisted we stop, though we were short of our planned nightly stop in Sault St. Marie and the motel was not on the AAA recommended list. My father booked two rooms, placing the four kids at one end of the motel and he and Vivian at the other end. It didn't end up that way. At first, we kids tried to be very quiet. I cried first, then Brian, and finally our mother had to come down to our room where she spent the night.

The next day, in the morning fog that shrouded the highway as we crossed from Sault Saint Marie into Michigan, four state troopers and a road block suddenly appeared in front of us on the highway. There had been a prison break. The policemen did not smile or hide the shotguns at their side as they eyed us suspiciously. No longer in Canada, our Mounty on the window could do nothing to help. The policemen's gruff warning not to pick up any hitch-hikers was a rather irrelevant piece of advice to give a family of six in a shoebox Ford. My father drove on with his hands resolutely on the wheel as if he was escaping with family from the dangers of *True Magazine* back to the safety of *Life Magazine*.

THE FORD KEPT TO a serious homeward pace with a steady stream of cigarette smoke trailing from the driver's vent window. My father replied patiently with *It's just a couple more hours* as my brothers and I repeated the question that is the final children's chorus of every family vacation on the road. Finally, somewhere in Wisconsin, our radio picked up the scratchy sounds of the mellow voice of WCCO's "Hobbs at Night," and our father said we were nearly home. Hobbs put me to sleep. I awoke in my bed at Queen the next morning.

The story of my father's behavior at the Blind River Motel was retold so many times and to so much laughter that you would have thought he set the whole thing up in advance—a satire of the incorrigible father on the family vacation. I no longer cared that the other kids in the neighborhood had Polaroid snapshots of themselves and an American Indian chief taken at Mt. Rushmore. Half the kids on the block had photos like that. We had a decal of a Mounty in the window of our Ford who kept an eye on things and was looking out for us. Did the other kids hear about the prison break in Michigan? We had helped the police solve the case. We had memorized *bonjour* and *comment allez vous* which was enough French to convince kids in our neighborhood that, while "abroad" the Hayes boys had mastered a foreign language.

A few other stories stayed behind in a film canister in Uncle Keith's closet. The film would have revealed the landscape of Canada in my mother's smile, or my father shedding all pretence before the camera and losing himself in the simple joy of playing with his four young sons as they put a silly red beanie on his head. The 16 mm stories were all but forgotten until one of my own sons, on another family vacation, asked his Great Uncle Keith what was inside the canister in his closet.

THE FRIDAY NIGHT FIGHTS

We loved to watch Lucky Strike's *Your Hit Parade* on TV. Our mother never failed to mention that Dorothy Collins and Gisele MacKenzie were Canadian girls. She added that MacKenzie was from Winnipeg to let us infer that the singer and she had probably been friends. In 1955, when MacKenzie and Snooky Lanson did their duet of the Sammy Cahn song "Love and Marriage," the song's repetitive four-beat rhythm and simpleton's rhymes came off with a scolding, I-told-you-so tone.

In Lanson's delivery of the third stanza –

Love and marriage, love and marriage
It's an institution you can't disparage

he pointed and wagged his finger at the camera. He knew what the audience was thinking. Shame on you, don't even think it, he appeared to say with a smirk on his face. When you put a few things together—that gesture by Lanson, the observation that the dark-haired MacKenzie had a bit of the vamp in her, and the inevitable suspicions that went through your mind when a guy had a name like "Snooky"—you got the hint. Neither they nor the audience were as dumb as the song but nobody was going to say a thing. Even if the 1950s covenant of love and marriage happily ever after showed signs of strain, Catholics were not going to talk about it.

The troubles in Aunt Eileen's marriage started before the wedding. Whenever anyone in the family or from the old neighborhood spoke of her, they invariably shook their heads and said she was such a pretty girl. Nobody remembers how she met John Nevin. His father was a prominent lawyer and one-time gubernatorial hopeful in North Dakota. When

JD showed up at Dupont in 1946, Lucy confided to the Frankmans that she couldn't remember that North Dakota ever had a man that handsome. He knew women were easily smitten by him. His charm did not wear well with my uncles, Jim and John. They never understood why their future brother-in-law, on his first visit to their home, told them repeatedly that the future was in "cold steel rolls." A fast courtship hastened the couple down the aisle at Ascension. My father, whose role in the wedding was to give away the bride, showed up at the church early on the evening of the groom's dinner. Eileen was already crying. She had not heard from JD all day. He had not showed up for the rehearsal. Her brother waited a half hour beyond the scheduled time. *He's not showing up, forget it, don't marry him,* he said over the sound of his sister's tears. *I love him, you have to find him, Mark, please,* Eileen said through her tears. *Please find him.*

It was a long search, the evening spent combing the hotels and downtown bars of Minneapolis. It was late when, on his first stop on the other side of the river, my father found JD at the bar of the St. Paul Hotel. He paused for a moment. The phrase "cold steel rolls" went through his mind. He could lie. Tell Eileen he never found her groom. Too late. He was spotted. *Mark, what are you doing here? How about a drink, Mark?* JD parried as if this was just a chance meeting and ignored my father's cold stare. He lit up a Camel and began, *Are you going to marry her or not?*

Eileen's marriage was the subject of terse and oblique comments right from the start. The newlyweds bought a new rambler in Edina not far from our house on Queen. During her second pregnancy, when Eileen was expecting twins, my father brought her home one afternoon to our house. She was in her nightgown, soaking wet, and crying. *You don't have to go back to him. I'll get you an apartment,* he said with an anger I didn't recognize in his voice. My mother ushered me into another room. *What's wrong with Aunt Eileen?* I asked. It was nothing, she said. Uncle JD and Aunt Eileen were just having an argument. She did not tell me that Eileen had been hanging wash on the line that morning in her nightgown and sent JD off into a rage. He picked up the outdoor hose, narrowed the nozzle to a hard needle of a stream, and turned it on his pregnant, half-clothed, screaming wife.

The Catholic ban on divorce applied to our vocabulary. The word was never uttered in sentences about Eileen and John Nevin or any marriages in our family. Exceptions were made in references to Protestant marriages and my mother's side of the family. Always said in carefully guarded tones, the words "thinking about divorce" cropped up in grown-up conversations about our Aunt Eva and Uncle Keith. *You know Eva can't have children and they've decided not to adopt*, my

mother would say by way of injecting into the conversation a dispensation before the mandatory judgment was pronounced in the silence of her in-laws' minds. Much later, after the ban on discussing divorce had been lifted, my mother, her brother Norman, or Grandma Elsie would say that Keith was seeing someone with an emphasis on "was" as if the verb belonged in the past pluperfect tense.

I thought my mother got mad on Friday nights because I wasn't a good eater. I restricted my diet to wieners, peanut butter sandwiches, scrambled eggs, and pancakes. She would have

My Aunt Eileen

already served me one or more of these entries in the course of the day. Dinner, however, was another matter. No substitutions. Friday nights were the worst.

In my mind, there were few entrées more appalling than mock chicken legs, which were a staple of our weekday meals. Those breaded lumps of paste on a stick came alive on my plate. The crust had fur and the things purred. But they were nothing compared to the monster of the sea, the Friday night tuna casserole. Most nights I made some effort by pushing and re-arranging the entrees in such a way as to make it appear that I had eaten something. On Friday nights, I stuck fast to my principles and could often count on the solidarity of one, two or all of my brothers in the hunger strike at the kitchen table. Without a token gesture of interest, a prodding with a fork or spoon, I stared at my plate and settled in for the long wait at the table as my mother's anger boiled up and she laid down her rule. Alright, you have to sit there until you clean your plate.

I was usually still in the kitchen when the Friday night fights started at seven, a little after my father came home from Harry's. He entered the house through the kitchen door. *What's the matter, Nickelplate,* he would say to me with a laugh, *the blue-plate special not working for you tonight?* He didn't get a laugh from my mother. The routine was that they would have dinner by themselves after my brothers and I had eaten. A pitcher of martinis came out to fill the time between our meal and theirs. Our mother divided her attention between the ongoing tasks in the kitchen and an effort at a conversation with her husband in the living room where he had settled in on the couch, martini beside him on the table and a paperback potboiler in hand for extra company.

The signal came about the time when the martinis caused my mother to sneeze. She yelled, *Mark, the dinner's cold. When are we going to eat?*

Let's just finish our drinks and we'll eat, he replied. As her tone darkened and her voice rose a few octaves, she made it clear that this argument was about something other than dinner. *What are you doing at Harry's? You've got a perfectly good home to come home to. You and your friends! What's so great about Halvorson, Dunshee, Nelson? I wasn't born yesterday, you know. All those women sitting on your lap.* And so on, and so on.

Eventually Mark decided to stop going to Harry's on Fridays. After that, he was home about the time the evening ordeal at the kitchen table started for me and my brothers. Otherwise, the routine was the same. From his position on the couch in the living room, he would laugh and shout out barbs and jokes to his sons in the kitchen. And as we served our time at the kitchen table, the martini pitcher was making its third lap. Finally our mother would sneeze and her voice would explode in a sentence about dinner. Usually, our father remained quiet, pulling his punches and hoping to win on points, but one Friday night my mother threw a martini glass at him. It broke and cut him on the forehead. *I'm not taking this shit anymore,* he yelled and left the house, spending the night at a hotel. The next night Lucy stayed with us, and our parents spent the night at the Radisson downtown. Our mother stopped drinking martinis.

9

Mercy Needing

Quid sum miser tunc dicturus?
Quem patrononum rogaturus
Cum vix Justus sit secures?

What am I in misery saying?
What patron for me is interceding,
When the just are mercy needing?

— Dies Irae

It was the day after my First Holy Communion, one of those summer days when moist air from the south and hot winds from the west conspired to set Minnesotans dreaming about real estate in the Southwest.

Kevin Dolan returned to my house that morning on his bike, keeping his promise. It would be an ordinary day for George Crone, who remained blissfully ignorant of how others arbitrarily decided his fate. It was too hot for a fight, we decided, and he was too stupid for us to waste our time just beating him up. Instead, Kevin proposed we go wading in the Minnehaha Creek to cool off. The runoff from the late spring rains had engorged the creek from Lake Minnetonka downstream all the way to the Mississippi, and it was flooded over the banks just down from our house. Socks and shoes off, jeans rolled up to our knees, we waded into the flooded waters. Though the creek retained its "Song of Hiawatha" romanticism through much of the year, in the heat of summer it often took on a septic smell, with nests of nipping crayfish and the dead carcasses of carp strewn along its banks. Nobody wrote poems about it then.

As usual, our jeans refused to stayed rolled up. An edge would suck in a little water and the rolled-up cloth slowly but ineluctably sank lower until it had soaked in water to the knees and the thigh. The denim absorbed the creek's telltale summer smell, making it impossible to convince my mother that we had not been playing in it. I was not supposed to play in the creek when the water was high. Our plan was to wait in the sun until our jeans dried, but we hadn't calculated the heat of the sun and our lack of patience with nature's way of drying cloth. *I can make something up,* I said, *let's go back to my house.*

Some fast brake action and a few wheelies on our bikes announced our arrival. Just as we were setting our bikes against the evergreen in the front yard, young Mark came running out. *You can't go in right now,* he said. I forgot at the moment that my wet jeans placed me in a weak position for arguing against house rules. *Why not,* I said, *I need to change my clothes.* Young Mark said our mother had just waxed the floor. It had to dry.

Just then, our neighbor, old Mr. Wells, appeared in the driveway. My mother stepped out of the kitchen door. She said to Mr. Wells, *I'm afraid that Mark has passed away.* That's when my face began to burn.

That morning she had helped my father to a lawn chair in the backyard. She noticed he wasn't reading. A book lay in his lap. *Why don't you read, Mark,* she had said. She could only make out from his stutter that he wanted to say he couldn't see. She busied herself in her flower garden in the east lawn. She had transformed the half of the lawn up to the maple tree—the one with my swing—into rows of roses, gladiolas, cosmos, day lilies and irises. *Viv,* he yelled. A second time, *Viv.* What now, she thought.

He was silent. His back was toward her. When she came to him, she screamed, *Mark.* The second time, she screamed *Mark, you have to come here,* so her oldest son would know she wasn't calling her husband. *I can't do it,* she said to young Mark, *you have to carry him to the living room.* The father was so much taller than his oldest son. Gripping under the arms, young Mark walked backwards dragging his father's long, inert body. His feet bumped, thumped hard, and stiffly bounced on the steps leading down from the landing to the first floor. Several times young Mark paused for breath, braced his father's body on his knees, and feared that he would drop him. On the way down the steps, my father lost a shoe when the left foot, the one on the artificial leg, grated across the carpeted steps flipping off the beef-roll loafer. Young Mark got him to the couch and rolled him over, first pushing his face and chest flush against the back of the couch and then grabbing the shoulder to draw the body back down to fit. Our mother covered him with a white sheet. The left leg slipped out from under the sheet and dropped with a thud on the carpeted floor. Young Mark lifted the foot up and pushed it back under the covers. It fell out again. The leg was determined to escape and young Mark was reluctant to lift and re-arrange his father's body again. For an instant, he and his mother both stared at the foot on the floor, unable to utter a word in response to my father's last act of stubbornness until they heard the sound of the bicycles outside. *It's Nickey. Tell him not to come in the house,* she said to young Mark.

After she spoke to Mr. Wells, she looked at me and said I should go to my room and pray. When I saw the sheet on the couch, I tried to fix my eyes on the stairway to my left leading up from the living room. An involuntary tropism turned my head. I saw the contours of my father's long frame underneath the sheet and his leg and a shoeless foot sticking out of the white sheet, resting on the heel, and pointing upright on the floor. The familiar white wool sock told me it was really him under the sheet. In my bedroom on the second floor, I knelt beside my bed. My face was fire and the tears burned hot on my skin. I thought I should pray out loud. My voice croaked incoherently. A moment of apostasy overcame me. I could not remember what the word prayer meant. Then, I remembered things we called the *Our Father* and the *Hail Mary*. I remembered it was a good idea to say them nine times. One attempt to say the word "father" faltered and stopped at the first syllable. The word "Mary" stopped at the first consonant. The name was no comfort to me. The two half-spoken words released a rage that was not about to waste a breath on the routine words of the prayer and blamed them and their broken promises for what had happened. I heard a voice, a man's voice, repeating again and again, *Down, down, down.* A deep, low man's voice —*Down, down, down.* I gave up on praying. I left my room and went outside to investigate. I thought the voice came from the backyard by the incinerator. No one was there. The closer I came to the incinerator the further away and more faint the voice sounded. I went to the front of the house and sat on the curb at the street. People came to the house. Uncle John. Vic. The friends of my father who had always showed up for martinis.

KEVIN DOLAN REMEMBERED how my face turned a burning red when my mother told us what had happened.

Father Driscoll arrived at the front door. The appearance of a priest brought on an automatic reflex that made me follow Driscoll into the house, where I assumed my brothers and I were to sit across from him in the living room, politely answering his questions. At last, sixteen years after my parents' wedding, Uncle Jim and Grandma Lucy's wedding gift, the crucifix had a purpose. Driscoll opened the crucifix by the main entry way and from the secret place removed a small bottle of oil, a white cloth and a candle. The realization immediately settled in that this priest had not come as company for a visit. Whispering *May I be excused*, I quietly went back outside to sit on the curb.

Parish gossip cast old Driscoll as a priest with a drinking problem and a gruff disposition who typically greeted his parishioners by audibly clearing his throat and rarely by uttering their family names. On this day, he drew from a deeper well. He performed the Last Rites for my father. He stayed on for hours. He made the dreaded telephone call to Richard Gill. He spoke to my mother with a gentle voice that no one in the parish knew he had. Most of the time, he sat beside my father praying, remembering a boy called "Red" Hayes from half a lifetime ago when Driscoll was a young parish assistant and "Red" had the best jump shot at the Ascension Club.

It was late when Kevin Dolan returned. His mother Eleanor bucked him on his own bicycle. Sitting on the handlebars, Kevin carried on his lap a pie his mother had made for me. Eleanor presented me with the pie—a fresh strawberry pie with a warm criss-cross crust on top through the warp and weft of which large strawberries peaked out. It struck me suddenly that Kevin's mom was so young, pretty, and fun. I had never thought of it before. I would not say this to my mother who was older and didn't know how to ride a bike.

The funeral was the only time my father did not stand in the back of the church during Mass. Every pew was filled and men crowded into the vestibule and along the aisles by the walls. We followed the casket into the church, pausing for a moment in the vestibule. A man said to me with a smile that he was just about my size when my dad and he started playing basketball together. At the entrance to the church, men picked up prayer cards with the Sacred Heart on the front. The words

"In Memory of Mark N. Hayes," his birth and death dates, a prayer to the Sacred Heart, and Richard Gill's address and telephone were written on the back. There were also envelopes. Inside them, the men put checks and notes itemizing the number of prayers, novenas and masses that would be said. One was a memorial from my father's old nemesis of the Ascension playground, Swappach, who pledged a Mass and added a note saying, *It was only a lucky punch, Mark. God Bless.*

Donations came in for 79 Masses and two high solemn Masses. These did not include special devotions. The Benedictine Fathers of Benet Lake, Wisconsin, enrolled my father in their "Golden Book." Every day in perpetuity, my father's name would be listed among the names of dedication for the daily High Mass, prayers, good works, and evening "Holy Cross Blessing" undertaken by the monks. Five masses—three low and two high—would be said in his name at the Franciscan Monastery in Rochester. The Catholic Boys and Girls Home promised 25 Masses. Individual priests anted up. Father Luger led with a promise of 100 masses. Father Brietenbeck came in second with 30. The next, third place, was a surprise. Father Driscoll pledged 25 Masses.

Richard Gill rode with us in the limousine. He sat in the front seat beside the driver. My brothers and I sat with our mother in the next rows. When we entered the car, the driver pulled out two folding stools attached to the back of the front seats. I was already anxious to tell my friends later about how the inside of a limousine was like a sitting room and had secret seats. We followed the hearse carrying my father and his six pall-bearers. I kept turning around looking at the cars that followed us down 50th St. and pointing out to my mother that a line of cars without end was following us. She was irritable and snapped, *Sit still, don't look around.* I stared back anyway, knowing that something of my father was still alive in the long line of cars.

Father Driscoll led the Funeral Mass. Six other priests, all dressed in the black vestments I recognized from the Good Friday service, joined him at the altar. I knew five of the priests from their frequent visits to our house on Sundays. The sixth, Dunphy, was to me an ancient priest and a friend of Grandma Lucy's without a name. The priests took turns at saying a prayer, raising the incense, or another of the myriad acts that made the Mass last so long. Father Farrell from the Church of St. Joan of Arc gave the eulogy. It re-worked a lesson in church design the priest had learned from my father into a long-winded mixed metaphor about the church as a ship, my father as the shipbuilder, and a host of other names placed in sea-faring roles. Richard Gill kept looking at his watch. My father seemed more alive in the casket at the sanctuary than he had the night before at the wake with the distorted smile on his face, effeminate rouge on his cheeks and a rosary the undertaker placed in his cold hands that in life he had refused to say. An American flag covered the casket. The casket stirred. The flag fluttered. I wanted to say something to Richard Gill but then I saw the two large fans standing high on poles in each corner of the sanctuary. Looking at Christ on the cross, I remembered a movie we had watched in school. A little boy in a church prayed so hard to Christ on the cross that he turned his head and smiled. When the statue on the cross neither quivered nor turned its head toward me as it had done in the movie, I gave up and turned instead to St. Anthony, appealing to the saint's power for finding things lost.

Fort Snelling Cemetery is a suburb for the dead. Located about a mile from the original Fort Snelling, the veterans' cemetery is a mirror image of the subdivisions that had sprung up across the southern boundary of Minneapolis after the war. All the places were the same except they were in the form of white gravestones on plots of land rather than rows and rows of tidy ramblers. This was the end of an unbroken timeline for the lives of the veterans from their hometowns to the postwar sub-divisions that covered the far ends of Minneapolis and its suburbs and finally to this place.

My father was among the first to move into his area of the cemetery. The sod had only recently been rolled across the grounds, and it had turned brown and shrunk in the heat to expose long strips of dirt. There was a mound of black soil nearby. The nuns had taught us about dust and about remembering that from dust we came and to dust we would return. Dust for me was a fine powder found on basement windowsills. I didn't see the connection. What had dust to do with my father, the casket, the hole in the black earth, and moist, black loam piled up near his plot of land? I tried not to look at the casket and paid no attention to what Father Driscoll was doing. Small mulberry trees had been planted along the rows of graves, and I counted them from the beginning of the rows of graves up to my father's place. I needed to remember it was the third sapling. A small nozzle connected to a hose sprinkled water on it, reminding me of my father's digging and planting back at the house on Queen. He had insisted on planting larger spruce trees when friends said smaller seedlings grew better. My father replied that he wanted to live to see them as grown trees. Although he never saw his spruce trees fully grown, he would have plenty of time to see this small sapling grow into a full mulberry tree.

Grandma Elsie had come from Canada to help. After the cemetery service, it seemed to me that more people came to our house than even my father could have known. On the backyard picnic table, my mother had set up six bottles of gin, six bottles of scotch, mixers, ice and glasses. All those priests came. The guests went to the backyard, pulled up the lawn chairs and without hesitation poured their own cocktails. They were all smiles and laughter. *Let's drink to Mark in heaven*, Father Novak said, raising his glass. Elsie was shocked. She asked her daughter why all those ministers were drinking. *It's their tradition* was all my mother could say. As the realization set in that these were not the stern Lutherans of her youth, Elsie relaxed and enjoyed a few beers while she talked and laughed with the ministers.

My father's friends joined the priests in the backyard. It was such a good time. Father Dawson told the story again about how my father let the priest in Cooperstown pay for the new church by rolling dice until finally the priest won. More anecdotes and stories came out. The phrase—*such a great guy*—was heard again and again. When my mother stepped out from the house into the yard, Loevinger said to her, *Hey, Viv, why don't I set up the fly-catcher to take care of the bugs?* Someone else shouted, *Why not ask Mr. Lizard, Mr. Turtle, or Mr. Rabbit to do it?* Loud laughs and the clicking of ice cubes followed, honoring my father by the ritual that followed the joke. The jokes themselves were not re-told. The telling of them belonged to my father.

People stayed until late afternoon. From inside the house, I heard the sound of my mother and Elsie picking up the dishes. Elsie was laughing about something one of the ministers had said. Everyone was gone now, leaving the backyard a silent gathering of outdoor tables and furniture, empty glasses, plates, and paper napkins that occasionally rode on a gust of wind to a nearby empty chair. The simple aluminum lawn chairs with their criss-crossed tapestry of fiberglass tape sat empty and silent. The glasses for high-balls, old-fashioneds and martinis stayed on, patiently waiting for someone to return and tell another story.

Inside the house, Elsie raised her voice and said emphatically, *Vivian, you should marry one of those ministers.* My mother replied saying something about, *not when Nickey was still so little.* My Grandma adopted a tone that let her daughter know she had been thinking of her next point for a while. *Vivian, let Eva and Keith adopt him,* she said. Outside in the yard, I moved over the lawn chairs and sat in one with its back to the house. In a low whisper, I began *Mr. Tur-tel is at the well.*

Epilogue:
Walking with My Father

I learned early on that life is lived in the past. The city changed, even the Catholics changed, and yet, my father and his Minneapolis came back to my life like the rails of the old streetcar lines that appear every spring in the ruts and potholes of the city's streets. At our home on Forest Dale, I knew where to find him. As one summer passed to the next, we met in secret in our third floor attic. In the old navy trunk were the knives, carvings, postcards, and souvenirs from Africa and the Pacific. His gabardine suits, vests, and overcoats hung with the patience of the dead on a rack along the wall. Placing my cheek against a suit coat, I could still pick up the traces of my father's breath in the scent of the Camels that clung to every thread of his clothes. Standing alone, as if at attention and waiting for the order to walk, was his wooden leg.

At Christ the King grade school, the keeper of his memory was the ancient Sister Louis Gonzaga who had taught my father and his siblings at Ascension. When she saw me in the halls of my grade school, she would call me by my father's name or the name of an uncle, then shake her head correcting herself, and smile with tears in her eyes, repeating softly, *your father, your father.* The old nun understood what others did not. My fourth grade nun, Sister Rose Cecile, never smiled or laughed. The starched linen of the Sisters of St. Joseph's habit pinched her face into a taut pink grimace. Tortoise shell eyeglasses were the style but she kept to the thin metal-framed granny or "Mr. Peepers" glasses. One day in religion class she led a discussion of whom we should be praying for. A few gave the official answers—Pope Pius XII, Archbishop Leo Benz, and Father Driscoll. Katie Olsen said she prayed for her dead grandmother. Then, Sister Rose Cecile asked the class. *Is there anyone Nicholas should pray for?* She went on uncharitably, *yes, there is,* and turned directly to me. *You should be praying for your father, Nicholas. Do you ever pray for him?* She had exposed me. I had no father. I could not speak.

After grade school, I moved on to *D,* stepping not into my future but deeper into my father's past. By my time in the 1960s, *D* stood in the heart of the city's skid row. The city fathers constantly threatened to bulldoze the old district in the name of progress, Catholic parents driving their sons to the school muttered under their breath that the brothers should have moved the school to the suburbs long ago; the word "condo" as a cure for urban blight had not yet entered the vocabulary of Minneapolis. The old school hallways and the streets of Nicollet Island and lower Hennepin were strewn with images of my father like unclaimed luggage he had left behind.

My father's artificial leg had come from Northwestern Artificial Limb and Brace, which stood on First Avenue North. A century earlier, this area was the town of St. Anthony, named after the waterfall that drove the lumber mills. The whirring blades in those mills had severed more than a few arms and legs in their day. At the turn of the century, the city fathers did not see a problem with the working conditions that made cripples of its men, but did see an opportunity for promoting Minneapolis as a leader in the wooden arm and leg business. The ads featured drawings of smiling workers who stood firm on their artificial legs or waved with a wooden arm to the nation's readers.

In 1961, I knew nothing of this. I discovered the district early in my high school career by skipping classes. The class breaks between religion and history, when I had a pass to carry out my dutiful role of bringing our mission money to the principal's office, provided me enough cover to slip away unnoticed. As I slinked past the principal's office where my father's photograph from his basketball days hung on the wall, he gave me his half-smile and a wink before I darted out the door and into the streets. On First Avenue North, the warehouses for coat factories and women's clothes were on their last legs. The owner of Ribnick Furs had, in his high school days, been a boyfriend of my Aunt Eileen, and I nodded my head as I passed the store as if greeting an old family friend. I saw my father's suits in the display windows of the underpriced Jewish tailors—Nate's, Jake Jule's, and Bernie Berman's. He had continued to buy his suits in that neighborhood as his firm had prospered, rather than switching to Dayton's Northbriar Shop, Juster's, or Sims, where men of his income level were accustomed to shop. He had done this for the same reason he drove Fords when he could have afforded a Lincoln or Cadillac, though his friends teased him about the fact that his suits didn't have a brand label on the inside lapel.

I paused at one of the shop windows, listening as one of the suits retold one his old jokes and seemed to be suggesting we go to Harry's for a martini. Then something distracted me. I had stumbled upon the Northwestern Artificial Limb and Brace company and come face to face with the apparition of my nightmares. A replica of my father's artificial leg stood in the store room window. The sight brought on a horror and fear worse than I felt at the freak shows of the State Fair. The concept of "metaphor" was no longer for me just another easy question on a multiple choice test in English class. It was the artificial leg in the window. My father had walked on this leg in his descent into hell, his deformation from the tall, handsome athlete to his last days as something of a freak in the *Life* Magazine world of the 1950s. Again and again, I came back and forced myself to look straight at the wooden leg in the display window, in much the same way that I forced myself to keep my eyes open and watch the horror scenes from old Bela Lugosi and Boris Karloff movies.

One summer day while I was in the attic at home among my father's things, a man on crutches and missing a leg came to our front door to beg. My mother climbed up to the attic, picked up the wooden leg, and returned downstairs. She gave it to the man at the door. My father then smiled at me with that familiar slant to the left and his Kilrossanty eyes. He didn't need it anymore. *Well, Nickel-plate,* he said, *I guess that's about it, let's go for a walk. So you guys won the Hayes-Diehl wars.*

Acknowledgments and Sources

These stories have been told in other forms at other times by other voices. The responsibility for the way they appear here is entirely mine. In some cases, names have been changed where it was the considerate thing to do. Three voices in particular lie behind the story from its first to last page: Vic Gilbertson, who never tired of telling the stories of his friendship and collaboration with my father; John Hayes, my father's youngest brother and the last living member of the Hayeses on Dupont, who showed infinite patience toward my infinite questions; and, above all others, my mother Vivian, whose memories filled this book and have enough left over to fill a library.

For the details on the Hayeses in Kilrossanty and their emigration, I am in debt to Sean Ready, Chief Executive of the Dunbrody Project and Irish Emigration Data Base, New Ross, Ireland and James Rees's *Surplus People: The Fitzwilliam Clearances, 1847-1856* (Cork: Collins, 2000). Robyn Zuck and Elizabeth Bufton, Barrie Public Library uncovered the records of the family in Ontario. Debbie Miller, Reference Specialist of the Minnesota Historical Society, located long lost documents and church records of Ascension Parish. Ann Regan's *Irish in Minnesota* (St. Paul, 2002) helped me set the stage for my family's small part in the larger story of "the Minnesota Irish." Grandma Lucy's grand niece and my second cousin, Helen Burke, Minneapolis Public Library plowed through the archives of North Dakota and unearthed a trove of documents on the O'Brien's and especially the life of our Great Grandmother Anne Halloran O'Brien. Her work was supplemented by Leo Beauchamp who shares with me a distant family connection to the O'Brien's and brought to light their early history in North Dakota. In the 1970s, late in life, my Great Aunt Tess, Lucy's youngest sister, preserved memories of the O'Brien's early North Dakota days through a series of letters, carefully typed, re-produced in multiple carbon copies, and sent to her nieces and nephews. Among the memories, Aunt Tess saved from extinction the memory of Nick's appearance in North Dakota and his courtship with Lucy.

The stories of my father's boyhood on Minneapolis' North Side could not have been written without help from the following: Ed Gearty, who represented the old neighborhood in the Minnesota legislature for seventeen years and was *de facto* the official historian of Ascension Parish; Patty Stromseth and Louise Vossberg of Ascension Parish; Michael Collins, FSC, President of De La Salle High School; and Fr. Robert White who provided access to the records of the Archdiocese of St. Paul and Minneapolis.

Two works helped me put the details of my father's African diary into a broader picture: Capt. Edward Ellsberg's *Under the Red Sea Sun* (New York: Dodd, Mead & Co., 1946) and the privately printed *Middle East War Projects of Johnson, Drake & Piper, Inc for the Corps of Engineers, U.S. Army 1942-1943* (New York, 1943).

The late Ralph Rapson shared his insights into the history of modernism and the contribution of Hills, Gilbertson & Hayes. Alan K. Lathrop, Curator, Northwest Architectural Archives, University of Minnesota Libraries, guided me through the archives of my father's old firm. On Christ Church Lutheran, its Pastor Emeritus, Dr. Paul Rogers and the architect, Fredrick Bentz offered their insights into the theology behind Saarinen's design. Barbara Flanagan kept my memory honest in its depictions of Harry's, the Nicollet Hotel, and the Hennepin Avenue in its prime.

Nick Coleman, Mark Conway, Al Eisele, Noreen Herzfeld, Patrick Hicks, Killian McDonnell, OSB, Larry Millett, and James S. Rogers read earlier versions of the manuscript and offered suggestions that turned later versions into a far better work. My cousin, Sheila Hayes, who has inherited our Uncle Jim's fine editorial eye, put it to work on earlier drafts of the manuscript. I owe a special debt to my friend, the late Bill Holm, who told me that I had a story worth telling and helped me to tell it better. Bill, your copy of the book is waiting for you at your cabin in Hofstras.

My Administrative Assistant Norma Koetter never complained about the endless changes I made to the manuscript, skillfully formatted its text and images, and, along the way, became an expert in the history of my family and the Minnesota Irish. My research assistants, Rheanna Kado and Kathryn Holt discovered a gold mine of information. Two colleagues in the History Department filled in the wide gaps in my knowledge. Cynthia Curran directed me toward the scholarship that explained my family's experience in the tragedy of Ireland's Great Hunger. Ken Jones helped to place the details of my father's life from coping with Prohibition to his love of pulp fiction within the context of American social history.

Finally, thanks must go to my wife, Marcia who has lived with her dead father-in-law for the past seven years.

Nick Hayes is a professor, writer and commentator for the media. A frequent guest on television and radio, he has also published widely in newspapers, magazines, and journals. He has been the recipient of awards and grants from the Ford Foundation, National Endowment for the Humanities and the Fulbright Program and received an Emmy in 1991 for his work on TPT's *Television and Democracy in Russia*. Today, he is a professor of history and holds the university chair in critical thinking at Saint John's University in Minnesota and is a contributing writer to *www.MinnPost.com*.

For more information and speaking engagements, please visit *www.nickhayes.org*.